GIVE PEACE A CHANCE

PREVENTING MASS VIOLENCE

David A. Hamburg with Eric Hamburg

Paradigm Publishers

Boulder • London

Copyright © 2013 Paradigm Publishers

Published in the United States by Paradigm Publishers, 5589 Arapahoe Avenue, Boulder, CO 80303 USA.

Paradigm Publishers is the trade name of Birkenkamp & Company, LLC, Dean Birkenkamp, President and Publisher.

Library of Congress Cataloging-in-Publication Data

Hamburg, David A., 1925–
    Give peace a chance : preventing mass violence / David A. Hamburg with Eric Hamburg.
        p. cm.
    Includes bibliographical references and index.
    ISBN 978-1-61205-138-3 (hbk. : alk. paper)
    1. Violence—Prevention.   2. Peace.   I. Hamburg, Eric.   II. Title.
    HM1116.H35 2012
    303.6'6–dc23

                                                                                        2012030400

Printed and bound in the United States of America on acid-free paper that meets the standards of the American National Standard for Permanence of Paper for Printed Library Materials.

17 16 15 14 13   4 5

CONTENTS

PART II WHO CAN DO WHAT FOR PEACE?

Preface and Acknowledgments

This book was written under difficult circumstances: family illness; serious injuries; the necessity to move to Washington, DC, after nearly three decades in New York. Furthermore, the intellectual task was intrinsically difficult in seeking to synthesize decades of experience with exceedingly difficult, tragic, horrifying experiences: different varieties of war and mass atrocities including genocide. Would it be possible to formulate principles that cut across the major forms of mass violence and could lead to useful insights, wise policies, and institutional innovations? Could one draw on the intellectual, technical, and moral resources of the scientific and scholarly community, the best of the policy community, and personal experiences with violence at different levels of organization and in different parts of the world? The importance of this subject matter, and my unusual range of opportunities, made it a compelling necessity to try to answer these questions to the extent possible.

It would have been impossible to pursue this analysis and write this book without the deeply significant, enduring help and love of a very close family. My wife, Betty, a distinguished scholar, practitioner, and leader in child health, has been for sixty years a bulwark in personal and professional life. Her own remarkable contributions in adolescent health and development have recently been summarized and are currently in press. Her persistent support and adaptation to my adventures, such as the African hostage crisis, have made an immense difference in all of my work.

Our first offspring, Eric, though living across the country in Los Angeles to raise his extraordinary son (also David), has been deeply immersed with me in all aspects of my efforts to understand and prevent deadly conflict. He has played a major, highly constructive role in the work that made this book possible. He made an important documentary on preventing genocide. He is a lawyer; a distinguished filmmaker; and above all a humane, compassionate, democratic person.

Our second offspring, Peggy, has not only been highly supportive but has created a distinguished career in medicine and public health, most recently as a highly innovative, farsighted leader of the US Food and Drug Administration, an immense, complex, worldwide operation. In the face of these heavy demands, and raising two wonderful children, Rachel (now at Yale) and Evan (now in his final year of high school), she and her brilliant husband, Peter Brown, have created a lovely apartment for us in their beautiful home and made arrangements with great ingenuity and generosity to cope with the health issues and pursue the work of this book. Peggy's work, based first in New York and then in Washington, has had truly worldwide significance. She is a thoroughly good human being whose personal attributes contribute to her professional advances for the benefit of our shared humanity.

Jack Barchas, a great leader in medicine, chair of a unique department of psychiatry at Weill Cornell Medical College, has for a dozen years provided the professional conditions necessary for pursuing work on prevention of mass violence. His intellectual stimulation, personal encouragement, and institutional ingenuity have made a crucial difference and continue to the present day.

In the Department of Psychiatry at Cornell, the atmosphere was very positive and helpful. Two people who did a great deal of work on and around the book are Linda Newman and Emily Benedetto. I am exceedingly grateful to them. Moreover, this department, with my help, generated the unique Pritzker Consortium on the biology of mental illness.

Jack Rowe, a pioneer in geriatrics, health policy, and leadership of health institutions, has been helpful in many ways over many years, not least in facilitating this book. He has been an authentic leader on the medical scene, with special contributions at Harvard, Mount Sinai, Aetna, Columbia, and the MacArthur Foundation.

Two people have made an extraordinary contribution by having the patience to work closely with me at the Institute of Medicine, National Academy of Sciences; at Harvard; and for many years at Carnegie: Elena Nightingale and Susan Smith Santini. Their ability, dedication, and loyalty are off any scale I know.

Several organizations were extremely helpful in most or all of the sweep of work over the years on preventing mass violence. The Foreign Policy Association, headed by a person of rare vision, Noel Lateef, recognized our work on prevention when it was in its infancy, clarified its significance for the world, and provided platforms for its advancement.

A collaborative family: David, Betty, Eric, and the second David Hamburg.

Other organizations were also helpful. The Council on Foreign Relations, especially its Center for Preventive Action, has made a positive difference in the field. I am pleased to have had the opportunity to help establish this center and foster its work for some years.

Several major universities have given intellectual stimulation and cooperative efforts of the highest quality: Stanford, Harvard, and Rockefeller University. So too have the New York Academy of Medicine and the remarkable Mount Sinai Medical Center.

The American Association for the Advancement of Science (AAAS) has been an important source of stimulation and encouragement over many years, particularly during the time when I was an active board member, then president, then in close relation with Carnegie, and now as visiting scholar. It is a true umbrella organization, covering all of the sciences and making them better understood, especially through its publication of the great journal *Science* and its far-reaching annual meeting that is a major source of public interest in science and technology. *Science* is now edited by Bruce Alberts, with whom I worked closely on science and technology for development.

The other great umbrella organization of the sciences has been very good to me in more ways than I can describe here. Some of it is in this book. The National Academies' basic science, medicine, and engineering constitute one of the most respected scientific institutions in the world.

There is another "family" (sketched in this first chapter of the book) that has given me much education, support, and encouragement: Carrie Hunter, Barbara Smuts, Steven Smith, and Emilie Bergman Riss. Drawn together by the extremely stressful experience of the African hostage episode, we have been a mutual aid society ever since. This extended family includes remarkably insightful diplomats, Lewis Macfarlane and Beverly Carter, as well as leaders in research on human evolution, especially Sherwood Washburn, Richard Wrangham, and Anne Pusey.

Several decades of active participation in the life of Stanford University, as a faculty member, as a trustee, and as participant in many intellectual activities, carried forward my work in this field. Recently, I was deeply moved by the tribute paid to me as a "Founding Father" of the Human Biology Program on the occasion of its fortieth anniversary. My contact with this program was invigorating over the whole course of its continuing existence and vitality. Elsewhere, I have given a long list of superb people who were helpful along the way. Here, I can

A productive family: Evan Brown, Peggy Hamburg, and Peter and Rachel Brown.

only express my deep gratitude to Alexander George, Donald Kennedy, Joshua Lederberg, Bill Perry, Sidney Drell, Herant Katchadourian, Bill Dement, and Jim Mark.

Carnegie Corporation of New York, the original general-purpose foundation, celebrating its centennial year in 2011, played a very important part over more than two decades in my education in preventing mass violence. We were able to foster wide-ranging research and networks of scientists, scholars, and policymakers through much of the world. The interdisciplinary, international, and policy-oriented character of this work proved stimulating not only for me but for many remarkable people constituting various networks carrying forward the prevention agenda.

Among those most consistently involved (listed alphabetically) were Graham Allison, Jack Barchas, Al Carnesale, Ash Carter, Jimmy Carter, Hillary Clinton, Bill Dement, Larry Diamond, Sid Drell, Alex George, Mikhail Gorbachev, Melanie Greenberg, Lee Hamilton, Herant Katchadourian, John Kerry, Dick Lugar, Jack Matlock, Elena Nightingale, Sam Nunn, Joe Nye, Delores Parron, Bill Perry, Julius Richmond, Lee Schorr, Fred Solomon, David Speedie, John Steinbrunner, Ruby Takanishi, Melanne Verveer, Jim Watkins, John Whitehead, Elie Wiesel, and Edward Zigler. We formulated ways of reducing the nuclear danger, preventing mass atrocities, and fostering nonhateful personal development. My successor at Carnegie, Vartan Gregorian, gave me continuing encouragement.

Although I have had the very good fortune to lead a variety of commissions, councils, and the like, I have no experience to match the Carnegie Commission on Preventing Deadly Conflict. Cyrus Vance—a person of utmost wisdom, integrity, and decency—was the perfect cochair. And the same can be said for Jane Holl Lute as executive director. The three of us worked very closely together for five years, and the results exceeded anything we dared to imagine. Its significance was quickly seen by world leaders such as Kofi Annan, Hillary Clinton, Javier Solana, and several major democratic governments (especially Sweden). Its influence continues to be broad and constructive more than a decade after its completion. The main report and the seventy-odd associated publications constitute a unique resource. The mix of world leaders and great scholars turned out to be invaluable.

Opportunity to roam the corridors of the UN was very instructive, especially working with Kofi Annan, Boutros Boutros-Ghali, Desmond Tutu, Sadako Ogata, Francis Deng, and Bob Orr. For all its problems, the UN is a wonderful window on the world, and I learned a lot.

We seem to live our lives in conjunction with a set of "extended family." On a day-to-day basis in Washington, we are surely indebted to the Pascual family for their practical kindness and skill: parents Minda and Greg; daughter Grace; and daughter-in-law Sherry, who has been my excellent assistant in the preparation of this book.

As the years go by, one appreciates more and more the value of excellent medical care. In this context, I am deeply grateful to several distinguished and devoted physicians: Valentin Fuster, David Thomas, Elizabeth Cobbs, David Hansen, and Bill Dement.

There are so many people and so many institutions that deserve my heartfelt thanks that I deeply regret it is just not feasible to go on longer—with one exception. Jennifer Knerr has been a blessing as a superb editor for "my gang"—first Alex George, then the Carnegie Commission on Preventing Deadly Conflict, then several subsequent books culminating in this one. Though I have known excellent editors who have helped me and my friends, I have not known anyone like Jennifer: her scope of knowledge, her positive orientation, her sensitivity in identifying opportunities for improvement, her creative imagination in all phases of the work—from a broad intellectual framework to the beauty and nuance of a cover. Our respect for her has no limits.

An Invitation to Peace

There is a recent revival of serious analytical efforts to work toward preventing deadly conflict in general and the ultimate elimination of nuclear weapons in particular, examining both technical and political obstacles and intermediate steps toward overcoming them. Difficult as these problems are, there must be a serious, sustained effort to reduce the nuclear danger as much as and as rapidly as possible. Nongovernmental organizations (NGOs) worldwide could make a major contribution on the weapons problems. So too could the international scientific community. The US government has recently given this movement a strong boost. The tasks of prevention require sustained cooperation across national boundaries and among various institutions and organizations.

This book draws on a great deal of research, field observation, and careful descriptions of the paths to mass violence. War now has destructive capabilities almost beyond imagination, and hideous mass atrocity is recurring. Incitement to hatred and violence is easier, more vivid, and truly contagious, even at a global level. Moreover, "light weapons" and "small arms"—highly lethal beyond public understanding—are rapidly covering the world, area to area. We need no reminder that weapons of mass destruction have not gone away despite the monumental progress of the Nunn-Lugar program. No part of the world is so remote and no group so small that it cannot inflict great damage on people everywhere. Everyone everywhere is at risk.

We relate this most poignant body of information to the growing research literature on this subject by advocating for what we call *pillars of prevention*. These pillars of prevention are mostly long-term measures that are useful for prevention of all sorts of mass violence: war, genocide, and mass atrocities. They depend largely on the cooperation of international organizations, established democracies, and also excellent NGOs. Above all, building public understanding and encouraging action on a worldwide basis are essential. For this reason, our book is intended to reach an educated, nonspecialist general audience.

This book naturally draws upon the cumulative record of our experience. It is a synthesis of the authors' several decades of research and experience with preventing mass violence, including wars and mass atrocities. It builds on that prior work and draws on multiple sources of information from different disciplines and from various parts of the world. It presents basic concepts derived from the authors' work in a series of major enterprises, from the resolution of the Cuban Missile Crisis through the work of the five-year Carnegie Commission on Preventing Deadly Conflict to the publication of a series of subsequent books that probed crucial aspects of prevention, including *No More Killing Fields*, *Learning to Live Together*, and *Preventing Genocide*. In the course of this presentation, the senior author summarizes personal experiences that clarified for him principles, policies, and institutional innovations on several crucial issues. The concepts are further illuminated by insightful observations of world leaders and eminent scholars, many of them his close associates who are pioneers in the prevention of mass violence.

The emphasis is on building broad public understanding of ways to strengthen decent human relations; making people alert to emerging dangers and skillful in resolving differences; and establishing norms and institutions that support humane, compassionate, and secure living conditions.

At the core, these concepts delineate pillars of prevention: early warning and early action to help countries with deteriorating intergroup relations, the building of equitable socioeconomic democratic development, the protection and promotion of human rights, education for survival, and ways of diminishing the risks of the most dangerous weapons. To deal proactively with such dangerous and complex subjects, it is essential to pool the world's intellectual, technical, and moral resources from many disciplines, nations, and organizations.

The international community must make every effort to help countries or regions in trouble—manifested in growing hatred and violence. Many countries will benefit, some quickly, some slowly—yet over decades or generations, virtually all can benefit from building these pillars of prevention.

This will require organizations such as the UN, the EU, and the community of established democracies to keep in close touch with all regions of the world so as to respond with empathy and concern in offering help promptly—early, ongoing action to prevent mass violence—searching for decency in human relations and a sense of common humanity.

ONE

PERSONAL EXPERIENCES AS
PATHWAYS TO PEACE

Immersed in stress research since 1948, I began to realize more and more that stress responses were a kind of mobilization for action—but without producing action, in most contemporary circumstances. The energy metabolism of stress, cardiovascular responses to stress, and the role of various hormones in stress—all pointed in the direction of the body's getting ready for some intensive exertion. This anticipatory mobilization must have served adaptive functions over a very long period of time, under the conditions in which we evolved. Over millions of years, the human organism and its predecessors must have been able to take actions that would prepare them to do whatever was necessary to survive, but in contemporary circumstances stress does not often lead to intense exertion. To dig into this more deeply, I and other researchers in the field studied the brain and hormones in clinical and experimental conditions, focusing especially on the adrenal cortex.

FROM STRESS RESEARCH TO HUMAN AGGRESSION

The people we were studying in the 1950s and beyond were, for the most part, in sedentary situations and, for that matter, largely lived sedentary lives. In

1

just a moment of evolutionary history—two hundred years of time since the Industrial Revolution—the human way of life changed drastically as compared with the millions of years in which we've evolved. The human experience probably carried over these stress responses from an earlier time based on genetic predispositions shaped by cultural changes. So the old responses in alarming situations might no longer be adaptive. In fact, that view became a general orientation of ours, certainly about aggressive behavior. Much of what was adaptive earlier was no longer adaptive in contemporary circumstances and might well have influences on today's diseases. That led me and my colleagues to get directly into some evolutionary studies and ultimately took us on quite an intellectual as well as physical journey.

PIONEERS IN THE STUDY OF HUMAN EVOLUTION

This field has gone far beyond where it was in the beginning because genetics, then incipient, has made fantastic progress. I have always felt deeply grateful to my original mentor in genetics, Tracy Sonneborn, and to my long-term colleague, another great pioneer in modern genetics, Joshua Lederberg. Our research group was able to show major genetically determined variations in the way individuals processed the stress-related hormones. Jack Barchas and Roland Ciaranello pursued this line of inquiry very effectively. They both became leaders in neuroscience and psychiatry. Genetics has become very important in the stress field and in psychiatry generally at the present time.

On the evolutionary side—closely related to genetics in fundamental terms—we wanted to understand how human stress responses evolved. In 1956, I got a letter out of the blue, inviting me to spend a year at the then-new Center for Advanced Study in Behavioral Sciences. It brought together fifty distinguished scientists and scholars from ten to twelve fields each year at Stanford (though it was then a fully independent institution). Each person was free to pursue his or her own scholarship in any way. It was a unique opportunity. The first or second day I was there, a wiry fellow appeared at the door and introduced himself. His name was Sherwood Washburn, and he was one of the great pioneers in the modern study of human evolution. So there began a multiyear collaborative review of the research literature on many facets of human evolution bearing on stress and aggression as well as attachment and child development. That eventually led me to go to Africa.

I went multiple times in the late 1960s and up to 1975, each time taking a family member with me and working with Stanford students in the field research unit we had established. Washburn had begun the new wave of primate studies in the natural habitat, just a few years earlier (in the early 1950s). I got interested in whether it would be possible to learn about chimpanzees in the natural habitat because of their very close biological relationship to humans. The new work in genetics was showing that 98 percent of the genes of chimpanzees and humans were identical.

In 1959, I sought to establish a research unit in the chimpanzee natural habitat, but it was very difficult because my best opportunity was in the Congo, and violence there blew up at the time of independence. About a year later, in 1960, Professor Clark Howell, a distinguished archaeologist, told me he was aware of my search for a young zoologist or medical missionary and had a good lead. Louis Leakey told me that he had started a young woman named Jane Goodall on studies just a few months before in Tanzania, on the other side of Lake Tanganyika from Congo. She was trying to get chimps accustomed to humans so that close-range observation would be possible. So I started corresponding with her. Then she came for a visit to the United States, and we became friends. She and her husband, a great photographer, Hugo von Lawick, had a treasure trove of film, even from an early point, of chimpanzees in their natural habitat.

After several years of intensive research at the National Institutes of Health, I moved to Stanford in 1961. I recruited into the department people with backgrounds in genetics and biochemistry and evolution, bringing the different disciplines together. Stanford had a lot of land, and the administration generously gave me about twenty acres set aside to build a seminatural laboratory for chimpanzees. They could live in groups, each consisting of several acres. But we knew very little about how they lived in their natural habitat. What's a day in the life of a chimp? Nobody knew at the time.

When I first went to Africa in the 1960s, Goodall was about to leave. She had finished the work for which she could get her PhD at Cambridge University, and it didn't seem a practical proposition to stay. Von Lawick needed to do filming elsewhere on other subjects. But it was clear that they really wanted to stay, though they had little support for doing it. So I offered to try to get funding and some organizational (especially academic) support and make a relationship with the Tanzanian government that would give them an official blessing. They were delighted to have this opportunity, and so we made a substantial research station out of it; it was a wonderful collaboration that lasted the better part of a decade. Over time, we were able to get graduate students and postdoctoral fellows and remarkable undergraduates in human biology, so at any given time we had twenty or so people working there from Stanford, from Cambridge University in England, and from Tanzania. It was international and interdisciplinary. The methods became much more systematic and, to the extent possible, quantitative observations of the behavior of chimps in their natural habitat moved from studying a single community to studying two adjacent communities so the interaction between the communities could be clarified. That turned out to be extremely illuminating because of the violence between different communities that was discovered.

At the seminatural laboratory at Stanford, we wanted to be able, for example, to train the chimps to hold out their arms to have blood drawn, which it's possible to do. Training in behavioral science methods was emphasized, with the excellent leadership of Helena Kraemer. So we had the seminatural laboratory at Stanford and the natural habitat studies. People went back and forth, students working first at one place, then the other. There are different things you can do in a laboratory than in a natural habitat. Each has its own limitations, each its own strengths. It was unique in the world at that time. It came to an end with a hostage episode in 1975. Now let me sketch this bizarre episode.

A LIFE-CHANGING EXPERIENCE

On May 19, 1975, I received many urgent messages in California that four of my students had disappeared in Africa. There were calls from the State Department, the press, families, and others. All we knew was that about forty heavily armed men had come in off Lake Tanganyika into our camp on the lakeshore on the night of May 19, 1975, taken four people, and disappeared on the lake. A few shots were heard, and nobody had any idea what had really happened. Were they killed and dumped in the lake? Who was it? Who took them? What was it about? We knew nothing.

So I decided I immediately would go over there and see if there was anything I could do, even though I hadn't the foggiest idea of what. We were all quite scared. It was just a bizarre experience, the kind of thing that you may read about but that doesn't happen to "real" people.

It was some days before we found out that these were rebels against the government of Mobutu Sese Seko, the longtime dictator in Congo. These rebels lived very high in almost impenetrable mountains, perhaps nine thousand feet in elevation, rising dramatically out of Lake Tanganyika on the other side of the shore from our camp. They sent a letter of demands to President Julius Nyerere of Tanzania. They had taken these young people and were holding them hostage. The point was that they earlier had a secret supply line for a thousand miles from the Indian Ocean at Dar es Salaam, the capital of Tanzania, across Tanzania to Lake Tanganyika. That supply line had been shut down by Nyerere, the leader of a very poor and well-meaning country, in a trade deal with Mobutu, who was blessed with valued resources but not with any sense of decency. They were furious with Nyerere. We were pawns in an African political conflict. We were meant to bring pressure on Nyerere. We were somehow supposed to get their people back who were operating the supply line and get the supply line reopened. But that proved to be impossible.

So we set out to do whatever we could: first of all to find out who had taken our students, and then to make contact with the hostage-takers. How to do that? Eventually we made contact and then looked to see if we had any conceivable negotiating leverage. We did this mostly in very remote areas and with some cloak-and-dagger experiences. It became possible to figure out different strands of negotiating possibilities, and that led, over a period of a couple of months, to three of the students being freed. But they were still holding the fourth student, and they conveyed their intent to kill him if necessary for political purposes. Then President Nyerere helped us. That was absolutely vital and a vivid lesson in the value of benign leadership.

These people believed that the ends justified the means, and they committed many human rights violations in the process. Because they wanted some recognition, I was able to use this as bargaining leverage: making clear that I could *not* endorse them in any way, but letting them explain their outlook to the world. With difficult negotiations, they agreed. In due course, they were persuaded by other incentives to release the remaining three hostages. But I knew that they were not to be trusted and that they would in fact try to trick us.

We devised a very complicated mid-lake fail-safe transfer, which failed because Mobutu had located our group and set up heavily armed gunboats in the lake. So it was Mobutu who blocked off the transfer this time, not the rebels against him. The only option that remained was to meet the hostage-takers on their beach at night. So under their guns, they released all but one of the hostages—a male student, Steve Smith. He was extremely vulnerable for political reasons.

The only way to free this student was to involve President Nyerere. As luck would have it, his official Tanzanian representative (an anti-American bureaucrat) went out of town, so the American ambassador made an urgent plea for a meeting with Nyerere, which was readily granted. The Tanzanian representative had proved to be a real obstacle who misled us into believing that Nyerere would be of no help. The opposite was in fact true. Nyerere was determined to help free Steve if necessary and made necessary concessions— which were not made public—to these rebels.

When Steve was finally released, the students organized a reunion celebration that evening and gave me an "Honorary Degree in Contingency Planning" written on the only available piece of paper they had. I have many honorary degrees, but this one is the best and will always recall the courage, affection, and ingenuity of these students.

To conclude, after two and a half months, all four were free. It was a very important experience. It was the end of our work in Africa, and it certainly influenced the rest of my life. Those years were extremely stimulating and an opportunity to get some insights into human evolution. I wrote several papers with Washburn and Goodall and others, but more importantly, inspired students, some of whom are now professors at Harvard (Richard Wrangham), Michigan (Barbara Smuts), Duke (Anne Pusey), and elsewhere and are making important contributions to the field. So I view it as a fantastic set of dreams. I never dreamt of going to Africa in the first place. I never dreamt of doing primate research. I never dreamt of dealing with a hostage problem. But there it was.

Ambassador Beverly Carter challenged me, after that event, to think about using my capabilities in spheres beyond the university, particularly to relate the scientific and policy communities to address the dreadful problems of hatred, violence, ignorance, malnutrition, and disease that I experienced so vividly in the hostage crisis.

A few weeks before the hostage-taking, I had a tentative invitation to become president of the then-new Institute of Medicine, National Academy of Sciences. Or to put it another way, the search committee, looking for a president, wanted me to be the lead candidate. The academy is a very special place in the American and indeed world scientific community.

Yet at that pre-hostage moment, I felt I couldn't leave Stanford; I couldn't leave the work in Africa. I had developed a configuration of responsibilities that was unique to me, and I thought if I pulled out, it probably wouldn't be sustained. In any case, I loved what I was doing. Our children with whom we have always been very close had grown up on the Stanford campus. I never envisioned leaving at all.

That offer was made early in May 1975. On May 19, the students were taken. Two and a half months later, it was over. When I got back to Dar es Salaam at the end of it, there was a letter from the president of the National Academy of Sciences that essentially said something to the effect that an experience such as this can be deep. It can affect your whole life. It can make you rethink what you want to do. So let us reconsider the Institute of Medicine.

Thus I was, in a way, a changed person, and from then on, both in that position and later at the Carnegie Corporation of New York, I was fundamentally trying to find ways to do something useful on these dreadful problems. Moving on to become president of the Institute of Medicine was one powerful way to address them at the level of policy. We were able to lay out a program for dealing with major issues, including diseases of poverty, primarily in developing countries, and created an international health program.

One further point on the life-changing influences: the courage and integrity of the student hostages (Emilie Bergman, Carrie Hunter, Steven Smith, and Barbara Smuts). Fortunately, they were allowed to stay together, and their *mutual support* was of inestimable value. Moreover, and deeply touching, they were convinced that I would immediately come to Africa and find some way to get them freed. While that was a hope-sustaining fantasy because I had so little preparation and so little leverage, it taught me an unforgettable lesson in *human solidarity*. The themes of this experience in Africa echo through the remainder of this book.

AN EVOLUTIONARY PERSPECTIVE: INSIGHTS FROM OUR WORK IN AFRICA

My initial focus in our Laboratory of Stress and Conflict at Stanford was on *individual and small group* levels. It then expanded to include the *community* and then larger *intergroup* and *international* conflict. So, over a period of decades, it was possible to develop an unusually broad view of human conflict and its resolution.

From an evolutionary point of view, I had done research and field work and come to the conclusion that group membership is fundamental to survival. It

David Hamburg with the four hostage students and Professor Don Kennedy. October 2011 at Stanford.

is so important for humans to identify with a valued group that we sometimes end up justifying our worst atrocities in the name of loyalty to that group. "Holy wars" begin from this point of view.

Many people have a vaguely formulated assumption that the genetic heritage of human nature makes mass killing inevitable. It is a matter of great importance whether human nature inevitably leads to catastrophe. Therefore, it is vital to consider what we know about the elements of human nature that bear upon mass violence. If there are genetic tendencies of this sort built into our ancient heritage, then we must consider what else is built into that heritage pertinent to protecting against such violence, helping us to survive as a species. Therefore, we worked on elements of biobehavioral sciences that illuminate such questions.

Of special interest are our closest genetic relatives, chimpanzees, who share 98 percent of our genes. Their patterns of threat, attack, and submission are similar to some of the aggressive and conflict-resolution patterns observed in our own species. They raise their arms in threat; hit, punch, and pound with the arms and kick with the legs in attack; brandish and throw objects to intimidate opponents; scream when frightened; crouch and whimper to express submission; and reach out to touch, pat, or embrace in order to reassure an uneasy subordinate.

There are also some similarities between the contexts in which threat and attack behavior occurs in nonhuman primates and humans. Monkeys and apes are particularly likely to engage in such behavior in the following situations:

1. When competing for scarce or valuable resources that promote survival and reproductive success—e.g., food, and for males, access to fertile females.
2. In competition for high status within a group; severe aggression is particularly likely during periods of unstable dominance relationships and is particularly prominent when maturing males are involved.
3. When protecting close friends or relatives, and particularly infants, from threat or attack by other group members.
4. In response to threat or attack by higher-ranking animals; in this case, redirection of aggression toward subordinates is common.
5. Toward strangers trying to enter the group and toward members of other groups, always for territory and particularly when groups are in competition for access to mates or high-quality, clumped foods.

Thus, the evolutionary contexts in which aggression occurs most frequently are those in which an aggressive response seems likely to *promote an individual's survival and genetic fitness* by (1) increasing access to resources, (2) protecting relatives, and (3) defending relatives of "friends" with whom the aggressor has affiliative bonds that promote cooperative efforts to achieve mutually beneficial goals. Similarly, submissive patterns of behavior that often serve to inhibit attack can be viewed as adaptive responses by subordinates who would lose more through aggressive competition than they could gain. There are indeed conflict-resolution patterns among chimpanzees.

Intercommunity Aggression

Our group discovered that chimpanzee males are organized into distinct communities that occupy ranges. When males from different communities come into contact, mostly they avoid each other. But when a large party encounters a lone stranger or small group, violent fights may occur. Adult males and infants may be seriously injured or killed by violent males from other communities, and rarely even females can be killed. Several studies in different locations establish the systematic patrolling of community boundaries by groups of males who behave in highly antagonistic ways in such encounters. Females rarely take an active part in intercommunity encounters except to defend themselves and their offspring.

Males of one community, closely related because they remain in their groups of biological origin, regularly gather together to engage in such patrols. Moving silently in contrast to their usual noisy habits, these males move toward one edge of their range, frequently stopping to climb trees and view the distance, looking and listening for signs of strange chimpanzees. If the party of strangers is outnumbered, the patrolling males move forward with extreme caution until they are just a few yards from the chimpanzees of the other community. At this point, they charge, in a powerful display of violence. The small groups may be brutally attacked and endangered.

Richard Wrangham and Luke Glowacki have extended this research. They systematically reviewed intergroup fighting in chimpanzees and nomadic hunter-gatherers living with other nomadic hunter-gatherers as neighbors. They believe that intergroup aggression evolved according to the same functional principles in the two species, that is, selection favoring a tendency to kill members of neighboring groups when killing could be carried out safely.

What is the function of such intercommunity violence? By extending and defending community boundaries, a group of males achieves access to a greater number of females and other resources such as premium food. The larger chimpanzee territory is established and defended by groups of males cooperating with one another. This is consistent with other evidence from research on higher primates, suggesting that the evolution of *cooperative* behavior is related to the evolution of *aggressive* behavior in primates.

The systematic, organized, brutal, and male-dominated attacks of chimpanzees are the closest phenomenon to human warfare observed in any nonhuman primate—though a very long way from contemporary war. When the chimpanzee evidence is considered along with information on responses to strangers in a variety of nonhuman primate species, there are probable links with the human tendency to react with fear and hostility to strangers. A fundamental question is whether there are genetic predispositions in our ancient past to *in-group/out-group distinctions*. Mahajan et al. present very interesting evidence of rhesus macaques having cognitive tendencies to make in-group/out-group distinctions. Human tendencies to respond aggressively in particular situations may well be partly the result of natural selection operating during our species' evolutionary past. Emotional response tendencies that may have been highly adaptive under ancient circumstances may become maladaptive when environmental conditions change drastically, as they have in the most recent phase of human evolution. In learning to cope with violent tendencies, we need to take into account both negative and positive patterns inherited from adaptive efforts of long ago.

Today, a few remote people subsist mainly by hunting and gathering. These remaining populations are the only living representatives of a way of life that characterized all human populations until the invention of agriculture about ten thousand years ago. Hunter-gatherers are fully modern humans genetically, although they are different from our ancestors in important respects. They are the best models we have for reconstructing the way of life of the long human hunting and gathering past. They have been studied with increasing sophistication in recent years.

In early humans, a sense of personal worth is predicated on one's sense of belonging to a valued group; a sense of belonging depends on the ability to undertake the traditional tasks of that society with skill and to engage in social interactions in ways that are mutually supportive. These experiences occur within the context of a small, face-to-face group that provides the security of familiarity, support in times of stress, and enduring attachments throughout the life span. In our view, this set of relationships is crucial in the *evolutionary and historical success of human adaptation*.

Relationships between Attachment and Aggression

In nonhuman primates and humans alike, the first contexts in which distress, frustration, fear, and anger are experienced are those in which the bond to a primary caregiver is threatened. Fear serves to promote the infant's attempts to reestablish contact with the caregiver, and anger heightens the infant's ability to overcome obstacles to achieving this goal.

In monkeys and apes, attachments to other group members are often developed and protected through aggression. One of the most frequent contexts of aggressive behavior is protection of close relatives and friends. The most vivid example is a mother's protection of her offspring, even against dangerous, high-ranking males.

In addition to the strong bonds that develop between particular individuals, nonhuman primates are attached to the social group itself with its distinctive attributes. Opportunities to be engaged in one's social group are usually pursued with determination. In the wild, monkeys and apes accidentally separated from their groups often become agitated, vocalizing loudly and repeatedly. They appear to be searching persistently for their lost companions. Excitement and pleasure have been observed in monkeys and apes upon reunion after brief separations. These pleasurable emotions are the positive counterpart to the negative emotions of anger, fear, and grief experiences when contact is disrupted. Such evidence is strong in chimpanzees.

So, our ancient ancestors lived in small groups in which they learned the rules of adaptation for survival and reproduction. They were vulnerable to natural stresses—lack of food or water, weather, predators, infections, other humans. Then very gradually came the onset of agriculture, and after thousands of years, another change of profound significance—the Industrial Revolution two centuries ago, with *transformative implementation* in the twentieth century. Science and technology have played a profound role in this transformation. In this moment of evolutionary time, the human species has drastically changed the world of its ancestors. Natural selection over millions of years shaped our ancestors in ways that suited earlier environments. We now have new adaptive challenges and opportunities.

Humans existing now, after our long evolution, have incorporated biobehavioral patterns that have worked in survival and reproduction in the past, transmitted both by genes and by culture. Among these are linked patterns of attachment and aggression. For millennia, it has evidently been important to *belong* to a group, to *believe* in a group, to be *loyal* to a group, and to be ready to *defend* one's group. In the process, it has been common to dehumanize members of other societies. Aggression via groups has been used in implementing adaptive requirements. Yet group membership has great potential for protection and security. These are elements of the ancient human legacy that we must cope with in the transformed circumstances of contemporary life if we are to avoid the dangers of complacency. The immense danger of this situation is also a powerful stimulus for using humans' extraordinary learning, problem-solving, and survival capacities to diminish great risks as we accomplished in the wind-down of the Cold War and now seek additional modes of *mutual understanding* and *early, ongoing conflict resolution*. All this is novel, difficult, and risky, yet there is evidence of progress in the twenty-first century and creative innovations for more to come.

ANOTHER PERSONAL EXPERIENCE ON PREVENTING MASS VIOLENCE

Crisis Prevention

In 1978, under the auspices of Pugwash, I convened a small group of US, Soviet, and Western European scholars in Geneva to learn about crisis management principally by examining what had been learned by American scholars studying the Cuban Missile Crisis—especially Graham Allison and Alexander George. In 1978, the emphasis on crisis *prevention* was a largely new way of thinking, and there was an element of surprise for those at the meeting in thinking in terms of crisis prevention rather than management. The Soviets were suspicious. Essentially, what was said to the Soviets is that it is simply not in our national interests to go to the brink of nuclear confrontation because it's too hard to manage, and ground rules should be worked out for prevention. One example during the Cold War was the establishment of the hotline between Moscow and Washington and then its upgrading. In this and other prevention efforts, we were geared toward procedures and arrangements that could reduce the likelihood of a nasty surprise. Following the 1978 conference, the focus was on practical ways of avoiding a nuclear confrontation in the context of an ongoing Cold War.

Reducing the Nuclear Danger

In 1982, when I arrived as president of Carnegie Corporation of New York, I systematized this approach with the help of a fine staff, board members, and outside consultants—great scholars and international leaders. They began to map out what it might look like to create a program on avoiding nuclear war. Several strands emerged: (1) How can nuclear war actually happen? We convened and funded scholars and scientists to answer this question. (2) What are the paths to prevention? Different bodies of knowledge and skills brought together in a continuing way were needed. A special focus of understanding the adversary was also initiated.

Once the interdisciplinary groups of US scientists, scholars, and other experts were working together in several foci, we connected them with Soviet counterparts, chiefly through the Soviet Academy of Sciences, to begin a process of reasonable communication. The Soviet invasion of Afghanistan

Historians now agree that the Cuban Missile Crisis was the single most dangerous moment in human history. Kennedy said at the time he thought the chance of it rolling to war was somewhere between 1 and 3—that's what he said to his brother quietly. Where could this end? In 1962, maybe there would have been 100 million people killed; but in the mid-1980s, maybe we would have succeeded in killing everybody—so just completely out of proportion with any conceivable purpose, objective or otherwise, and so the fact that I think I became personally more persuaded that these guys for sure didn't want to go there.
—Graham Allison, Harvard University, from Eric Hamburg/ Rick English documentary, Preventing Genocide, *2009, Stanford University Library*

in 1979 greatly worsened the Cold War and led to talk in government circles in Washington, DC, and Moscow that perhaps nuclear war was inevitable or that one side could "prevail." Nuclear war was arguably the most important problem in the world, and if a foundation could make a difference, even marginally, then it was very worthwhile. This was consistent with Andrew Carnegie, who was obsessed with war and peace questions.

In early 1984 (about a year before Mikhail S. Gorbachev took office), I planned a conference with Jack Matlock, Ronald Reagan's principal adviser on the Soviet Union, and James Billington, an expert scholar on Russia (now the Librarian of Congress). The topic was US-USSR scientific and scholarly exchanges with Soviets. Could they be usefully revived, and if so, how? On his own initiative, after courteously asking our permission, Reagan spoke to the entire group in the spring of 1984. It was one of his most forthcoming messages to the Soviet Union, saying he was going to revive the exchanges on a selective basis, relying on the judgment of this group. He wanted to revive not only some of the scientific exchanges but also his own idea to extend it to the arts. Reagan and some of his closest colleagues found this conference to be a useful step toward peace. This experience gave me strong encouragement to pursue these problems.

Recognizing an Authentic Opportunity

A landmark of authentic historic significance occurred when Gorbachev assumed leadership of the Soviet Union in 1985. As it turned out, he was far more receptive to the kinds of ideas we were working on than leaders before him. Some of our Soviet scientific counterparts had ready access to him. So there was a unique opportunity created by this study group to facilitate links among independent experts from the United States with both US and Soviet leadership. This group served a kind of "brokerage" function for getting Western people, ideas, and information to Gorbachev and his closest advisers. In fact, Gorbachev stated publicly that these kinds of contacts helped him to shape his new thinking and to move closer to accommodative international policies and more democratic outlooks. He expressed publicly his gratitude to us for facilitating this process and for the substantive benefit of these discussions.

As soon as Gorbachev came to power in 1985, we explored whether he differed greatly from previous Soviet leaders in his willingness to face serious domestic problems. He stopped the ritual incantation of the perfection of the Soviet society and the emergence of a new Soviet man. While he retained pride in his people and their (unfulfilled) ideal of social justice, he was in our personal communications from 1985 onward an extraordinarily penetrating and pervasive critic of his country's shortcomings. He called attention to the stark reality of an unproductive economy. He was keenly aware of the contrasts of his country with those more technically advanced and with the middle-tier developing countries as well. He was offended by the evidence around him of rigidity in thinking; deceitful practices; widespread corruption, including in the Communist Party itself; and repression.

To an unprecedented extent, he turned to the scientific and scholarly communities to help himself understand the difficulties and to seek ways of modernizing the Soviet economy and society. He asked for my help in this process regarding the international scientific community. Several insights became recurrent themes in his speaking and writing: (1) the world is rapidly being transformed by advances in science and technology; (2) the consequences of nuclear war in the Soviet Union would go far beyond the horrendous damage of World War II; (3) there is a continuing danger of inadvertent war based on human or mechanical error, and the effects would be exceedingly devastating even if the war were limited to conventional forces, which is very doubtful; (4) Soviet foreign policies since World War II have been unwise and in some ways counterproductive—as in the invasion of Afghanistan; and (5) decades of Soviet military buildup have imposed a serious drain of money and talent from the civilian economy.

For these and other reasons, he was inclined toward an accommodative external policy. He sought to diminish not only the economic costs but also the political and psychological costs of continuing on the path of his predecessors. He was keen on earning Western respect and obtaining Western expertise in a cooperative mode. He sought intellectual, technical, and economic resources to modernize the Soviet Union. He explored with me and others whether he could expect some reciprocal attitudes from American leaders. We were reassuring along these lines in terms of our own judgments.

How NGO/Government Collaboration Can Help

Gorbachev's years in power were characterized by a good deal of "new thinking." His contacts with Western leaders and independent experts contributed to this creative process, as he explicitly realized on numerous occasions, even early in his term of leadership.

- I formed a relationship with Gorbachev that continued for many years. This relationship facilitated the contribution that Western scientists and scholars were able to make via the joint study groups and in other ways to diminish the nuclear danger.
- A key part of our strategy was (1) to get clusters of US scientists and scholars and other experts to work on avoiding nuclear war; and (2) once up and running in the West, to establish or strengthen joint study groups with Soviet counterparts (working largely through their Academy of Sciences).
- The three most important of those were up and running before Gorbachev: (1) arms control, (2) crisis prevention, and (3) behavioral science. They were endorsed by him in due course.
- On the topic of arms control, I helped to create at the National Academy of Sciences a Committee on International Security and Arms Control (CISAC) and served on this committee for several years. I learned a great deal about arms control from such great physicists as Wolfgang Panofsky and Charles Townes. CISAC has been creative and constructive since 1980. We alternated meetings twice a year in Moscow and Washington.
- As a piece of luck, the Russian chair, Evgeniy P. Velikhov, was a distinguished physicist and a pragmatic problem-solver. I met with

him as usual during a break at a meeting of CISAC in Moscow, and I said to him something like this: "I know you have a new leader. I have no idea whether he is sympathetic to arms control or not, whether he is committed to the cause of peace or not, whether he's potentially friendly to the United States or not. I hope he'll be all of those things, but I don't know anything about him. For all I know, he might represent a setback. But I do know this: that new leaders like to have some distinctive contributions, a distinct ecological niche that they can carve out, that, 'I as a leader have made this unique contribution.'" And I said, "While he's new in office, is there anything we could do, either through this arms control group or in some other way that would be helpful?" Velikhov seemed quite interested. He said, essentially, "Let me think about it and I'll get back to you tomorrow."

Now, what I didn't know then was that he and his friend Roald Z. Sagdeyev—also an eminent physicist, who later became a member of the Carnegie Commission on Preventing Deadly Conflict—had easy access to Gorbachev. Gorbachev had a set of advisers before he became the highest leader, and he used them very intensively afterward. What Velikhov did was to contact Gorbachev that evening, and when I came in the next morning, he was looking for me. He was very excited. He had concrete suggestions—for example, pursuing peace-oriented communication between Soviet and American scholars, and initiating computer-based friendly communication between Soviet and American children. I told Velikhov quite frankly that I would need to run it by the people in our government because I didn't want in any way to get into a hassle where people might say we were transferring technology that was inappropriate.

I came back and considered it with Matlock, a wise foreign service professional. He later became ambassador to the Soviet Union. He was very supportive and urged me to go ahead. So that was one project of interest to Gorbachev and the US government.

Then there was another project, and this time Velikhov came—it was in Washington, it was actually a special trip. This was a few months later. Gorbachev was interested in creating an international foundation that would be a vehicle for more contact with the outside world, that wouldn't go through the Foreign Ministry or the Defense Ministry or the Communist Party, but would be a way of widening his contacts, and quite possibly enhancing his stature in the outside world.

The three key people initially instrumental in forming the International Foundation for Survival of Humanity were Jerome B. Wiesner, who was the president of MIT and had been President John F. Kennedy's science adviser, Velikhov, and myself. The actual drafting of the charter and bylaws was done in Carnegie's offices, when Velikhov and Sagdeyev were here. We had lawyers looking at it and tried to do it in a way that would strengthen the hands of democratic reformers in the Soviet Union. We constructed a distinguished board with scholars from North and South America, Asia, Africa, and Europe as well as Russia.

I was president of the American Association for the Advancement of Science (AAAS) at the time. Gorbachev said, "You should be actively supporting social science. How can we make rational policy when we don't have any social facts we can believe?" It was all distorted by ideology and dishonesty. He said, "You have a great scientific community. You should set an example. You should help our people develop serious data collection in the social sciences."

I was stunned and didn't know how to interpret it. I did feel that he'd have to be an extraordinary actor to be playing the part. When we got to talking about nuclear weapons, he was trembling. He basically said, "Nuclear weapons are insane and don't serve any useful military purpose. What kind of aim could be fulfilled by destroying our two countries and much of the world?"

So I began much more actively encouraging individuals and delegations to go and visit with him. The most striking occasion was a time in March 1988, when I took a delegation of five leading members of the Senate and five leaders of the scientific community. We had essentially a week there in half-day blocks, meeting with his defense chief and his foreign minister, leaders of the scientific community and the like, and then finally a half-day session with Gorbachev. Among other things, we were able to bring up, I think with some sensitivity, very delicate issues such as the loosening of the yoke on Eastern Europe and why that would be in the Soviet interest. So I tried to be, in a way, a broker for Western ideas and Western people, directly and indirectly, to his close advisers and to him personally.

Gorbachev gave me remarkably frank critiques of the problems in the Soviet Union as well as the earlier oppressive regimes. Yet he was proud of its history and culture in important respects. He emphasized the Soviet people's intelligence but said that their system was one that warped their development.

> *You asked me if I would go with you and Senator Nunn and Richard Lugar on a trip to Russian Ukraine. The Cold War was now over, but we had these tens of thousands of nuclear weapons still in the former Soviet Union—some in Russia, some in Ukraine, some in Kazakhstan. And the country was in a state of economic, social, and political turmoil, and the question of course is, what will happen to the weapons in those conditions? Our visit confirmed our worst fears, that the danger of those weapons getting loose was very high indeed. And on the airplane trip back, we all sort of conceived what became the Nunn–Lugar program as a way of trying to prevent that tragedy from happening. I think it was at that stage that I became focused on the importance of prevention.*
>
> *After I became secretary of defense, I concluded that I should put a very high priority on trying to deal with these nukes as we saw them in the former Soviet Union before one of them got seized by a criminal gang and terror gang against the United States. So the focus was clearly on preventing the tragedy before it happened, and the tool for that prevention which was already available to us with the Nunn–Lugar program.*
>
> —**William Perry**, *former Secretary of Defense, from Eric Hamburg/Rick English documentary* Preventing Genocide, *2009, Stanford University Library*

His central task was to free the creativity of the Russian people. He knew this would be difficult and dangerous for him but vitally important for his country and the world.

Later, when he left office, I urged him to visit the Carter Center, to see what former president Jimmy Carter (1977–1981) was doing and to set up some similar functions. He did that. Carter was very good with him, inviting him to come and spend a year there if he wanted. Gorbachev tried to emulate some aspects of it, and Carnegie gave him some support, because here's a man who had played an enormous role in ending the Cold War and bringing freedom to his own people, to the people of Eastern Europe, and to the Soviet empire. I knew he would have a difficult time after leaving office and felt we should keep his ideas and his persona active on the world stage because he was deeply respected throughout the world.

We believed that the behavioral and social sciences could help to avoid nuclear war even in the darkest days of the nuclear era and took note of Gorbachev's interest in social sciences as a way of conducting rational policy. We encouraged the US National Academy of Sciences to set up a committee on contributions of behavior and social sciences to avoiding nuclear war, and it proved useful for years. Alexander George, the distinguished political scientist at Stanford University, was a major contributor.

While still in office, Gorbachev acknowledged in a speech he gave at Stanford University that the new thinking did not arise just in the Kremlin, that outsiders were enormously helpful, and he pointed to people such as Sidney Drell, Bill Perry, and George Shultz at Stanford. During another speech at the Council on Foreign Relations, Gorbachev gave specific credit to Carnegie Corporation of New York's contributions and endorsed the Carnegie Commission on Preventing Deadly Conflict (CCPDC).

Later, I worked with Jane Holl, executive director of the CCPDC, to get five distinguished world leaders to do personal essays on leadership for preventing deadly conflict: Gorbachev, Boutros Boutros-Ghali, Desmond Tutu, Jimmy Carter, and George H. W. Bush (first of the two Bush presidents). Although each essay is different, they generally address the contours of the leadership question. The crosscutting themes are *vision, courage, ability to articulate a mission*, and *ability to stimulate others to share that vision*.

Gorbachev's essay was distinctive. He was terribly impressed with the historical tendency of leaders, particularly national leaders, to validate what he calls "brute force." He thought it was a primitive concept and very dangerous. Contrary to what many of his colleagues wished him to do, he gave the signal that the Soviet Union would *not* use force again against Soviet bloc members as they had in Hungary and Czechoslovakia in earlier times.

Thus, it was possible for NGOs such as these to foster communication at the highest levels between the United States and the Soviet Union in the most dangerous depths of the Cold War. It became clear that both Reagan and Gorbachev had deep concerns about the immense danger of nuclear war, and it was at least marginally useful that we were able to encourage their thinking about this critical danger and to facilitate their communication about it, first indirectly and then in a series of summits that came to have a profound effect on the prospects for a better world.

PART I

PILLARS OF PREVENTION

EDUCATION FOR PEACE

Overcoming Complacency, Ignorance, Prejudice, and Wishful Thinking

Unfortunately, we have too many societies where young people, where the youth have been completely neglected, where [there are] bright, intelligent, inquisitive children hungry for knowledge who want a chance to develop themselves but have no opportunities. So [it is] the responsibility of the international community and international governments to really make it a priority . . . I would say next to almost none invest in young people, invest in their rehabilitation, invest in their education. That's one of the best things we can do to ensure not just durable peace in a society but to prevent major conflict.
> —**Olara Otunnu**, *United Nations, Children in War,*
> *from Eric Hamburg/Rick English documentary*
> Preventing Genocide, *2009, Stanford University Library*

One of the greatest opportunities we have for creating a better world is to actively educate for peace. Learning to live together amicably is neither simple, nor easy, nor anything we can take for granted. Yet substantial, sustained education for this purpose is not only important for economic benefit and good health but also fundamentally for human survival. What conditions favor constructive results in child and adolescent development? What can shift the odds away from rotten outcomes such as hatred and youth violence? How can our children grow up healthy and vigorous, inquiring and problem-solving, decent and cooperative? How can adults, including political, governmental, religious, and business leaders, follow this path? Pivotal institutions powerfully shape child and adolescent development: family, community, media, health, and education systems.

There is a sense in which this whole book is about *education*. If humanity cannot come to understand the immense dangers of mass violence, the prospects for well-being and indeed for survival will be poor. Yet this field has largely been devoted to post-violence efforts to pick up the pieces. Our approach is to learn as early as possible how to *prevent* disaster.

The formal educational system is one important element—indeed, a gaping hole through most of history and most of the world. So we address it here, while keeping in mind that both the preceding and following portions of this book strive to provide understanding and stimulation for the vital task of preventing mass violence. Thus, education is a fundamental pillar of prevention, now weak because of neglect and poor social priorities, but potentially strong in a profound and pervasive way.

PROSOCIAL BEHAVIOR IN LIFE SPAN DEVELOPMENT

One key place to begin such crucial education is with *leaders*—not only political but those in all the powerful sectors of human societies. Another, perhaps more fundamental in the long run, is work with *children and youth* to build a solid foundation through education so they can shape a peaceful life that embodies mutual understanding and cooperation among human groups throughout the world. They can grow up to develop a strong constituency for prevention of mass violence, supporting leaders who are peacefully inclined—and generating leaders in various sectors who are informed and skillful in minimizing disputes.

There has long been complacency all over the world about prejudice and ethnocentrism—taken for granted like the air we breathe. Yet the dangers of hateful outlooks are likely to be great in the twenty-first century—as we saw on September 11, 2001. Although teaching attitudes and beliefs of hatred to children occurs—all too often in so many places—and has been virtually automatic—conveyed by many parents, reinforced by clergy, enshrined in textbooks, and inflamed by political leaders—it has been widely ignored or rationalized. All this has been conducive to terrible harm in the past.

We are now facing the emerging realities of our exceedingly interdependent world, which throws us humans together more extensively and dramatically than ever before—for example, international travel, information transmission for better and worse, highly valued economic transactions, and large-scale immigration. Our species has a very long history of distrusting strangers, despising out-groups, fighting each other in many ways and many places, and using the most damaging technology available at the time. Today, the capacity for incitement of hatred and violence is much more powerful than ever before. Not only does radio cover the most remote areas of the world, with its ready capacity to become "hate radio," but the Internet provides unprecedented large-scale opportunities to vilify out-groups and describe ways of making weapons of all kinds for their destruction.

Mainstream efforts to modernize education largely neglect these topics even in the established democracies—not to speak of oppressive states. Yet there are many promising examples of research, educational innovations, and visionary leadership emerging in various parts of the world. We have devoted most of our earlier book, *Learning to Live Together*, to promising lines of inquiry and innovation that promote humane, democratic, and prosocial development in childhood and adolescence.

It is extremely important that the human tendency to generate intergroup conflicts—perhaps adaptive long ago but now exceedingly dangerous—be widely understood. All groups have probably inherited malevolent tendencies along with benevolent ones, as we see from evolutionary and historical research. The human future depends on the way these tendencies are clarified through education over the entire life span.

We must now find a basis for fundamental human identification across a diversity of cultures in the face of manifest differences and overt tensions. Modern humanity is a single, interdependent, crowded, worldwide, weaponized species, vulnerable to pervasive stress from severe poverty, from harsh disparities, from drastic climate events, and much more. So we must cooperate in our own self-interest. This should be crucial in modern education. How can we provide decent life chances in every country for a quality of life compatible with human dignity and make arrangements within each country to protect human rights; respect pluralism; avoid oppression; give children and youth a decent start; respond cooperatively to stressful events; reinforce decent, humane leadership; and make use of what science tells us about a better humanity? Peace education goes beyond goodwill and exhortation to substantive, fundamental information, ideas, aspirations, and relationships.

THE LONG HISTORY OF INTERGROUP CONFLICT

The study of human evolution and history shows that a sense of personal worth has long been based on one's sense of belonging to a valued group; a sense of belonging, in turn, depends on the ability to competently undertake the traditional tasks of that society, to engage in mutually supportive social interactions, and to participate in the emotionally significant shared experience of group rituals. The enduring group offers guidance, protection, and satisfaction. A key concern for the human future is how to extend the psychological group of human survival to a much larger world community.

Altogether, kin-based group membership has been crucial in human evolution. But strong group membership can also make us susceptible to hatred and violence. We inherit through genes and customs a strong need for *belonging* in a primary group, and all too easily our primary group may render us hostile to other groups. Everywhere in the world, hostility toward other people has been facilitated by a pervasive human tendency toward harshly distinguishing between positively valued "we" and negatively valued "they." We have more to say about this in Chapter 1.

Research from several disciplines, in field and laboratory, shows that human beings are readily able to learn in-group favoritism or in-group bias. People are remarkably prone to form depreciatory distinctions between their own and other groups, to develop preferences for their own group, to discriminate against other groups, to accept favorable evaluations of the activities of the in-group, and to accept unfavorable assessments of other groups that go much beyond the objective evidence or the requirements of the situation. Experiments show how easily hostility can form and become deeply entrenched between groups and how unfairness can aggravate such tensions. It is vital that schools and other child-rearing institutions—for example, religious ones—provide a setting in which young people from different backgrounds can overcome the in-group bias and then reach *valued common goals* in an atmosphere of *collaboration*. The same principle applies in the formation of governments and international organizations: mutual aid for mutual benefit.

The world transformation in which we are now immersed involves so much widespread frustration, it may be transformed into virulent prejudices against minority and foreign populations as well as infidels. Ethnocentric and nationalistic inflammatory politicians as well as religious fanatics have long understood the human tendency to seek someone to blame under circumstances of intense frustration. Now there is heightened danger, when incitement to violence have become so vivid and readily amplified by advanced technology. Social media has great potential for worldwide sharing of human experience, but they may also be readily transferred into *anti–social media*.

A "holy war" tends to provide a strong sense of mutually supportive solidarity within the group, but it also generates hostile exclusion and glib justification of mass violence toward the other group. Yet religious nationalism is not entirely closed to pluralistic tolerance. In fact, some movements hope to implement tolerant governance if given the opportunity. This gives the international community an opening to reach out in friendship to moderate leaders and democratic reformers. With substantial help, such reformers and their associates may over time change their societies. One crucial set of changes in the strengthening of education is understanding how democracy actually works, educating girls and women, teaching science and technology for shared prosperity, and practical understanding of nonviolent conflict resolution.

OVERCOMING INTERGROUP HATRED

Education for hate is an all-too-pervasive part of human experience. And various media often provide reinforcement for hate messages. We are often weak in the domain of preparing children for decent human relations and creating nonviolent ways of addressing serious grievances. This deficiency is at its peak in repressive societies but is also prevalent in dogmatic, extremist elements of democratic societies.

Intergroup contact under favorable conditions can overcome the lethal obstacles of the past. If groups are strange to each other and therefore fearful or hostile, why not bring them together so that they can get to know each other and become friendly? This is promising but not easy. A variety of field and laboratory experiments indicate that intergroup competition tends to strengthen social relations within each group and to disrupt relations between different groups.

Research suggests the importance of overlapping group memberships in the modern world. There are myriad possibilities of large-scale international contact that have recently emerged. People who belong to groups that cut across ethnic, national, or religious lines may serve a bridging function among people who differ in many ways.

How can early, ongoing conflict resolution occur through personal contact, and how can mutually beneficial cooperation be achieved? There is a strong, positive effect of friendly contact in the context of equal status, especially if this contact is supported by relevant authorities, is involved in cooperative activity, is encouraged by a mutual aid orientation, and provides tangible benefits to both groups. This leads to improved attitudes between previously suspicious or hostile groups as well as constructive changes in their relationships over time.

In cooperative learning, the traditional classroom of one teacher and many students is reorganized into heterogeneous groups of four or five students who work together to learn a particular subject. The research literature clearly reflects the favorable impact of cooperative learning techniques on achievement in secondary schools as well as in elementary schools. They are applicable also to military and political training institutions. There are several aspects of cooperative learning that have practical importance: learning to work together, contributing in some way, learning that everyone is good at something, appreciating diversity, complementing skills and dividing labor, and acquiring a mutual-aid ethic.[1]

Beyond the classroom, this orientation can unify different groups in the search for a vital benefit that can *only* be obtained by their cooperation. In experimental research, strangers were made into enemies with isolation and harsh competition, but then transformed into friends when exceedingly valuable superordinate goals were introduced that could only be achieved by cooperation. There are beneficial effects of working cooperatively so that people *formulate a new, inclusive group* that goes beyond narrowly oriented groups with which they enter a situation. Such positive effects are particularly strong when there are tangibly successful outcomes of cooperation. We emphasize mutual benefit in mutual aid.

Despite all the identity distinctions that have so long separated peoples, the world is now one in which friendly personal contacts on an equal footing and mutually beneficial cooperative ventures can occur more readily than ever before. We have the opportunity to identify superordinate goals and organize cooperative efforts to meet them in issues of human survival: avoiding nuclear war, minimizing terrorism, achieving sustained prosperity, and establishing decent intergroup relations within and among nations. The place to start is in education at every level—from the youngest children to mature would-be statespeople. This is an adult as well as a child's enterprise because the contemporary economy relies heavily on working effectively in groups.

The public health approach to adolescent violence is similar in principle to behavior-related health problems such as smoking. Violence prevention programs train service providers in a special curriculum, especially in hostility-prone communities. They then translate this curriculum into practical services for adolescents and enlist the support of the community in preventing such violence, building norms of early, ongoing conflict resolution. Besides curriculum development, the need is for community-based prevention education in schools and community organizations, including religious ones, clinical treatment services, and media campaigns sponsored by reasonable organizations and supportive institutions.

All this is crucial for high-risk youth in impoverished communities. They need social support networks and life skills training. Both can be provided in schools and school-related health centers as well as in community organizations, including faith-based youth activities and sports programs. Communities must make special efforts to create attractive, safe, growth-promoting settings for young adolescents during the out-of-school hours—times of high risk when parents or other responsible adults are often not available to supervise their children. Such programs have diminished smoking, violence, and teen pregnancy—and in the same mode have diminished intergroup hostility. Success of such efforts diminishes the susceptibility of youth to hate-promoting political demagogues and religious fanatics.

Cooperative, nonviolent problem-solving in childhood and adolescence is a developmental sequence of experiences and opportunities that can promote decent, constructive behavior in relation to other people—from the simplest interactions to worldwide communication, from small intergroup relations to large identity groups.

EMPHASIZING PROSOCIAL BEHAVIOR

Prosocial behavior refers to decent consideration for others as well as oneself, to the capacity of finding satisfaction in functioning cooperatively with others. Starting with the family, mutually respectful social support networks are essential for a satisfying and productive life span. Democracies seek a decent respect for the experience of humanity beyond self-centered preferences.

Research on this topic operationally defines prosocial behavior as helping rather than hurting or neglecting, respecting as opposed to denigrating, being psychologically supportive and protective rather than dominating or exploitative. Precursors appear early in life. Newborns, who make distress cries in response to cries of other infants, are already showing signs of empathy. Children in their second and third years show emotional distress and take positive actions in the presence of distress of others. Family settings in which consistent expectations orient to prosocial behavior do in fact strengthen such behavior. This is the path to prosocial behavior. Experimental research clarifies this development. Children exposed to adult models of prosocial behavior, when compared with similar children in control groups lacking pro-social orientation, show the positive behavior manifested by the models, whether it is honesty, generosity, or helping or rescuing behavior. There is also evidence from naturalistic study of toddlers' prosocial actions that delayed imitation by children of their mother's ways of comforting and helping occur spontaneously in children's efforts to help others. The combination of early attachment, primarily to family members, plus abundant modeling over the years of growth and development leads to prosocial behavior that becomes firmly established, strengthens human relationships beyond the family, and contributes to a sense of personal worth.

Longitudinal field-experimental studies have been done to strengthen children's prosocial orientation and behavior. The results show that children in such intervention programs are more supportive of each other, more spontaneously helpful and cooperative, and more concerned about others than those in the conventional classes. In addition, they are able to resolve conflict in less damaging ways, with more compromise, planning, and attention to the needs of the various individuals engaged in the conflict. They also manifest more democratic values. Effects clearly go beyond the classroom, and academic achievement is *not* compromised—for example, they do well in mathematics.

Parents, teachers, and religious educators can be consistent models of sharing, helping, and comforting behaviors. Prosocial classroom activities such as role-playing are enjoyable to children. They promote feelings of sympathy and build self-worth in helping others, all the while fostering nonviolent problem-solving. Parents and teachers can also organize to press for responsible media programming that exposes children to more altruistic behavior and to less violence. Community organization and mutual efforts are needed to influence the media in prosocial directions.

Empathy is vital in the development of helpful behavior, and it is associated with relatively low levels of aggressive behavior. For these reasons, empathy training has been undertaken in elementary school–aged children in order to regulate aggressive behavior, promote prosocial behavior, and formulate strategies useful for classroom teachers of children from the ages of seven to eleven. Interestingly, as we shall see later, successful diplomats see empathy as a crucial first phase of their work.

Role-playing exercises can enhance one's ability to understand other ethnic, religious, and national groups. Delineating similarities between individuals in tense situations is a helpful strategy. Beyond the classroom, there is a fundamental need to grasp our common humanity in everyday human relations.

Families and schools are the two most important institutions in democracies that shape children's attitudes and behavior toward different groups. Both are taken into account in teaching conflict resolution. Such programs include cooperative learning, conflict-resolution training, constructive use of controversy in teaching, and creation of dispute resolution centers. Students need a serious curriculum with repeated opportunities to learn and practice cooperative conflict-resolution skills. Joint problem-solving is a basic element of lifelong learning that has useful applications in economic as well as social contexts. Professor Morton Deutsch, a great pioneer in the study of conflict resolution, and his colleagues at Columbia University have shown how this works in many schools of New York City.

School mediation programs are spreading rapidly, stimulated significantly by the success of peer counseling as developed in the 1960s and 1970s by Beatrix Hamburg. Research suggests that school mediation programs have positive effects in reducing violence and enhancing self-esteem as well as social skills of the mediator. What is learned in school needs to be transferred to supportive homes and communities. School programs can actively encourage this transfer of learning, especially to parents as well as to staff members of community organizations.

In cooperative learning, competition is not eliminated from students' experience. In fact, healthy competition often inspires greatness, whether it is building a better instrument or developing gifted athletes or creative scientists. But excessive and harsh competition, especially in the classroom, can create a destructive atmosphere of winners and losers, breeding feelings of isolation, depreciation, and alienation that can readily slide into hatred and even violence.

There is a growing trend in education that fosters constructive, unselfish behavior during adolescence: *community service*. This can be organized effectively not only by schools but also by community organizations and religious institutions, businesses, governments, and universities. It can provide opportunities for learning, skill development, economic opportunity, and social respect. It should generally not be seen as punishment.

THE WORLDWIDE SIGNIFICANCE OF EDUCATION FOR PEACE

The problems of prejudice, ethnocentrism, hatred, and violence are still low on the priority list of the world's activities in education and science, in the media, in the business community, in places of worship, and in governments. Why not move this subject to a higher place on the world's agenda? Scientists and educators, through their most dynamic organizations, can use their deep knowledge and strong influence to enhance research and education on prosocial child and youth development, on ways to minimize the growth of prejudice and ethnocentrism, and on acquiring skills of *early* conflict resolution. Orientations from our ancient past often hinder efforts to enhance our understanding and use of scientific knowledge when it is available. Educational institutions from early childhood to graduate education have a vitally important role to play in the human future, more so than ever before as the people of the world are drawn together in unprecedented ways. Can we use our unique learning capacities that made the human species so successful during the course of its evolution to adapt now to immense dangers? How can human beings learn more constructive orientations toward those outside their own groups while maintaining the values of primary group security? We are gradually learning constructive approaches, which recur throughout this book.

INTERNATIONAL EDUCATION

We humans must of necessity find decent ways to interact with strangers, move beyond stereotypes, and even turn potential adversaries into friends.

This largely exceeds the prior experience of humanity. Now we have to learn how to transcend virulent prejudices, learn how to live together with people who are initially strange and implicitly threatening. We can widen the horizons of education from childhood onward and learn about other peoples, cultures, and ways of life. In this process, strangeness can be converted to familiarity, suspicion to fascination. Thus, international education bears not only on economic well-being in a world of technoeconomic globalization but also on the vital issues of preventing mass violence. It extends beyond schools and even universities to involve businesses and religious, media, and community organizations.

Most teachers are not adequately prepared to teach global studies, and those who have the necessary motivation or skills need help with implementation. Among the useful steps are to increase the opportunity for teachers to travel and bring the outside world back into the classroom, provide intercultural experiences at home, and use the Internet to give students insight into other cultures.

Links in *peace education* between (1) higher education institutions and (2) elementary and secondary schools are essential for training teachers to be knowledgeable about global issues and intergroup conflict resolution, within and between countries.

Foreign language study can usefully be serious work at all levels of education. Competency in another language is exceedingly helpful in opening windows to the world. Advanced technology can aid this process, including, importantly, a modicum of understanding of the history and culture of other peoples. Such skills have economic utility and can diminish prejudice.

Educational institutions can respond to this need in several ways. They can integrate international and global perspectives into the curriculum in a substantive way. This can be reinforced in admissions requirements for higher education. Students should show competence in a second language. Higher education institutions can emphasize the importance of knowledge about the entire world and promote skills for communicating across cultural barriers. This includes studying abroad and making it feasible for the full range of students—including minority and low-income students—to take advantage of the opportunity. By fostering diversity in the student body, there are opportunities for students to engage with people from different parts of the world.

Technology can be used to full advantage. The Internet is accessible and provides a virtual international exchange with the ability to connect classrooms around the world. The nature of the content is vitally important. It can range from empathic understanding of diverse cultures to the construction of nuclear weapons—there is also a dark side to the Internet. Teachers are central to bringing international perspectives into the classroom, and they need preparation for the task. Real leadership in schools, business, government, international organizations, and philanthropy will be necessary to generate constructive international education. The consequences can be beneficial in a variety of sectors.

SCIENCE, TECHNOLOGY, AND THE NEW WORLD

Altogether, these high aspirations will require major educational adjustments, public policy changes, and governmental and community support. Nowhere is this more urgent than in substantive *education for peace*. What is distinctive about education for peace? It draws heavily on the basic concepts and educational processes for violence prevention as described in this book. It illuminates crossing adversarial large-scale intergroup boundaries and hostility across *national* boundaries as well as across *ethnic, religious,* or *political* boundaries within a nation. So we must study international war, civil war, and mass atrocities. The large-scale hostilities have not been so much the focus of attention in recent education as interpersonal and community education for conflict resolution. Education for peace goes beyond goodwill and exhortation, even in interpersonal conflict resolution. But the likely dangers of the twenty-first century make education for peace a vital subject throughout the world for in-depth study.

The aim is for people in different cultures to grow up committed to finding alternatives to violent conflict. The need to build peaceful societies is one of the world's most pressing problems. This fact constitutes a powerful stimulus to the education community to formulate curricula, materials, and school environments conducive to peaceful living. Likewise, it challenges religious institutions and community organizations, the media, and governments and international organizations.

Human beings can indeed learn to work cooperatively. Modern technology has made warlike behavior a form of *mass suicide*. We can find ways in which all of humanity can legitimately be treated as potential allies. This is a matter of practical adaptation, indeed of human survival.

PROVIDING EDUCATION FOR PEACE
AND SHARED PROSPERITY

Personal development–shaping institutions such as the family, schools, community-based organizations, religious institutions, corporations, governments, and the media have the power to mold attitudes and skills that favor decent human relations at every level of personal and social development. They can make constructive use of findings from research on intergroup relations and conflict resolution. We must learn from infancy through our life span how to achieve *mutual accommodation* among individuals and human groups. This cannot be taken for granted, even in democracies.

In the twenty-first century, it will be necessary in child and adolescent development to put deliberate, explicit emphasis on developing prosocial orientations and a sense of worth based not on the deprecation of others but rather on the constructive attributes of others as well as oneself. In counteracting our ancient tendencies toward ethnocentrism and prejudice, we will need to foster reliable human attachments, positive reciprocity between people, friendly intergroup relations, a mutual-aid ethic, and an awareness of superordinate goals requiring cooperation. This fundamentally extends beyond youth and beyond the formal educational system. It bears on economic well-being, environmental protection, personal security, and indeed human survival.

THREE

---✦---

EARLY WARNING

Taking Prompt Action to Protect Peace

I was in Kenya in 2008 trying to negotiate the very serious conflict between the opposition and the government. The groups I met with, the civil society groups, the churches, and the business community, were extremely well organized but perhaps weren't able to focus their energy and influence the way that they ought to have. I met a group of business men who represented 85 percent of the GDP [gross domestic product] in Kenya. So I told them, "This is influence, this is power. How do you use that influence? How did you try to influence events, talk to the politicians and the governments before the explosion?" There was silence, and so when we got the agreement, I brought all of them together: the civil society, the churches, and the business community.

I met each group and told them, "Look. Now we have an agreement. It's an agreement that can work, but don't leave it to the politicians alone. This is your society too; the society belongs to all of you, and you have to be active, you have to be vigilant, you have to ensure that these agreements are honored."

—**Kofi Annan**, *former UN Secretary-General, from Eric Hamburg/Rick English documentary* Preventing Genocide, *2009, Stanford University Library*

What is distinctive about the *early prevention* approach to mass violence? (1) It emphasizes *proactive help* to countries in trouble—if possible, prior to any killing.

(2) Because danger signals are typically evident years before the carnage, there is *ample warning time* to act before blood flows. (3) It recommends the formulation and dissemination of *specific response options* and contingency plans to deal with early warning signals. What to do till the doctor comes? (4) It draws together *many tools, strategies,* and *practices* to prevent mass violence—information, ideas, and policies from many intellectual and geographical sources. And (5) it clarifies what international organizations can use those tools, strategies, and practices most effectively, and emphasizes the *role of the established democracies.*

POINTS OF ENTRY FOR COOPERATIVE HELP IN EARLY CONFLICT RESOLUTION

A peaceful world, free from genocide, war, and terrorism, will depend on an international community, and especially the *established democracies* (a growing community), to be ready and willing to be on the alert for sister countries in trouble and to apply skills, attitudes, and mechanisms in extending help to these countries to prevent bad outcomes. By "countries in trouble," we refer to such attributes as intergroup hostility, governmental repression of vulnerable groups subject to prejudicial stereotypes, rising hate speech, systematic violation of human rights, and inclination to deal with problems by violence. The conundrum is that no favorable outcome can occur without substantial changes, and these are unlikely to happen without outside help. Yet those countries most in need, and especially those with repressive leaders, are most likely to be suspicious of, and resistant to, outside help. And often these negative manifestations are detectible at an early stage, well short of mass violence. Yet there are many countries and sizable groups within almost every country who find tendencies toward hatred and violence dangerous and unwelcome. Thus, there are serious, thoughtful, constructive possibilities for nations in an early stage of intergroup trouble.

What are some examples of points of entry for proactive help?

1. Offers of tangible *economic development* linked with *internal conflict-resolution mechanisms* throughout the development process, helping to build national capacity for early, ongoing conflict resolution—with international help as may be necessary and acceptable.
2. Cultivation of relations with *moderate, pragmatic, emerging leaders*—preferably *democratically inclined* to the extent possible.

3. Fostering relations with civil society insofar as the governing regime permits it, showing the regime that the development of a constructive, problem-solving civil society is in its own interest.

4. Promoting *mediation*, preferably at an early stage before revenge motives become severe. Offering such mediation with explanation of its benefits for the nation itself, urging it if necessary, and even pressing with international cooperation to make clear the *incentives for accepting such mediation*.

5. Encouraging units, such as those of the United Nations Development Program, in a troubled country to *build strength in mediation*, illuminating the prospect of economic incentives and the major gains from following a peaceful path.

6. Recognizing that organizations such as UNICEF, which exist in many countries, have valuable *activities for healthy child and adolescent development* as well as education. The offer of extra support for such constructive units can be very attractive, especially in light of the almost universal human attraction to the well-being of their own children.

7. Health units in each region, especially the World Health Organization, can offer immediate help along with a *vision of long-term health improvements*. Given the virtually universal yearning for good health, and especially the health of children, there is an opportunity here for health diplomacy. *Health can be a bridge to peace.*

For all such points of entry, there are modalities that are likely to be accepted as tangible help and prevention of disaster. These modalities include *sympathetic interest, empathy for suffering, respect for human potential*, and *a vision of better opportunities*. Indeed, they can illuminate options that would lead to a better life for the whole society that is getting into trouble.

The most pervasive need is for the international community to be prepared and proactive in helping nations or groups in trouble rather than waiting for disaster to strike. It starts with listening. Empathy is the core of early opportunity to help. In the short term, this makes it feasible to put out fires when they are small. In the long term, this essentially means help in acquiring attitudes, concepts, skills, and institutions for resolving internal and external conflicts. It means help in *pointing the way toward political and economic institutions of democracy*—recognizing multiple steps that will be required and clarifying the potential benefits. There can be—and of necessity will be—many different international configurations through which such help can be provided. And it can be done in a way that is sensitive to cultural traditions and regional circumstances. This orientation respects a group's history but draws the line at war and mass atrocity.

There is a considerable convergence of research and carefully considered experience in suggesting constructive modes of negotiating that offer real promise of meeting basic needs, addressing grievances seriously, and finding paths to mutual accommodation through joint problem-solving. This approach to negotiation has much promise for preventive diplomacy, whether used by governments, intergovernmental organizations, or nongovernmental organizations.

There is a growing tendency in the diplomatic world to begin with dialogue on whatever subjects may be of shared interest and not inflammatory—from the wonder of child development to the beauty of nature or whatever. Problem-solving then involves a gradual, shared effort to find a mutually acceptable solution. The parties to a dispute move from neutral topics to reflect tentatively on their interests and priorities, work together empathetically to identify the core differences dividing them, open their minds creatively in search of alternatives that bridge their opposing interests, and jointly assess these alternatives in the search for mutual benefit. The impact of problem-solving on the outcome of conflict can be highly positive, especially the development of an integrative solution derived from reformulating basic questions and putting problems in a different, more hopeful context.

CONFLICT PREVENTION AND HEALTH: AN ARRAY OF OPPORTUNITIES

Since the 1990s, individuals and institutions have made substantial efforts to understand the development experience of the second half of the twentieth century and to learn from both its successes and failures. One major feature of these efforts has been to take a broader view of the development process, recognizing the crucial importance of *human development* and linking social and economic considerations—not least a heightened appreciation of health in development involving equality of females and males. Now, proactive help can be facilitated by communicating prospects of good health through intergroup cooperation across adversarial boundaries—for example, preventing diseases, which only can be done through regional cooperation. This requires an early vision of what is possible. So, for example, the pervasive desire for good health provides a point of entry for joint problem-solving.

The technically advanced democracies can provide tangible help so that diagnosis, treatment, and prevention of disease draw upon the strongest possible knowledge and skill. To do so, health must be a vital part of education for reasonable leaders in high-tension poor countries as well as rank-and-file citizens—that is, another point of entry for proactive help.

International cooperation on a mutually respectful basis is essential for the effective implementation of such policies. It is crucial to build local capacity by promoting individual and group competence; generating directly relevant discussion to the situation at hand; promoting new knowledge; diffusing information to potential users and refining it through local application; creating institutions to support education, research, and knowledge dissemination; and enhancing the capacity of public and private organizations to reach sound decisions based on objective analysis. Thus, the offer to help has no "neo-imperialist" implications but rather compassionate, respectful, and effective actions as a powerful source of hope for the general population, especially the children.

Overall, health has a special role to play as an incentive for cooperation. *Health is a shared value* that is profoundly important to people around the world. Cooperative health interventions have both an immediate impact on people's lives and long-term benefits. They can inspire trust, confidence, and hope: the vision of a better life. Health care is largely nonideological and free of the political and emotional baggage that other programs are perceived to carry in certain parts of the world; thus, it can become readily acceptable even to adversarial parties. Indeed, health programs can foster broader foreign policy and diplomatic goals in important—and sometimes unique—ways by illustrating the rewards adversarial parties can achieve by peaceful cooperation for mutual benefit in pursuit of a *superordinate* goal that can only be attained by such means and by placing emphasis on the welfare of children, whose health and safety have a special value across cultures, religions, and national boundaries. International cooperation in the eradication of smallpox during wars, as occurred in the 1970s, illustrates what is possible.[1]

MEDIATION SUPPORT UNIT: A PROMISING INNOVATION

In Kofi Annan's tenure as secretary-general of the UN, he encouraged the creation of a professional unit to foster effective mediation—a mediation support unit for field operations. His successor, Ban Ki-moon, endorsed this approach and moved to strengthen the significant Department of Political Affairs (DPA) into "a more proactive and effective platform for preventive diplomacy, including mediation, at the service of Member States."[2]

In an unusual report to the General Assembly, Ban emphasized: "Now focus must be put on the Organization's capacity to prevent and resolve conflict—a better investment than dealing with the costly aftermath of war and a critical investment to ensure the billions of dollars spent on development by Member States, the international financial institutions and the United Nations itself are not wasted when armed conflict or war erupts."[3] This clearly echoes the Carnegie Commission on Preventing Deadly Conflict and the subsequent reports generated in Annan's search for "a culture of prevention."

Even the most talented and persuasive mediators cannot get far without resources that include a practical and professional support staff with knowledge specific to the occasion. Military means may be useful in the short term for checking a particular conflict, but only political solutions achieved through negotiations offer hope of putting a definitive end to a conflict—and to do so without an intervening disaster.

The Mediation Support Unit is designed to be a locus of expertise, best practice, and knowledge management on mediation-related activities world-wide. It serves the United Nations as a whole, regional and subregional organizations, and other peacemaking bodies.

The support takes a variety of forms, including organizing dialogue, workshops, and training for parties in conflict; researching and advising on substantive and technical issues (for example, border demarcation); structuring cessation of hostilities agreements; encouraging civil society participation, amnesty provisions, minority rights, confidence-building measures, and natural resource sharing; implementing peace agreements and other matters; participating in peace talks in an advisory capacity, on a short-notice standby basis if necessary; funding and participating in fact-finding and mediation missions; and identifying, deploying, and funding external experts.

An established roster of experts can be called upon regularly, and they can link with skillful external resources. This unit also identifies accomplished mediators who have served in the past and who agree to provide advice on an ad hoc, even if short-term, basis—though longer-term availability is preferable. It has mobilized donors and created partnerships with training institutions to illuminate general mediation techniques, as well as more specialized aspects of mediation. All the training courses are open to the UN system and to partners in regional and subregional organizations.

Indeed, the secretary-general submitted a special report to the Security Council in April 2009 on enhancing mediation and its support activities. The report covers the experience of the United Nations and regional organizations in mediation. It deals with such crucial topics as resolving disputes in a *timely* manner, establishing a lead actor, selecting the most appropriate mediator/mediation team, engaging the parties *early*, structuring mediation to address the root causes of conflict, managing spoilers, accommodating peace and justice, mediating throughout implementation, providing mediation support for difficult groups, building *regional* capacity for mediation, and strengthening national/local capacity for conflict prevention/resolution—in essence, capacity-building for peaceful development, an approach that in the long run can offer powerful initiatives. Such work need not be limited to the United Nations.

EDUCATION OF POLITICAL LEADERS FOR PREVENTION

Education for *preventing* mass violence should include governmental and political leaders as well as civil service and foreign service officers. They have potentially heavy responsibilities in this sphere. They need to prepare for early warning and early action through interdisciplinary, international cooperation.

We reiterate a novel example of what can be done: the Aspen Institute Congressional Program, established on behalf of the Carnegie Corporation, a nongovernmental, nonpartisan educational program for members of the US Congress. It provides strong factual basis for understanding critical public policy issues by convening high-level conferences in which legislators from both US political parties and both houses of Congress are brought together with internationally recognized independent experts and other highly respected leaders. From 1983 onward, this work extended to include European parliaments and then members of the Russian Duma. Its focus was reducing the nuclear danger and finding paths out of the Cold War. There are many examples of useful influences of these meetings: preparation, participation, follow–up, and continuing relations among participants in a problem-solving mode and feedback loops to presidents and prime ministers. Such meetings could be extended regionally and in due course extended globally by the community of established democracies.

INTERNATIONAL CENTERS FOR THE PREVENTION OF MASS VIOLENCE

Early warning is valuable. The UN, the European Union, and some democracies provide examples of building pillars of prevention of mass violence. Together with an international coalition of democracies, a broad-based network intensely focused on preventing mass violence could create a critical mass of knowledge and skill by assembling a permanent core of professional staff drawn from scientists, scholars, diplomats, lawyers, political and military leaders, and specialists in the fields of conflict resolution and violence prevention. It could collect and constantly update reliable information from all sources about circumstances in troubled countries or regions that would predispose them to violence. It could monitor these potential conflict situations, especially in "hot spots" (and even "warm spots") where threats of mass violence are emerging. It could also establish an *integrated warning-response system* in which experts would analyze and evaluate early warning indicators of human rights violations. It would then link them to a full array of constructive responsive options, based on its reservoir of knowledge and skill in prevention. This approach fosters over time a network of cooperating regional organizations—including the EU, the Organization for Security and Co-operation in Europe, the North Atlantic Treaty Organization (NATO), the African Union, the Organization of American States, and the Association of Southeast Asian Nations—that use the centers' intellectual and moral resources and aid each other in the process of proactive help.

COMMUNITY OF ESTABLISHED DEMOCRACIES

Established democracies have special responsibilities concerning these critical issues, both within and outside international organizations. They can influence cooperating states and organizations to make their development aid, trade agreements, investment transactions, and other incentives conditional on the recipient's commitment to promoting education for early and ongoing conflict resolution, overcoming prejudice, and preventing mass violence in order to change norms away from violent pseudo-solutions. They can emphasize the role of *superordinate goals*: that is, *mutual aid for mutual benefit.*

This orientation facilitates cooperative networks of like-minded institutions of civil society—especially scientific and scholarly communities; educational and religious organizations; businesses; the media; and NGOs oriented to promoting democracy, human rights, intergroup tolerance, and equitable development. It offers training to people already engaged in, or preparing to enter, professional positions in national or international bodies likely to be involved in prevention of mass violence, with the goal of building a worldwide cadre of professionals who will make such prevention an integral part of their work. This would include development and distribution of textbooks, curricula, and documentaries, as well as constructive use of the Internet. Training in mediation, negotiation, and intergroup accommodation can have a high priority. Grants to universities and research institutes to support research on factors that cause, exacerbate, mitigate, and prevent mass violence would be helpful.

Above all, the community of established democracies must get its act together, preferably with the creative and cooperative participation of the United States. That can be done only if the democracies are able to relate to others on a basis of mutual respect and genuine collaboration. It means sustained help in building political and economic institutions of democracy. Collaboration can be done in a way that is sensitive to cultural traditions and regional circumstances.

As a practical matter, international cooperation is essential to ensure the pooling of strengths can provide adequate financial, technical, and human resources to help the process of socioeconomic development over decades, working toward a responsibly regulated market economy and fully open society.

The democracies working together can build capacity for nonviolent conflict resolution in economic matters and in relations between ethnic and religious groups. This is feasible when most people in a society feel that they have decent life chances: when they are not oppressed; have their basic needs met for child and adolescent development; and live in a social environment conducive to hope, physical security, and a reliable standard of living.

For many of the world's people, democracy is not just a new political system but also a new way of life. Citizens of oppressive regimes operate in a closed, stifling environment, without the experience of publicly sharing opinions

on political matters or learning the arts of compromise and mutual accommodation among ethnic, religious, and political groups. All this takes time,
solid advice, and security on the ground. Representative government brings
with it freedoms and responsibilities that are unforeseen by newly liberated
peoples, and democracy cannot prosper without the responsible use of these
freedoms on an individual and a local level. Friends of transitioning nations
must help newly free citizens to realize the full benefits of the democratic
way of life and ways of decently taking advantage of their unprecedented
opportunities. Helpful outsiders can foster modes of compromise and learning to value cooperation for mutual benefit. This approach is pertinent to
the difficult Arab Spring and to the emerging, struggling post-Communist
countries of Eastern Europe and parts of Asia.

NGOs AND EARLY PREVENTION

Such groups as the Center for Humanitarian Dialogue, the Nuclear Threat
Initiative, the Crisis Management Initiative, and the Carter Center are part of
an array of nongovernmental organizations around the world working to build
peace at every stage of the conflict process, from *early prevention* through later
phases. They operate across a range of peace and security issues, from preventing
sexual violence, to fostering sustainable communities, to working with industry
to prevent the spread of conflict minerals such as diamonds, to promoting
human rights everywhere. They are developing partnerships with public and
private entities to strive for sustainability of their efforts. Governments are
becoming more skillful at working with many NGOs to promote peace and
security, with special attention to early prevention as opportunities to help in
conflict resolution arise. These organizations at their best are not threatening
to different groups or nations. They have the flexibility to move quickly into
situations of emerging danger and to work side by side with potential adversaries even over long times if necessary to move toward mutual accommodation.

CRUCIAL ELEMENTS OF PREVENTIVE DIPLOMACY

In the past several decades, scholars have undertaken a wide range of inquiry
having to do with real-world negotiation in a variety of settings as well as

experimental studies on simulated negotiation—and links between the two.[4] A problem-solving orientation is useful rather than putting down the adversary or rigidly adhering to egocentric/ethnocentric positions. To implement this approach, mediators and negotiators need extensive knowledge of the situation in conflict, including its social context, and creative thinking about different ways in which the parts might fit together. Negotiators need to guard against premature closure; commitment to a single royal road to virtue; an assumption that there is necessarily a fixed pie that must be carved up; and leaving the solution of the adversaries' problem to the adversaries alone, even though they have the prime responsibility.

Overall, the financial and human costs of early preventive action are likely to be much lower than those of putting Humpty-Dumpty together again after he has been smashed. The Carnegie studies converge on key points of success in preventive diplomacy. They send a to-whom-it-may-concern message to the international community: governments, intergovernmental organizations, nongovernmental organizations oriented to peace and justice, and leaders in different sectors. Some recurrent elements of the preventive diplomacy message emerging from worldwide research and experience are reiterated here because of their importance in preventing mass violence. What do these in-depth studies recommend?

Recognize dangers *early*; beware of wishful thinking. Get the *facts straight* from multiple credible sources, including the history and culture of a particular latent or emerging conflict. *Pool strengths*; share burdens; and divide labor among entities with the capacity, salience, and motivation to be helpful. Foster widespread *public understanding* of conflict resolution and violence prevention. This gives a basis for hope of just settlement. Offer mediation early; a fair-minded third party with legitimacy can facilitate problem-solving by adversaries. Formulate *superordinate goals*—a recurrent essential theme in this book—that is, goals highly desirable to both adversarial groups that they can only obtain by cooperation. Use *economic leverage*: what can be gained by peaceful settlement, and what can be lost by violence? Clarify incentives for conflict resolution. Support moderate, pragmatic local leaders, including emerging leaders, especially democratic reformers. Buffer their precarious position. Bear in mind the pervasive need of negotiators and their constituencies for respect and dignity. Help negotiators strengthen the cooperation among the constituencies within their own group. Maintain an attitude of shared humanity and possibilities for mutual accommodation. Upgrade preparation for preventive diplomacy in relevant entities—for example, governments, the UN, regional organizations; established dedicated units for preventive diplomacy that combine knowledge and skill in early conflict resolution and knowledge of the region; specific training for staff, updated in light of ongoing worldwide experience and research; and a roster of experts on call for leadership organizations such as the UN, the EU, and democratic governments. Ubiquitous human conflicts largely can be resolved high on the slippery slope that might otherwise lead to mass violence.

FOUR

DEMOCRACY AND PEACE

Preventing Mass Violence with Best Civic Practices

So what does democracy do? First of all, democracy provides a set of rules of the game that institutionalize peaceful competition over policies, over resources, over opportunities to lead . . . that ensure that there's going to be a repeated game in which over time the opportunity to lead and to pursue an alternative set of policies or different distribution of resources will be open . . . so there can be circulation of a lead, circulation of a power, in a sense kind of a circulation of policies. If people get the sense that there's no hope for them to achieve what they want by peaceful means, that the avenues of peaceful, lawful, in a democratic sense constitutional competition and pursuit of their interests are closed to them, they are much more likely to use violent means. They are much more likely to take this feeling of exclusion and develop a sense of deep enmity and resentment that there is some "other" out there— some other group, some other set of elites that are responsible for their exclusion—and to feel that their grievance can only be relieved by some violent means.
—**Larry Diamond**, *Stanford University, from Eric Hamburg/Rick English documentary* Preventing Genocide, *2009, Stanford University Library*

The attitudes, beliefs, and procedures typical of democracies are valuable in dealing with intergroup conflict at all levels, within or beyond state borders. These include informal dialogues, third-party mediation, and organized negotiation between hostile groups; at least moderate tolerance and respect for the viewpoints of other people; and agreement on the practical value of mutual accommodation.

Democracies, whatever their faults, certainly protect human rights better than nondemocratic societies. Fairly elected leaders are much less likely to engage in large-scale, egregious human rights violations that create intense fear, severe resentment, and a desire for revenge that leads to massive violence as the only way to redress grievances.

PRINCIPLES OF DEMOCRACY

A preference for democracy is not a sentimental matter. It is a set of opportunities for humanity. The basic principles of democracy are attractive all over the world, even though entrenched autocratic powers resist them. Professor Robert Dahl of Yale, a leading scholar on democratic governance, points out some of its principal advantages.[1]

Democracy offers defenses against vicious autocrats. It guarantees fundamental rights that other political systems do not grant. It ensures a broader range of personal freedom than any feasible alternative. It provides ways for citizens to protect their fundamental interests. It provides the fullest possible exercise of self-determination as compared with all other systems—that is, freedom to choose the laws under which one lives. It encourages the exercise of moral responsibility. It fosters human development more fully than any existing alternative. It encourages political equality, despite large financial disparities. It has built-in checks that deter modern representative democracies from warring with each other. It has a relatively free economy that strives to generate widely shared prosperity even in the face of formidable obstacles. All of this is very difficult at times—especially ways of coping with undue concentration of wealth and power, ways to overcome large disparities that are damaging in various ways. We suffered through this in the Great Depression of the 1920s–1930s and again in the Great Recession of the 2000s. Tools of democracy help to overcome these serious obstacles, though often too slowly.

All democracies seek systematic, fair procedures of governance that are based on the consent of the governed. A system of representation is essential, but no single kind will work for every group. Around the world many different arrangements for democratic representation exist—parliamentary or presidential, centralized or federal, single-member districts or districts with proportional representation, the requirement of exceptional majorities for certain purposes perceived as particularly vital, plebiscites for constitutional change, and special arrangements to protect the rights of vulnerable minorities. These variations share the common themes of seeking *fairness*, *widespread participation*, and *broad involvement in decisions* important to the lives of the population.[2]

PROBLEMS OF DEMOCRACY

Nevertheless, many obstacles stand in the way of sustaining well-functioning democracies. Even with the fundamental advantages they possess, democracies remain imperfect and require constant vigilance and ongoing adjustments to avoid erosion of democratic values and practices. The need to raise large sums of money in order to conduct modern, media-based campaigns besets a growing number of democratic states. The persistence of prejudice in one form or another impedes democracy in every society. Freedom of speech, crucial as it is, can tragically be converted to hate speech or ruthless, unscrupulous election tactics. Powerful special interest groups can damage the democratic process. The inability of some parliamentary systems to form governing coalitions can make pluralism unworkable. Even the oldest and most powerful democracies require vigilance in maintaining authentic democracy—nonviolent struggle to uphold the basic values and decent practices. This emphasizes the continuing need to readjust the balance of power among the elements of the society, especially the balance between majority rule and protection of minorities as well as between rich and poor.

PROSPECTS OF DEMOCRACY

A highly centralized, command economy is not compatible with true democracy. There is simply too much power concentrated in a government that employs everyone, controls all resources, and can readily abuse human rights. Much the same is true of private concentrated wealth and power. Pluralism is at the heart of a lasting democracy; it permits and fosters the dynamic interplay of ideas and enterprises by parties and by a great variety of nongovernmental organizations on the basis of reasonably clear, agreed-upon rules—rules that reflect a fundamental attitude of social tolerance and mutual respect among individuals and groups, as well as commitment to human rights in practice.

Democracies with strong market economies operate best when they guarantee safety nets for the seriously disadvantaged and make public arrangements for such vital human requirements as education, health care, and the protection of public health, as well as unemployment insurance. They employ progressive taxation in the interest of public fairness and foster equality of opportunity. Indeed, almost all modern democracies make deliberate efforts, however imperfect, to balance market efficiency with social justice.

Civil society bolsters democracy by giving a practical demonstration of how democratic values evolve through nonviolent disputes. Groups compete with each other and with the state for achieving a better future and the power to carry out specific agendas. Civil society creates coalitions of individuals that initiate valuable political activities in the service of equal opportunity, protection of human rights, and pathways to equitable development. Political parties are crucial components of civil society; they are vital mediating institutions between the citizenry and the state. They avoid bigotry, dogmatism, and all fanatical actions. This requires public understanding of the dangers that interfere with fair, national problem-solving. These norms can be reinforced in many ways, not least through the educational system and the media.

DEMOCRACY AND INTERNATIONAL COOPERATION

The established democracies, overcoming many obstacles, have learned lessons from the hatred and dreadful violence of the twentieth century and are seeking to expand the opportunities for better human relations, internally and externally. This impulse to fulfill the promise of democracy with informed, proactive, sustained efforts to prevent deadly conflict through just solutions and improved quality of life is not easy. What will come of the Arab Spring of 2011? The cry is for democracy and also a cry for help. Remember the Weimar Republic when the emerging post–World War I German democracy was treated shabbily by the existing democracies? Its failure paved the way for Hitler.

Can the international community of democracies formulate a decent minimum of democratic facilitation for most countries? A worldwide democratic orientation would mean a vigorous, sustained effort through the media, formal educational systems, social media, and popular movements to educate publics about the essential democratic experiences. What attitudes, practices, and institutions are vital for the emergence of a vibrant democracy? How can the international community make them widely known and understood? The vaguely formulated aspiration for democracy that has swept the world in recent decades can lead to the reality of democracy—not quickly or easily but with great potential.

Those nations that have well-established, clear-cut democracies include most of the nations of the world that are strongest economically, militarily, scientifically, and technologically—not to mention most successful in protecting human rights and preserving decent human relations. This fortunate community has a moral imperative to facilitate democratization around the world—in a systematic, deliberate, long-term empathetic way. Their own differences make it apparent that they cannot adopt a rigid approach but rather one that considers historical circumstances, cultural traditions, and human ingenuity in democratic governance. New media are not just exciting and inspiring but practical in their potential to efficiently disseminate democratic ideals and processes.

Although governments certainly have a major role to play, efforts to spread democracy are not purely governmental. They can usefully draw upon intergovernmental and international institutions as well as nongovernmental organizations. The more international cooperation, the better for knowledge, skills, and solidarity.

What are the most useful means for promoting democracy? In the case of new, emerging, and fragile democracies, it is valuable to strengthen the sense of mutual responsibility. This involves technical assistance, long-term solidarity, and financial aid to build the requisite processes and institutions, including widespread education of the public about the actual working of democracy. Building the means to conduct elections at both the national and local levels along with the establishment of legislative bodies at those levels is a good start—but not enough. Preparation, implementation, and follow-up of elections are crucial. The vote itself is central but only the end of the beginning.

Cooperative international efforts include the rule of law, embodied in an explicit legal framework. This includes an *authentic democratic constitution*, an independent judiciary with real capacity for interpreting laws fairly, along with oversight institutions to provide for public accountability. It is essential to create high-integrity public administration of a professional nature that *minimizes corruption*. Civilian institutional capacities can be created to analyze security questions, both within and beyond the borders of the country, to have civil/military relations that buffer aggressive tendencies while maintaining responsible military strength. Special measures to protect individual human rights, minority groups, and vulnerable sectors can evolve, including early, ongoing mechanisms to deal with conflict that are effective in preventing violence and accepted as striving for fairness to all. Intellectual strength on these matters is essential and calls for cooperation among universities and research institutes in various countries, linked to aspiring democracies on a consistent basis at least in the early years.

Toward these ends, it is useful for the democratic community to establish, preferably in joint efforts for practical sustainability, special funds for economic assistance that will be used to strengthen emerging democracies. But money is not enough: technical and organizational help is needed, and norms of decency between groups need strengthening. These various forms of respectful assistance must be sustained over a period of years to support the complex processes of building a democracy.[3] This means strong multilateral ties among the helping countries and organizations—pooling resources in various ways and sharing necessary assets.

ELECTION MONITORING AND DEMOCRACY

A remarkable step that is largely a product of the 1990s is the international monitoring of election campaigns—their *preparation, conduct,* and *aftermath*— to guarantee that they are not an empty show of democracy. Democratic governments, the UN, regional organizations, and NGOs have all contributed here and are strengthening their capacities to help.

With former president Carter's leadership, the Carter Center has been a pioneer in election monitoring. One major aim of these initiatives is to encourage a genuinely inclusive process for drafting a permanent constitution. To this end, the Carter Center objectively observes and comments constructively on the processes of political transition. Carter Center reports benefit other democracy initiatives such as local advocacy groups and international technical support initiatives. These efforts foster informed dialogue and encourage the development of a state with democratic values of *inclusiveness* at its core. The first year of an aspiring democracy is crucial. The Carter Center's continued presence as a neutral observation body to monitor the transition is valuable. It points the way to necessary international cooperation to help in building democracy.

The center's *collaborative* activities with an aspiring democracy provide a credible and impartial assessment of the political transition, promoting understanding among key domestic and international stakeholders and the public at large. It clarifies the successes and shortcomings of the political transition, informs challenges of the political transition, encourages resolution of issues through transparent measures, and provides recommendations that demonstrate international interest and support for sustainable peace and democracy. These methods have been applied on several continents in a cooperative spirit.

Standards for monitoring elections are emerging and shared internationally. But the advance preparation for elections is also very important, as was the case in South Africa after Nelson Mandela's release from prison. Communities and organizations need practice in working out compromises, understanding each other, clarifying their shared needs, and understanding what they want, but that can only be achieved through cooperation. Nonviolent joint problem-solving is rewarding—economically, politically, and psychologically. All this can be facilitated not only by the experience of advanced, established democracies but also by peer learning through the similar experiences of recently emerging democracies.

FOSTERING DEMOCRACY AFTER REPRESSION: THE CASE OF SOUTH AFRICA

A novel initiative contributing to the end of apartheid in South Africa was the Carnegie Inquiry into Poverty and Development in Southern Africa. Based at the University of Cape Town throughout the 1980s, it was directed by Dr. Francis Wilson, a distinguished labor economist, joined in due course by Dr. Mamphela Ramphele, who had been banished to a concentration camp by the South African government for her close association with Steve Biko, a hero of the freedom struggle. After we organized a senior group of Carnegie people who visited the "resettlement" camp where she was held (essentially imprisoned), the government lifted her banishment. At our urging, she was allowed to return to the University of Cape Town, but only in a minor position at first. With her great ability, she joined Wilson as codirector after a while and, in a dramatic turn of events, became the vice-chancellor of the University of Cape Town in 1996. Archbishop Desmond Tutu, who had called Ramphele to my attention, chaired the Carnegie Task Force on Religion and Poverty and provided wise guidance for the whole enterprise: the Carnegie Inquiry into Poverty and Development in Southern Africa. Many brilliant, courageous South Africans from all social backgrounds also contributed to the effort for equality of opportunity, the rule of law, and nonviolent conflict resolution in building democratic institutions. Ramphele was a symbol in the world of the regime's oppression of blacks and women and later became a major official on health and development at the World Bank.

The inquiry was unprecedented in its inclusion of persons from all sectors and races in South Africa. It drew upon the knowledge and research of a network of scholars and professionals in law, medicine, economics, religion, and other fields throughout the country, as well as community leaders, teachers, and social workers with firsthand knowledge of poverty at the local level. Twenty universities in the region participated in the study; it was a rare opportunity at that time to train black South Africans in research and leadership skills. Poverty was studied in relationship to land use, law, food and nutrition, health care, education and training, transport, housing, social welfare, and other quality-of-life indicators. It was also studied for its effects upon families, migrant workers, women, children, and the elderly. Overshadowing all else was the impact of apartheid. The inquiry made many practical recommendations to overcome *human impoverishment*, by which I mean not only low income but also harsh disrespect. Fundamentally, the inquiry focused on opening the doors of opportunity in the context of human rights, seeking ways to improve health and strengthen education for the oppressed.

Professional publications, international meetings, and media coverage—even a traveling photographic exhibit—were used to disseminate the inquiry's findings and practical recommendations widely. The recommendations as outlined above became influential in South Africa, Europe, and the United States, and their aspirations were fulfilled when Nelson Mandela was freed and democratic development ensued. Desmond Tutu, then and now, has personally been a source of inspiration (for me as he has been for so many others) throughout the world in the continuing promotion of democratic development.

The example of South Africa is important for several reasons. One is its status as a worldwide symbol of prejudice and ethnocentrism, as well as its emotionally charged efforts at democratic reform and conflict resolution. The Carnegie experience in South Africa shows the value of nongovernmental institutions in pursuit of peace and justice—and of disseminating throughout the world the lessons learned in that pursuit. There was much benefit from "depth on the bench" of leadership for nonviolent, democratic negotiations at the community level as well as at the highest levels. The leaders consistently pursued policies of fairness and reconciliation, not revenge.

NGO/GOVERNMENT COLLABORATION
IN VIOLENCE PREVENTION

In the early years of the twenty-first century, I undertook both a synthesis and an extension of the work on the prevention of mass violence, based now at the Weill Cornell Medical Center in New York. One strand was to help the Swedish government plan a pan-European conference of heads of state and government on prevention of genocide in January 2004.

Sweden was the first government to appreciate the significance of the Carnegie Commission on Preventing Deadly Conflict. They saw its implications for their own government and for the European Union. Similarly, Kofi Annan was the first leader of an international organization to see the wider significance, in this case for the UN. Thus, I had the good fortune to make many presentations at meetings of UN and EU activities as well as Swedish governmental and nongovernmental units. Much of this work led cooperative activities and durable prevention efforts over several years. Collaboration and friendship among people with deep commitment to humane, democratic, problem-solving values and openness to ideas for implementation— these are a vital part of the opportunity in all these matters of prevention. The democracy-building agenda is a difficult one because movement on it requires education of the general public of democratic countries as well as various sectors—scientific, policy, business, religious, media, and friendship networks— all the while stimulating better ideas and building institutional strengths.

An important example of conflict-oriented NGOs is provided by the Project on Ethnic Relations (PER). It is dedicated to reducing interethnic tensions in a region that has seen some of the most violent, intractable, and destructive conflict since the end of the Cold War. PER's neighborhood encompasses the culturally and politically diverse space of the former Communist bloc—from Russia and the Baltics through Central and Eastern Europe and the Balkans. But PER deals with a universal problem: how to temper the powerful emotions of ethnic identity with the political self-restraint that is essential to democracy.

With the support of the Carnegie Corporation and its active involvement, PER was founded in 1991 by Allen Kassof, who had a distinguished record as the founding director of International Research and Exchange (IREX), which fostered exchanges of scholars between East and West during the Cold War. His excellent deputy, Livia Plaks, was very helpful with languages, history, culture, and conflict resolution. PER provides an excellent example of how imaginative, persistent intervention by a small NGO can achieve significant and practical results. PER has the unusual attribute of combining direct involvement as mediator at the highest political level with work in community settings. PER's experience shows that with insight, patience, and durability, it is possible to modify the behavior of antagonists even in intense, historically rooted ethnic disputes. Yet the international community is weak in supporting such organizations financially.

Those who would encourage interethnic coexistence must find the means to dissuade or prevent political leaders from fomenting or exploiting ethnic tensions. Toward this end, PER has developed relationships with political and other leaders throughout the region. PER's flagship mediation efforts require intensive and continuous networking with the leaders on both sides of interethnic disputes—for example, Hungary and Romania. This is the single most time-consuming activity of PER's Princeton-based president and its executive director Plaks, who moved up to president when Kassof retired. She faces the ubiquitous problem of adequate funding for NGOs in the conflict-resolution world, but she has the advantage of excellent knowledge of key leaders in Eastern Europe.

PER convenes and chairs roundtables for the antagonists, sometimes in their own countries, but sometimes in neutral locations, usually Switzerland and occasionally the United States. Many of the roundtables draw senior participants/observers from the US government, NATO, the European Union, Organization for Security and Co-operation in Europe, and the Council of Europe. Although the roundtables are informal dialogues, in practice they can serve as venues for major negotiations.

Although high-level women politicians were always present at the PER roundtables for the entire period of our twenty-plus years of activities, in 2004, with a generous grant from the US Department of State, PER undertook a special effort to bring to the table a group of women from the governments and parliaments in the Balkans to discuss the issue of how to prevent ethnic conflicts and how their role could be made more important in this field. The discussion, which took place in Tirana, Albania, was a real eye-opener. The women who came to the table first said that they were not at all like their male counterparts and would not fight about ethnic relations, but within minutes of starting the discussion were in conflict across ethnic lines. At the end of two days, they were much more concerned about issues related to women and how they could help each other overcome obstacles in their countries to make more of a mark in the political system. Based on this emerging success, PER invited some of the women to Slovenia to write a short policy analysis from the point of view of women in the specific countries, how they see the interethnic dialogue, and what could be done to improve relations between communities. All of this information is available on the website www.per-usa .org under the label "Women in Governance and Interethnic Relations."

DEMOCRACY AS CONFLICT RESOLUTION

Democracy at its best has institutional mechanisms to cope with conflict in early, ongoing ways. Generally accepted rules are updated periodically by common consent. Its explicit concern for the dignity of individuals and protection of basic human rights makes it attractive to virtually all cultures, provided they understand individual dignity and basic human rights, and here again we see the importance of education.

Nongovernmental organizations have increasingly engaged in using democratic principles and mechanisms to help nations on the precipice deal with conflicts within their borders, particularly those arising from the resurgence of old, lingering prejudices and the political exploitation of ethnic nationalism. Democratization was at the core of virtually all the comprehensive peace settlements in which the UN has usefully participated in recent years. Although each region has its own legacy of cultures, languages, and religions, fundamental democratic principles, applied in ways that fit local circumstances, are useful everywhere in resolving intergroup conflicts and preventing their escalation to violence.

Preventing mass violence in societies that have been harshly constrained by authoritarian regimes also calls for the development and spread of strong civic organizations—another element crucial to enduring democratic governance. This takes decades, perhaps even generations, and requires both homegrown work at the grassroots level and collaboration with corresponding groups from countries with solid democratic experience. The public of previously nondemocratic countries learns what is involved in democracy: its rights, responsibilities, opportunities, and institutions. The community of established democracies can engage in high-level collaboration to stimulate the development of parties, parliaments, and responsible leadership to ensure a stable democracy in which a broad range of citizens participate actively in important decisions.[4]

In the short run, democratic transitions require frequent, and often informal, mediation by impartial outside parties to help contending groups acquire the ability and decency to reach common ground. It is particularly important for mediators to guide opponents toward developing a shared consensus about practical procedures to resolve difficult problems, and then to move toward creating institutions that give all citizens reliable access to those procedures. Antagonists can be persuaded that cooperation will lead to greater benefits in the long run, and that superordinate goals of compelling value to adversaries can be achieved only by cooperation. The successful examples of other countries and regions can provide emerging leaders with site visits and respectful meetings to engage in *peer learning* about coping with similar experiences.

Multiethnic societies can sometimes manage intergroup relations and maintain social cohesion by simple majority rule. But such democracy is difficult in societies with deep ethnic divisions and little experience with inclusive self-government. These conditions can lead divisive political leaders to bring about voting along strictly ethnic lines and so a tyranny of the majority. A better choice in such societies may well be the adoption of mutually agreed-upon power-sharing arrangements that encourage broad-based governing coalitions.

In the Carnegie Commission on Preventing Deadly Conflict, we were eager to explore options for various paths to democracy. Timothy Sisk, a scholar in democratic engineering, showed that power-sharing arrangements are most likely to succeed when a critical number of moderate political leaders, genuinely representative of the groups they claim to lead, agree to embrace pluralism and guarantee equitable distribution of resources. Over time, such measures of power sharing can move toward a more integrative and liberal form of democracy, especially with respected international help.[5] This process can decrease the chance of intergroup violence.

DEMOCRACY, POVERTY, AND POLITICAL IMPROVEMENT

The content and process of democracy building vary immensely. But one common feature is closely related to development, as noted in the next chapter. Those interested in promoting democracy and development try to help the recipient country's accountability to its poor. Elected governments can achieve the first step of such accountability. Democratic systems have this powerful long-run advantage in development: they can effectively encourage citizens' participation in policy formulation and implementation and are therefore likely to be responsive to citizens' needs. Because the very poor are so numerous and at the same time so susceptible to disease, malnutrition, violence, and social pathologies, the promise that democracy building holds for bettering their condition is a strong argument for making it an essential building block of socioeconomic development. Toward a humane and peaceful world, there must be intimate linkage of democracy and development.

UPS AND DOWNS: OVERCOMING SLIPPAGE

Professor Larry Diamond of Stanford, one of the world's leading scholars of democratic transitions, points out that since 1974, democracy has struggled through several phases. After the widespread trend toward democracy in the late 1970s and early 1980s, the democratic transitions became stronger and reached a climax with the collapse of communism in Eastern Europe and the former Soviet Union. Can the emerging democracies remain democracies, and can they achieve a level of democracy that their people truly value?

Many of the new democracies performed poorly, hardly justifying democratic status. Even with serious competitive elections, and sometimes peaceful shifts in power, much disappointment ensued. What most citizens actually experienced was a mix of abusive police forces, domineering local oligarchies, incompetent state bureaucracies, corrupt judiciaries, and harsh ruling elites.

Yet there are real democracies and regional neighborhoods where democracy is growing, even flourishing—in Latin America, South and Southeast Asia, and parts of Africa. Among the Arab states, Morocco is a good place to negotiate the path to democracy, and the Arab Spring in 2011 opened major new possibilities despite exceedingly harsh repressive behavior of established rulers, as we have seen in Libya and Syria.

The prospect for resurgence of democracy will depend primarily on three factors. The first is gradual economic development that lifts levels of education and information, offers real autonomy to citizens, promotes civic organization, and offers an authentic basis for hope of shared prosperity for the next generation. The second is the gradual integration of countries into a global economy, society, and political order in which democracy is a highly valued norm and the most attractive political system for general populations—one that delivers tangibly on improving quality of life.

The third factor is whether democracy takes deeper root where it has already sprouted. This has intrinsic value and also encourages neighbors and peers. The new democracies of recent decades must solve problems and meet citizens' expectations for freedom, a fair society, and widely shared prosperity—at least on the horizon. The whole society can come to believe in the norms of a democratic constitution, as is largely the case in South Africa. Thus, the strong, established democracies reach out in friendship, develop a cooperative agenda for reform, and strengthen their own institutions for democracy promotion, at home and abroad. This is not democracy at the point of a gun; not premature, unprepared elections without experience in compromise and mutual accommodation among political and other groups; and not walking away. Elections are crucial but not enough. They require serious preparation, monitoring, and follow-up. This in turn requires strong international cooperation for genuine helpfulness. In the long run, genuine democracy requires opportunity and fairness in both the economic and political domains.

All too often, predatory societies have no shared commitment to the public good, and no respect for law. Those who capture political power tend to monopolize it and derive benefits at the expense of ordinary citizens. The rich forcefully derive wealth from the poor, neglect public goods, and establish norms of corruption. The rank and file have little opportunity to move ahead toward better lives. This trend is conducive sooner or later to mass violence and is morally unacceptable. It is not only grossly unfair but very dangerous.

The advance of democracy and widely shared prosperity crucially involves restraining the abuse of power, opening up access to political and economic opportunities, and constraining the predatory tendencies by fair, impartial rules and institutions. Major innovations are necessary to make this possible— variations on cultural themes in light of history. Relations of mutual trust and cooperation must be constructed, moving across ethnic, regional, political, religious, and national divisions. Personal repressive rule must be restrained in the context of a vigorous civil society with independent organizations, open media, intellectual centers, and norms of mutual aid for mutual benefit. Sustained support of the international community is vital for such achievements.

HARD CASES

Russia is a special case especially because of its nuclear and bacteriological power and its long authoritarian traditions. The democratic reforms so remarkable under Gorbachev have eroded to a considerable extent—yet some democratic efforts persist, and in late 2011, visible opposition to Vladimir Putin's authoritarian tendencies became public. Russia's membership in the Council of Europe provides a significant opportunity to make that body a focal point for pro-democracy initiatives. In Moscow, the Gorbachev Foundation and the Carnegie Endowment for International Peace are useful for offering economic, political, social, and legal knowledge for pro-democracy initiatives; we have tried to help them over a good many years. Arms control efforts, in the spirit of the Nunn-Lugar Cooperative Threat Reduction Program, are singularly important in this regard, especially because they provide opportunity for mutually respectful discourse among influential people on pragmatic problem-solving that goes beyond weaponry.

The largest share of funds to support civil society in emerging democracies—however fragile—goes to NGOs, especially to the large human rights organizations. A typical arrangement involves a large international NGO working with a few promising human rights NGOs in a particular country or region. Much political aid is focused on basic human rights issues—opposition to torture, the death penalty, exclusionary hypernationalism. Comparatively little goes to broader political reform, even though human rights cannot be protected over the long term without solid democratic institutions.

BUILDING DEMOCRACY GOVERNMENT
TO GOVERNMENT

Within fifty years, it might well be possible to achieve a world in which every government is a democracy—not easy but doable. In a cross-cultural review of the world's areas, Diamond finds that most Muslims, similar to non-Muslims, support democracy. Democracy is now becoming a universal value of fundamental importance. The great strengths of the United States, the EU, Japan, Canada, South Korea, South Africa, Brazil, and others can provide powerful reinforcement for democratic behavior. Both individual nations and international organizations are now more seriously promoting democracy and challenging the sovereignty of authoritarian regimes that perpetrate or permit serious violations of human rights.

FOSTERING DEMOCRACY BY NONMILITARY MEANS

President Jimmy Carter launched a new and lasting emphasis on human rights in American foreign policy. It succeeded in pressuring a number of Latin American dictatorships to return power to elected civilians. President Reagan pressed for democratic transitions among American allies—the Philippines, Korea, and Chile. Thus, Carter and Reagan changed American foreign policy by establishing new and lasting institutions for promoting democracy and human rights. President George H. W. Bush (1989–1993) then further institutionalized democracy promotion by making it a major purpose in American foreign aid and solidifying the emerging democracies of Central and Eastern Europe. The case for promoting democracy is moral and very practical.

The established democracies have multiple instruments—diplomacy, aid conditionality, and sanctions—and all can pressure autocratic states to democratize and respect human rights. Some can be effectively applied by international democratic coalitions, as well as international or regional organizations. If necessary, external pressure can include economic ties (trade, investment, and credit); security ties (treaties and guarantees); social ties (tourism, immigration, overseas education, elite exchanges, NGOs); and religious institutions and democratic media.

By publicly documenting and denouncing human rights abuses in Latin America, and then coupling these denunciations with reductions in military and economic aid, President Carter and Cyrus Vance contained repression and accelerated momentum for democratic change in the region.

These policies were effective because they linked strong, moral positions with reductions in economic and military aid for human rights abuses. Similar events were highly significant in their impact on the apartheid regime in South Africa. Economic sanctions from the United States and Europe, as well as disinvestment by private corporations and institutions, intensified pressure on the apartheid regime and the white population in South Africa during the 1980s. When gold prices declined and domestic debt and inflation escalated, the result was severe economic deterioration and social isolation.

Political parties reflecting various interests get training on how to develop volunteer networks, campaign organizations, local branches, public opinion polling, and other practical measures. Thus, the world's democracies are trying to expand their community by helping aspiring democracies to develop their capacities.

CLUES TO DEMOCRATIC SUCCESS

In 1974, the overthrow of the dictatorship in Portugal began a rapid, worldwide expansion of democracy. By 1987, democracy had spread to nearly two-fifths of the world's states, although Eastern Europe, Africa, and the Middle East were still largely untouched. The fall of the Berlin Wall in 1989 and the collapse of the Soviet Union in 1991 changed the picture in Europe. Africa also began making a significant shift toward democracy with a 1990 "sovereign national conference" in Benin and the release of Nelson Mandela from prison in South Africa in 1994. By 1997, with strong pressure from external and internal donors, most African states allowed opposition parties some open space for civil society and free elections, though often limited in practice. But dangerous rulers like Omar al-Bashir in Sudan, Robert Mugabe in Zimbabwe, and both Laurent and Joseph Kabila in Congo resisted the trend. "Leaders" often precipitated violence by refusing to accept the results of election and/or by creating crooked elections—as in Kenya. Help is badly needed here and can be done in the way that Kofi Annan intervened with an excellent team of Kenyans and non-Kenyans.

Today nearly three-fifths of the world's states are democratic. Of the 125 states that became democracies in the 1990s, only fourteen have returned to authoritarian rule—and democracy resurfaced in nine of them.[6] Robert Dahl has noted a striking fact: if a modern democracy has lasted twenty years (one generation), it has an excellent chance of continued survival.[7] In principle, even the poorest of states have a chance to succeed in building a democracy. The fact that some of the world's most underdeveloped countries could achieve democracy is truly remarkable.

Amartya Sen, who won the 1998 Nobel Prize in economics in part by showing that democracies do not have famines, also demonstrated that impoverished peoples need to have a political voice and that democracy should not be thought of as a luxury only for the rich. Sen argues that something is of universal value if people all over the world have a reason to see it as valuable. Thus, democracy is indeed becoming a universal value.

There is little evidence that poor people would reject democracy if given the choice.[8] Surveys across cultures show that ordinary citizens everywhere value democracy. Democracy was the preferred form of government for two-thirds of the Africans surveyed by the 2001 Afrobarometer poll in twelve (mostly poor) countries.[9] Latin Americans have had time to become dissatisfied with the way democratic rule works in their own countries, yet 57 percent still find it preferable to an authoritarian regime. Only 15 percent believe a caudillo would serve them better.[10]

In 2001 in five countries of East Asia—Taiwan, Korea, Hong Kong, the Philippines, and Thailand—more than two-thirds of the population agreed that authoritarian rule should be replaced by democracy. The same is true for the ten formerly Soviet countries that have sought membership in the European Union.

Moderate Muslims, including intellectual leaders, promote a relatively liberal interpretation of Islam that downplays the literal meaning of holy texts. They emphasize the moral teachings of Islam that are compatible with such democratic ideals as accountability, freedom of expression, and the rule of law. Moderate Muslim religious leaders increasingly favor the separation of mosque and state.

The Arab Human Development Report of 2002 noted with regret that Arab states have largely failed to participate in the "global wave of democratization"[11] and insisted on the need of comprehensive political representation in effective legislatures to liberate human capabilities and make governance fully accountable.

The European Union joined the United States in the quest for democracy after the Cold War, working in post-Communist Europe with financial and organizational cooperation. All states that wanted to be a part of the EU and share in its prosperity were required to adopt truly democratic practices and respect for fundamental rights and freedoms. Over more than two decades, the EU has provided political and technical assistance to help these candidate states achieve free political and economic conditions. Membership in the EU, with its economic, political, and cultural advantages, depends on meeting these criteria. So adopting democratic policies and building democratic institutions have provided steps to peace and prosperity, a strong attraction for these states: a "magnet" effect.

The biggest transformation of recent years has been the focus on human rights and on democracy itself as a right for all people. It has become a world-wide norm that all countries seeking cooperation with other nations should adopt a democratic ideology—in other words, govern with the *consent of the governed*. At the very least, this progress has led to increased acceptance of democratically oriented intervention by friendly organizations and bolstered by internal advocates of human rights and democracy.

In today's world, about seventy countries still remain authoritarian. Professor Diamond examines the reasons, progressing from the least to the most common:

1. Dictators can claim the credit for rapid, recent economic prosperity under their authoritarian regime. Examples are Singapore, Malaysia, and in some ways China.
2. Dictatorial states that have large revenues from natural resources, such as oil or gold, and a fairly small population can buy off their people and/or support their internal structures of security and control. But even in these cases, the people show an eagerness to govern themselves, especially since the concentration of power is so readily abused.
3. Old Communist regimes persist through repression and isolation. Examples are Cuba, Vietnam, Laos, and North Korea. Even here we see that Vietnam is learning from China's gradual opening to the outside world, though China is a long way from democracy. As a region opens to the rewards of globalization, its citizens become better educated, and the international community offers both pressure and incentives, authoritarian control weakens. In 2012, Burma offers some basis for hope.

The chief impediment to the spread of democracy is not its rejection by the people but its rejection by their ruling elites, who have seized control of state structures and state resources. Dictatorships offer rulers total power and the accumulation of immense personal wealth that goes with it. Typically, these regimes rely heavily on outside assistance and loans because they are not willing to encourage a free economy that will generate internally the resources a government needs to survive. The international community must make its substantial aid conditional on humane, responsible, and increasingly democratic rule.

CAN IT BE DONE?

Democratization of the whole world is possible through international cooperation of governments and multilateral institutions. A respectful and inclusive manner of leadership by the established democracies working together can exert powerful influence. The time is ripe for concerted efforts toward global adoption of democracy, especially some near-term progress, but preparing for decades, even generations, of sustained, informed, and organized efforts. We must keep economic integration and growth alive as we encourage making freedom an important priority in our diplomatic and other international engagements— including development aid. Democracy is at the heart of this book because it involves the knowledge and skills to keep ubiquitous human conflict below the threshold of mass violence and to link peace with justice.

FIVE

---ﾐﾒ---

DEVELOPMENT AND PEACE

Fostering Socioeconomic Equality

The question is now that the challenges are political ones, not material ones. It's very interesting because you know I get asked all the time, "how do you prevent deadly conflict?" It's very interesting when they ask this question because it's predisposed. And I believe that the answers are complicated ones and of course it is: but I invariably respond, "You want to prevent deadly conflict? Educate young women, employ young men."...

Structural prevention was designed to put in place those kinds of deep-seated and long-lasting sorts of institutional and social forms that would give disputes a way to go, so people could manage the change that they were invariably confronting in relative peace.

—***Jane Holl Lute***, *Deputy Secretary, Department of Homeland Security,*
from Eric Hamburg/Rick English documentary
Preventing Genocide, *2009, Stanford University Library*

Democratic socioeconomic development on a worldwide basis offers humanity its best hope for producing conditions favorable to peaceful living, truly civilized relations, and mutual accommodation among rival groups—in short, for preventing war and mass atrocities.

This is a much more practical goal today than it was a few decades ago, even in the face of serious obstacles. Investment in human and social capital is now generally accepted as a central part of development, especially in promoting the health and education of girls and boys (and women and men) alike, thus making constructive use of the whole population. There are aspirations for a vigorous population that is well-informed, capable, fair-minded, intellectually curious, and mutually supportive in times of personal and social stress—also for social support networks in communities tackling their local problems constructively. The essential features of development—*knowledge, skills, freedom,* and *health*—can be achieved by sustained international cooperation—regional and global—that draws upon the unprecedented advances of modern science and technology.

HOW TO UNDERSTAND DEMOCRATIC DEVELOPMENT

Firmly grounding new democracies with fair-market economies requires decades or even generations so that their older and more established counterparts, chiefly those in the affluent West but also such recent democracies as Japan, India, and Brazil, are persistent and resourceful in working all over the world with democratic reformers dedicated to fairness in economic growth. The gradual increase of democratic and prosperous countries will reduce the likelihood of catastrophic wars and even genocide. Thus, considerations of socioeconomic development strongly overlap with our preceding discussion of democracy.

Development assistance, especially in the form of *capacity building* for meeting basic human needs through knowledge and skill, is crucial for very poor countries; their efforts to create decent living standards through development benefit from significant outside help that is not dominating but rather in the mode of *mutual problem-solving*. Fundamental, long-term solutions hinge on a state's own development policies, attentive to its society's particular economic and social opportunities and to careful management of its natural and human resources. They also hinge on developing the human assets to improve a society's quality of life, partly through international cooperation in adapting the world's knowledge, and on strengthening intellectual and technical resources.

Many nations in the Southern Hemisphere, those from the former Soviet bloc, and now in the Middle East have had difficulty in taking advantage of opportunities available for economic and social development. They are struggling to move away from repressive regimes, in the Middle East, as reflected in the massive protests of 2011 and 2012, and in Russia, having lost much of what was gained in the Gorbachev era. It is surely in the interest of more fortunate countries, near and far away, to facilitate the expansion of knowledge, skills, freedom, and health in these countries so they can become constructive members of the international community and less susceptible to social pathology, severe disease, and mass violence. A serious obstacle in some countries is egocentric, ethnocentric, brutal, and corrupt dictators. The "big man" or "permanent president" syndrome of poor governance and contempt for rule of law is a deadly internal enemy of development.

In this context, the Carnegie Commission on Prevention of Deadly Conflict emphasized that a country whose development does not include *broad participation* in the benefits of economic growth will be prone to violent conflict. Indeed, the intense resentment and unrest that grossly unequal economic distribution provokes can create a seedbed for hatred, bloodshed, and terrorism. This reinforces the case for offering poor countries international cooperation in political as well as economic development in the quest for new opportunities that meet basic human needs in a spirit of fairness and solidarity. Thus, we need not only to offer more economic aid but to do so in a way that diminishes the role of authoritarian "leaders."

During the 1990s, substantial efforts to understand how development occurred in the second half of the twentieth century resulted in a broader view of the development process that recognized the crucial importance of *human development*, and the firm link between *social and economic advances*. The human development reports of the United Nations Development Program (UNDP) in the early 1990s (under the remarkable leadership of Mahbub ul Haq, and with the eminent economist Amartya Sen as a major adviser) employed hard data and close, decades-long observation to make the case for the human factor in development.

Sen carried this approach further in his book, *Development as Freedom*, in which he emphasized the removal of major obstacles to freedom: poor economic opportunities due to systematic social deprivation, inadequate public services, social intolerance, tyranny, and state repression. In his 2006 book *Identity and Violence*, he clarified the importance of broad-based identities that overcome narrow, often hateful identities based on a single attribute that can violently disrupt development.

Analyses issuing from the World Bank reflect considerable agreement with this outlook. A series of important papers by Joseph Stiglitz (another Nobel Prize–winning economist, who in the 1990s was senior vice president of Development Economics and chief economist at the World Bank) examined the dramatic advances in much of the developing world during the last quarter century. But although remarkable gains in life expectancy and per capita annual incomes have occurred, significant regional differences exist, with sub-Saharan Africa lagging far behind. Stiglitz develops his analysis further in a new book on achieving fairness, hence broad prosperity, in better international trade. He notes approvingly that the European Union's "everything but arms" initiative has put a "human face" on globalization of trade in striving to grant the poorest countries free export into Europe of all goods except arms. Stiglitz recommends moving toward a new multilateralism. His visionary observations preceded the deep recession of the first decade of the 2000s.

He foresaw that the democracies should cooperate in designing a new coordinated global financial regulatory system, without which markets are at risk of fragmentation in an era of instability with profound economic weakness. Fundamentally, such cooperation strengthens the *international rule of law*, which makes economic progress possible.

In essence, Stiglitz implied several fundamental aims for economic advancement:

1. Widely shared prosperity;
2. Empathy and fairness in human relations;
3. Multilateral cooperation for an effective trading system; and
4. Moral commitment to decent human and environmental relations.

GOOD GOVERNANCE AND CONFLICT RESOLUTION

Good governance has recently emerged as a distinct component in development. What is it? First, the state must have the *capacity* to serve the public good, with a sound understanding of reasonable policies to accomplish that mission. To do the work, the state needs professional civil servants and state officials who are well prepared—often with international help—who follow established principles, and who are rewarded for doing so if they visibly *contribute to the public good.*

This commitment needs positive and negative reinforcements. It must be strengthened by institutions that penalize betrayals of the public trust and linked to *transparency* in the conduct of state affairs, providing freedom of information about how the government makes its decisions, conducts its business, and spends public money.

Transparency along with *accountability* enables society to monitor the responsibility of public officials. Thus, different institutions check and hold one another accountable, compelling them to justify their actions. Power is thus constrained, bound not only by legal constraints but also by public attention and concern. High levels of secrecy in government are invariably linked to abuse of power. A crucial hallmark of good governance is the *rule of law.* To achieve all of these criteria of good governance is very hard, but they must represent a level of aspiration for which democracies strive, keeping their own houses in order and using their influence externally to offer technical, organizational, and financial help in a friendly yet disciplined context.

An exceedingly important dimension of good governance is early, ongoing *conflict resolution*—with multiple mechanisms. Broad participation of diverse groups (and both sexes) is important here. Democratic development involves difficult choices in intergroup relations—the source of much potential trouble. What is in the public interest? A fair, ongoing process of dialogue among groups can help greatly to reconcile conflicting interests. A decent minimum of opportunity for all—moving in the direction of equal opportunity to the extent possible—makes for solidarity without intimidation in a diverse society—and most societies are more diverse than we usually recognize. Conflict resolution requires a general sense of fairness, justice, and transparency—and such resolution must be an early, ongoing process in democratic development.

In sum, when good governance of these dimensions—a sense of the public interest and decent human relations—takes place over years, it fosters *social capital*: associations that draw people together in relations of trust, reciprocity, and voluntary cooperation for common aims and mutual benefits. Thus, meeting these criteria is vital as the established democracies offer help to developing countries. They provide an enabling environment for economic growth, using the full range of talent in the society, both male and female.

HEALTH AND DEVELOPMENT

Health has been curiously neglected until recently in economic development efforts, as if it were a benefit to be achieved only in an advanced stage of development. But a healthy, vigorous population is essential to building a dynamic, equitable, growing economy. The benefits of globalization are potentially great, through increased exposure to new ideas; practical innovations; life-saving technologies; and efficient production processes, for example, access to effective medications and safer food. Yet these benefits are not yet reaching hundreds of millions of the world's poor.

Improving the health and longevity of the poor is a valuable end in itself, a fundamental goal of economic development. But it is also a *means* to achieving the other development goals. The links of health to poverty reduction and to long-term economic growth are powerful. A heavy burden of disease in low-income regions stands as a stark barrier to economic growth, and any comprehensive development strategy implies early, ongoing improvement.

The main causes of avoidable deaths in the low-income countries are HIV/AIDS, malaria, tuberculosis (TB), childhood infectious diseases, maternal and perinatal problems, micronutrient deficiencies, and tobacco-related illnesses. Effective programs to control these conditions, in conjunction with enhanced programs of family planning, would allow families to have longer, healthier, and more productive lives. Secure in the knowledge that their children would survive, parents usually choose to have fewer children and could therefore invest more in the education and health of each child. Improvements in health contribute to higher incomes, reduction of overpopulation, and improved intergroup attitudes in the context of opportunities and fairness. The highest yields come from addressing serious health problems that are amenable to prevention, such as cigarette-related cardiovascular diseases and cancers. Education for disease prevention is essential over the entire life span.

International scientific cooperation facilitates biomedical and public health research in low-income countries. Improved surveillance and reporting systems are essential to enhance knowledge of who suffers and dies of which diseases under what conditions. In public health, such knowledge is essential for disease prevention. One practical program is training of community health workers throughout the low-income countries in such a way that useful lessons from one country can be used in others, and new skills can be assimilated into practice. The World Health Organization, the World Bank, and international science academies such as the new InterAcademy Council have a great opportunity to spread useful knowledge and best practices rapidly, facilitated through the low-cost methods of the Internet.

EDUCATION, HEALTH, AND DEVELOPMENT: THE PROMISE OF AFRICA

In the 1970s, 1980s, and 1990s, nearly all Africans lived under dictatorships, and millions suffered through brutal civil wars. As if that were not enough, the HIV/AIDS epidemic exploded in the 1990s. Media coverage gave the impression that Africa was essentially hopeless.

Yet in the first decade of the twenty-first century, Africa's prospects changed remarkably. Across the continent, economic growth rates (in per capita terms) have been positive since the late 1990s. Democracy has advanced too. The majority of African countries held multiparty elections for the first time in the 1990s since the post-independence period. The extent of civic and media freedom on the continent today is much improved. Although Africa's economic growth rates still fall far short of Asia's extraordinary levels, the steady progress that most African countries have experienced is very encouraging. Why did it occur? Steven Radelet's insightful 2011 book, *Emerging Africa*, explores seventeen countries that have made significant advances. He analyzes hard statistical data, case studies, and a careful narrative that clarifies both Africa's earlier decline and its recent rebound.

He sees five main factors that have helped African conditions of life. Expanding democratization has prepared creative opportunities, and economic policies have curbed the unfair tax and regulatory policies that had damaged African households and investors. Resources for education and health care have been increased. New technologies, especially the cell phone, have increased Africans' access to markets. And the rise of a new generation of energetic leaders has brought new ideas, attitudes, and initiatives into hopeful action. Individual Africans have been crucial to these changes, often at great personal risk, but with constructive determination. Of all these considerations, the emergence of democracy is probably the most crucial.

Politicians rightly perceived that competent macroeconomic management and fiscal policies would benefit them at the polls, and so they began to give up their kleptocratic ways. Increasingly open political systems created new opportunities for well-educated "cheetahs," energetic political newcomers who were often trained abroad, to outcompete the slow-moving "hippo" holdovers from the anticolonial struggle. Newly democratic regimes have also been more eager to embrace, rather than suppress, new information technologies that can make markets more efficient and grassroots political organizations easier to form. Although social scientists are still debating the relationship between democracy and economic performance, Radelet makes a robust case that *democratic reform* was a necessary precondition for many of Africa's other recent advances, not least socioeconomic development.

Radelet highlights the role that the end of the Cold War played in creating more breathing room for real political competition in the 1990s. The political advances have, among other things, fostered education that has been vital in this progress. It raises labor productivity and contributes to faster economic growth. There are now many more skilled economists, technical professionals, and policy experts in Africa today than there were a few decades ago.[1] One of the fundamental underpinnings of successful socioeconomic development is *comprehensive education*, from preschool through graduate school, and including women on an equal basis, not only as a matter of equity but also as a matter of economic stimulus.

There are no illusions about the continuing damage of dictatorial leaders, but they may well be on the downward course over the next decade. The stereotypes of Africa are changing, and the international community is making more serious, informed, determined efforts to foster development in Africa.

SOCIOECONOMIC DEVELOPMENT TO PREVENT WAR AND MASS ATROCITIES

To develop research capability, especially pertinent to its own problems, it is essential for each developing country to connect its emerging scientific community with the international scientific community. The role of an effective technical community in moving toward *prosperity* is clear and consistent with democratic development—witness India with its high-tech production. Moreover, the international ties that develop in this way can be helpful in other ways, especially in fostering democratic norms and helping to sort out interstate conflicts without violence because cooperation among diverse scientists sets a good example and often generates creative ideas for dealing with intergroup or even international problems. This was a significant feature of coping with the awful dangers of the Cold War.

Several recurrent themes have emerged from world experience and scholarly examination of development cooperation and violence prevention. In order to quench fires before they become unmanageable, an early warning system needs to be developed to alert policymakers to key areas of potential violence. Development strategies for a particular country or region must take into account ways that aid can exacerbate or ameliorate ongoing tensions. In a particular situation, aid (financial, technical, educational) can be used in ways that foster mutual understanding and mutual benefit among adversaries and provide nonviolent means of addressing grievances by building capacity for ongoing conflict resolution—for example, a fair justice system and public knowledge of violence prevention in communities and ultimately prevention of mass violence.

Development cooperation must help to build capable states that can construct (with friendly outside collaboration as needed) conditions of *security*, *well-being*, and *justice* for all citizens. Moving toward these vital desiderata greatly diminishes the risk of mass violence, both within developing countries and beyond. It is the intersection of these three conditions that is crucial for prevention of mass violence.

- *Security* is about safety, from fear or threat of attack. But it is also about mutual accommodation so that different people can live together with a sense of fairness and mutual respect and of *mutual benefit from cooperation*.
- *Well-being* is about health, and also about equal opportunity. This means opportunity for education, training, preventive health care, and constructive employment. Young people without skills or decent prospects are very susceptible to demagogic incitements to violence.
- *Justice* is about the right of each person to have *a say in how one is governed*, and the right of each person to exercise that voice without fear of reprisal. Justice is also about accountability of those in power, bearing in mind that grave abuses of power manifested in widespread human rights violations can readily lead to war, mass atrocities, and even genocide.

It is crucial for the international community to identify and support those elements of civil society, as well as governmental entities, that can reduce intergroup antagonism; enhance attitudes of concern, social responsibility, and mutual aid within and between groups; and provide the technical and financial resources they need to operate effectively—including international norms of democratic development.

LEARNING AS WE GO: DEVELOPMENT AND VIOLENCE PREVENTION

The great value of the Marshall Plan and its evolution into the European Union was humanitarian in the post–World War II shambles. It was a deeply cooperative plan for regional economic development leading to prosperity and then a defense cooperation plan to deter dictatorial aggression. It was a serious, sustained effort that mobilized the creative energy of the smashed countries and thus prevented recurrence of mass violence. For more than half a century, it has demonstrated the profound value of *deep cooperation* for overcoming poverty and preventing war. That is the principle for rich and poor countries to apply in tackling these problems more than a half century later.

In a globalized world of rapid transportation, instant communications, and multinational commerce, no country can cut itself off from the problems of the poor countries. When violent conflict disrupts health systems in a disintegrating country, rich countries as well as poor face an increased threat of infectious disease. When violent conflict creates forced flows of refugees, it strains its neighbors' resources and exports discord along with disease—and the threat to the international community grows. When violent conflict fragments weak states, they become havens for terrorist groups that grow powerful on the chaos at home and threaten other countries.

When violent conflict undermines a country's economy, it creates chain reactions that aggravate economic loss by discouraging investment, domestic and foreign, and precipitating capital flight. When violent conflict destroys a nation's physical capital—roads, bridges, and power systems—past investments are nullified and future recovery impeded. Years of economic development can be destroyed in a few months—or in a few days if weapons of mass destruction are used. When violent conflict subverts a state's educational infrastructure, it destroys a foundation for progress in other areas, such as health, nutrition, civic responsibility, and preparation for employment in a technological world.

"Multi-stakeholder dialogue" is a technique for sharing concerns and grievances under reasonable conditions and is used widely in Latin American attempts to deal with conflicts between groups and regions by rebuilding political confidence. The discourse, often with peer learning, is spreading in Africa. Some European development-oriented institutions are supporting such efforts—intellectually, technically, and financially. Early dialogue on largely noncontroversial subjects is increasing. It can improve human relations and open paths to *preventive diplomacy*. This approach starts from the principle that peaceful resolution of conflicts can be achieved and sustained only through building trust and continued communication, but its success depends ultimately on effective government responses to the harsh social, economic, and political inequalities that originally produced the conflict.

When a state has undeveloped political structures and a desperately poor population but an enormous wealth of natural resources, it may become prey to what has been called the "resource curse." Ready cash from natural wealth allows political, military, and business leaders to accumulate vast resources while ignoring the needs of ordinary people and failing to develop healthy political and economic institutions. Control of the revenues from readily available resources often becomes a major cause of violent conflict between governments, rebels, and warlords. This is not inevitable. For example, Botswana has avoided conflict by fair revenue sharing and using its diamond wealth to produce high growth and rapid human development.

Whatever factors converge to fuel violent intrastate conflict, the consequences almost always become international in scope. In a violent conflict, as in public health, the first rule of success is that prevention is better than cure: the earlier the better; the more durable, the better. And the most effective strategy for prevention is equitable socioeconomic democratic development.

SCIENCE AND TECHNOLOGY FOR DEVELOPMENT

To participate in the global economy with reasonable prospects for prosperity, virtually every country in the world—and certainly every region—needs technical competence. The opportunities provided by science and technology in the coming century will be vast, reaching far beyond all prior experience. But how does this enormous potential become fulfilled equitably?

Mohamed Hassan, president of the African Academy of Sciences, observed that his continent's most serious problems—malnutrition, disease, and environmental deterioration—could be solved only by the efforts of a critical mass of African scientists, whose emergence and continuing existence depended on governments that provided them with both sufficient financial resources and unrestricted freedom of interaction with their colleagues at home and abroad.

How is a poor, developing country to succeed in diminishing the science gap? The scientific community is overwhelmingly located in and focused on affluent countries. Indeed, to say "affluent" is almost tantamount to saying "technically advanced." When Kofi Annan was secretary-general of the UN, he approached me about the possibility of addressing this critical problem. We joined with Bruce Alberts, former president of the US National Academies of Science, who then brilliantly led a movement in the global scientific community to focus much more intellectual and technical strength on the problems of developing countries. One of the most encouraging enterprises is the InterAcademy Council (IAC), a cooperative effort of eighteen major scientific academies, North and South, intended to provide the most penetrating, objective analysis of developing country problems—and global problems as well. Here leadership is vital on the basis of intellectual acuity, social responsibility, respect for the people of developing countries, and skillful diplomacy. New communications networks provide an opportunity for the world's scientific community to share its socially valuable knowledge and skill on an unprecedented scale.

The IAC is implementing an analytical program designed to improve access by all nations and peoples to the benefits of science and technology. Four major topics are being addressed—necessarily formulating specific foci within each one: (1) human resources, (2) research institutions, (3) scientific cooperation, and (4) global communications. Emphasis is placed on institution strengthening of the scientific and engineering communities in developing countries, thereby facilitating their ability to formulate and implement wise and effective policies. This work will also strive to be helpful to international organizations. Altogether, this remarkable social invention provides the opportunity to illuminate vital paths to development.

The first IAC report, *Inventing a Better Future: A Strategy for Building Worldwide Capacities in Science and Technology*, was presented to Secretary-General Annan at the UN in 2005. The IAC study panel that drafted this consensus report included experts from eleven different nations. The second report of the IAC was delivered to Annan at an African summit in 2005 and responded to his specific request for insight into ways to provide an adequate, sustainable food supply for Africa. After completing his ten-year tenure as UN secretary-general, he has taken up the implementation of this report in cooperation with African scientific and political leaders, as well as American foundations.

Bruce Alberts and Ralph Cicerone have used the intellectual and technical power of the National Academies to strengthen the capacity of numerous academies in developing countries. The IAC is one vehicle. The recent African Science Academy Development Initiative is another. This initiative directly engages African academies of science in building their capacity to provide independent, evidence-based advice to their governments and countries on health-related matters. Supported by a ten-year grant from the Bill and Melinda Gates Foundation, the US National Academies work especially closely with three science academies in Africa. The South African, Nigerian, and Ugandan science academies, competitively chosen on the basis of merit to participate in the program at the most intensive level, receive support and collaboration in advisory activities. The aim is to strengthen each academy's capacity in infrastructure, experience, and personnel, and also to encourage a relationship between each academy and its government so that the academy comes to be regarded as a trusted source of excellent scientific advice.

Several major health policy categories will be informed by science-based analysis in light of Africa's crushing burden of illness: (1) fostering research and development, (2) strengthening public health services, and (3) linking clinical medicine and public health. The African Science Academy Development Initiative is unfolding in the decade 2005–2015. Early activities included training each academy staff as necessary and establishing contacts with appropriate government agencies and other organizations. The objective is *long-term sustainability*, and the strategy will be modified as necessary to reach that target.

By the same token, the UN has held two unprecedented summit meetings on health and development in the past decade, one on HIV/AIDS and a second on prevention of noncommunicable diseases. It has also intensified its work on other infectious diseases. Much emphasis has been placed on disease prevention.

Calestous Juma, a distinguished scientist at Harvard, wrote in *Science* in 2011, "The role of science, technology, and engineering in solving Africa's most challenging economic problems—from telecommunications to agriculture to infectious diseases—is no longer in question. However, some leading international organizations undermine the role of innovation in development. The time has come for the scientific community to advance a new generation of international organizations that expressly promote scientific cooperation— agencies that can help foster technological cooperation for Africa's economic transformation."

The immense power of science and technology can be brought to bear on development throughout the world. The technically advanced democracies can make a major contribution in fulfilling the promise of this approach, working in concert with many others—not dominating but stimulating and cooperating in international efforts.

RECENT ADVANCES IN DEVELOPMENT: CHILDREN IN POOR COUNTRIES

UNICEF, the UN's children's agency, has recently illustrated the ingenuity of UN agencies by making some innovations for improving development. The agency conducted a careful study concluding that services for the world's poorest children in the most impoverished communities is the most cost-effective way of helping not only those at the bottom but also the less poor, what we nowadays refer to so often as the middle class. Of course, there is a strong moral element in this approach as well so that a major segment of the population is not dumped into a deep hole.

UNICEF analyzed statistical data from twenty-six countries and developed a computer model that was subject to independent expert peer review. The result shows that helping children five years old and younger, even in the most remote and disadvantaged areas of poor countries, can prevent 60 percent more deaths than the present situation. Thus, UNICEF recommends new policies, not only for its own work but for related agencies. These include training and deploying more *community health workers* who can use feasible modern technologies, provide basic health services to remote villages, and use mass communications to give poor people encouragement and guidance about seeking health care. In view of the long-standing, serious problem of maternal mortality, especially in Africa, they recommend maternal waiting homes near urban hospitals so that women from rural areas can readily get help in aid delivery as needed, especially emergency care that can prevent unnecessary deaths and serious damage to both mother and child.

BUILDING VIOLENCE PREVENTION
INTO DEVELOPMENT: UNDP

The United Nations Development Program (UNDP) has offices with professional staff in 166 countries—offices that make available to developing countries the world's knowledge, experience, and resources to help them work out their own best answers for equitable socioeconomic development. For this purpose, UNDP can call upon its worldwide staff and its many partner organizations.

The UN has increasingly recognized in recent years, especially during the era when Annan was secretary-general, that violent conflict can readily destroy socioeconomic development; therefore, it is vital to build conflict resolution mechanisms into development projects. Such dynamic leaders in UNDP as Gay Rosenblum-Kumar, Chetan Kumar, Kathleen Cravero, and Sakiko Fukuda-Parr have done much in recent years to *link prevention of violence with development*. They have provided a growing body of evidence that unless conflict is managed early and well in the process of development, it can lead to violence in ways that prohibit or destroy innovations for prosperity that development is intended to achieve. Indeed, even partially successful development can stir latent conflict because resources are reallocated, often unfairly even if inadvertently. This in turn can readily lead to tensions between class, ethnic, religious, or national groups. Thus, helping developing countries to build their own capacities for early, ongoing conflict resolution and indeed violence prevention constitutes a crucial part of development, much more than was recognized a decade ago. So, initiatives have been taken to build social cohesion in various countries, involving some combination of government, political parties, and institutions of civil society. The media and the military can play a constructive role in these efforts.

The UNDP's Bureau for Crisis Prevention and Recovery (BCPR) is becoming a storehouse of experience, methods, and tools for prevention of crises, for reducing the risk of natural disaster, and for recovery after crises. BCPR advises UNDP senior management on those issues and works in the field with UNDP country offices and, through them, with their host governments, providing technical help, expertise in best practices, and financial resources. BCPR incorporates opportunities for violence prevention into UNDP long-term development policies and programs. It promotes links between UN peace-and-security and development objectives, and helps governments develop their capacities to manage crisis situations.[2] A crucial test will be the extent to which it comes to focus on early prevention.

Rapid response is a priority in effective crisis prevention. In 2006, UNDP created an immediate crisis response initiative, nicknamed the SURGE Project. It dispatches trained and specialized UNDP staff to country offices within days of an emerging crisis. UNDP's international network of experts also contributes to drafting regular procedures for effective, immediate response. Online, they have placed and regularly update valuable tools such as checklists for prompt response and templates for planning as well as resource mobilization.[3]

The essential role of *women in development* has received increasing recognition—for reasons of equity, family solidarity, and economic advancement. BCPR now plans all its programs with a strong commitment to promoting women's equality and trains its professionals to promote women's inclusion. Special emphasis is given to (1) stopping violence against women, (2) providing justice and security for women, (3) involving women as decisionmakers, especially in peace processes, (4) encouraging men and women to work as equals in efforts to build and transform their society, and (5) including women's issues on national agendas—for example, opportunities for education.[4]

UN peace and development advisers, including conflict prevention specialists, are increasingly involved in UNDP operations, especially to construct a framework for crucial cooperation between UNDP and the UN Department on Political Affairs on the deployment of advisers and a methodology for country-specific collaboration at UN headquarters to support violence prevention efforts anywhere in the world. There have been recent examples of successful UNDP efforts in such prevention. UNDP helped Ghana set up its National Peace Council, which, at the request of Ghana's president, mediated internal conflicts and advised the major political parties on methods of choosing presidential candidates. In early 2009, Ghana completed a successful presidential election (including a runoff) with international monitoring and without violence.

The growing commitment to *including conflict-resolution mechanisms in development initiatives* has stimulated recruitment and training of specialists in planning effective conflict prevention initiatives; assisting aspiring democracies in building internal mediation capacities; disseminating specific, practical strategies for engaging reluctant national actors; and dealing with the complex historical, economic, ethnic, or cultural issues involved in emerging conflicts.

Another significant initiative is the emerging cooperation of UNDP and the large Japan International Cooperation Agency headed by a great leader, Sadako Ogata, with whom I worked for some years on refugee problems and on prevention of genocide. These are its basic elements: (1) addressing structural conditions oriented to root causes of conflict, (2) reconsidering development cooperation priorities to avoid unwittingly contributing to social tensions, and instead promoting peace-building incentives, and (3) filling a global policy gap by striving to meet advanced development goals in the new millennium. The initiative takes into account the important human security perspective in which Ogata has been a pioneer. This includes the root causes of conflict and the strengthening of fragile states.[5]

RECENT ADVANCES IN THE WORLD BANK: SOCIOECONOMIC DEVELOPMENT AND PREVENTION OF MASS VIOLENCE

From the onset of the World Bank, its presidents and senior staff believed that their mandate was only to focus on economic growth and to exclude political considerations. I had the privilege of meeting with each president from the 1970s onward. They were people of high ideals, exceptional capability, and substantial accomplishment. Yet they, like almost all of the financial/economic leaders of the world, could not bring themselves to cross the threshold of addressing prevention of mass violence despite its powerful relation to economic development.

Yet significant gains were made. For example, Robert McNamara established a strong unit on health and population. After leaving the bank, he worked with the Carnegie and other foundations to reduce the nuclear danger. Later, James Wolfensohn worked well with Kofi Annan to consider the dangerous relations of armed conflict and economic growth. They believed increasingly that we should think of socioeconomic development by way of diminishing intergroup and international violence, thereby enhancing the opportunities for constructive and sustainable development.

The 2011 *World Development Report*, under the guidance of the bank's most recent president, Robert Zoellick, is a powerful statement that looks across disciplines and experiences drawn from around the world to offer ideas and practical recommendations on how to move beyond conflict and fragility toward secure development. The key messages are important for all countries low-, middle-, and high-income—as well as for regional and global institutions:

1. *Institutional legitimacy is the key to stability.* When government institutions do not adequately protect citizens, guard against corruption, or provide access to justice; when markets do not provide job opportunities; or when communities have lost social cohesion, the likelihood of violent conflict increases. Countries need early established public confidence in a basic collective action even before rudimentary institutions can be created. Actions that can generate quick, tangible results help to establish confidence and intergroup cooperation.

2. *Investing in citizen security, justice, and jobs is essential to reducing violence.* Strong emphasis on early projects to create jobs is of great importance, as is the involvement of women in political coalitions and security and justice reform.

3. *Confronting this challenge effectively means that institutions need to change—not an easy process.* Partners from other countries and institutions must adapt procedures and formulate a long-term perspective. Development cooperation calls for donor coordination. Multidonor trust funds have proven useful in accomplishing these aims while lessening the burdens of new governments with very limited capacity.

4. *We need a layered approach.* Some problems can be addressed at the *country* level, others at a *regional* level, such as pooling resources for building capacity. Still other actions are needed at a *global* level, such as building new capacities to support justice reform and the creation of jobs, and forging partnerships between producer and consumer countries.

5. *The global landscape is changing.* Regional institutions and middle-income countries are playing a larger role. Thus, attention is needed to South-South and South-North exchanges and to the recent transition experiences of middle-income countries.

Zoellick makes a fundamental point in noting that, from the earliest times, the recognition that human safety depends on collaboration has been a motivating factor for the formation of village communities, cities, and nation-states. The twentieth century was dominated by the legacy of devastating global wars, bitter colonial struggles, and very dangerous ideological conflicts—all later stimulating efforts to establish international systems that would foster global peace and prosperity. To some extent these systems are successful—for example, wars between states are less common than they were in the past, and civil wars are declining in number. Yet, insecurity not only remains, but has become a primary development challenge of our time. One-and-a-half billion people live in areas affected by social fragility; violent conflict; or large-scale, organized criminal violence—not to speak of the spread of various highly lethal weapons and skill in their use.

The central message is that strengthening legitimate institutions and governance to provide citizen security, justice, and jobs is crucial to break cycles of violence. Building on the concept of *human security*, local, national, regional, and international partnership can stimulate an ongoing effort to deepen our understanding of the links between security and development and can foster practical action. Economic development must now be broadened in concept and action if it is to be effective in achieving goals of widely shared prosperity and decent living conditions for our common humanity.

The *World Development Report* summarizes several major lessons for violence prevention:

1. Community-based programs for violence prevention, employment, and associated service delivery, and access to local justice and dispute resolution. *Community policing* is a good example.
2. Complementary programs for institutional transformation in the priority areas of *security and justice.*
3. "Back-to-basics" job creation programs. These programs include large-scale *community-based public works*, such as those India and Indonesia use throughout the country, including high-tension communities.
4. The involvement of women in security, justice, and economic empowerment.

SCIENTIFIC COMMUNITY AND THE AVOIDANCE OF CATASTROPHIC DESTRUCTION

The problem of mass violence in the twenty-first century occurs in a world increasingly saturated with highly destructive weapons. We see in all parts of the world abundant prejudice, hatred, and threats of mass violence, even genocide. The historical record is full of every sort of slaughter based on perceived differences pertaining to religion, ethnicity, nationality, and other group characteristics. In this kind of world, the scientific community has a great responsibility to work in a reasonably unified way to address these profound and pervasive problems.

During the Cold War, the scientific community did much to cope with the nuclear danger. For example, leading scientists from the United States and the Soviet Union met regularly to seek ways to reduce the number of weapons and especially the likelihood of a first strike, to decrease the chance of accidental or inadvertent nuclear war, to find safeguards against unauthorized launch and against serious miscalculation, and to improve the relations between the superpowers through international cooperative efforts. It was also prescient in its exploration with the Soviets of biological terrorism. Moreover, the scientific community dealt effectively with behavioral and social aspects of reducing the nuclear danger.

These efforts brought together scientists, scholars, and expert practitioners to clarify the many facets of avoiding nuclear war. To generate options for decreasing the risk, they stimulated analytical work by people who knew various fields: for example, advanced weaponry and its military uses, in-depth knowledge of the superpowers and other nuclear powers, geopolitical flash points, the broad context of international relations and policy formation and implementation (especially regarding the superpowers), human behavior under stress (especially leadership decisionmaking), and negotiation and conflict resolution. Collectively these efforts provided needed depth and new options for dealing with very dangerous issues. A dynamic interplay between the scientific community and the world of policy evolved and influenced leaders such as Gorbachev and Reagan.

The scientific community is the closest approximation we now have to a truly international community, sharing certain fundamental interests, values, standards, and curiosity about the nature of matter, life, behavior, and the universe. Its shared quest for understanding knows no national boundaries and has no inherent prejudices, no necessary ethnocentrism, and no requisite barriers to the free play of information and ideas. Recent advances in telecommunications draw the quest for global understanding closer than ever before.

The scientific community, by increasing its attention to development, can provide a model for decent human relations and mutually beneficial cooperation that can help to transcend the biases, dogmas, and hatreds that have torn our species apart throughout history and have recently become so much more dangerous than ever before. Science can contribute to a better future by its ideals and its processes, as well as by the specific content of its research. These examples show vividly the great promise of international scientific cooperation for equitable development and the benefit of all humanity. The past decade has seen a remarkable expansion of scientific interest and organization to help in equitable socioeconomic development and the strength of these efforts to diminish the risk of mass violence.

SIX

HUMAN RIGHTS AND PEACE

Empowering People and Pragmatic Decency

> *For a very long time, [I was] influenced greatly by Gandhi's Satyagraha; so I wasn't a pioneer, I was continuing a tradition, a legacy that the apartheid government had sought to nip in the bud. As you know, they had had boycotts . . . sort of the traditional, conventional ways of trying to bring your plight to the attention of the authorities—and then you'd in fact have the passive resistance movement in the 1950s. And they had delegations going in to petition the powers that be. For some reason, actually, the media in South Africa for a very long time were favorably disposed, and so gave me the opportunity of putting across the plight of our people and the fact that we were committed to working through nonviolent means.*
> *—Archbishop Desmond Tutu, from Eric Hamburg/Rick English documentary* Preventing Genocide, *2009, Stanford University Library*

Prevention at its best involves creating a durable basis for peaceful living and decent intergroup relations. In the long run, we can be most successful in promoting and protecting human rights—and averting ethnic, religious, and international wars—by fostering democracy, equitable socioeconomic development, and the creation of institutions that protect human rights, both governmental and nongovernmental.

89

The founders of the United Nations were interested primarily in preventing another world war, and they perceived the Nazis' terrible human rights abuses—almost beyond human comprehension—as the early warning signs of aggression that never ceased. The UN founders believed that if the international community had acted early and firmly to stop Hitler and his followers from committing severe internal human rights abuses, it might well have been possible to prevent World War II. There is a strong link between human rights abuses and the path to war, mass atrocities, and even genocide.

Sadako Ogata, the distinguished former UN high commissioner for refugees, often reminds governments that today's human rights abuses may result in tomorrow's refugee movements with horrific dislocation and suffering. Gradually, since World War II and the Cold War, human rights have acquired greater political salience. Protection of human rights enters into preventive diplomacy and international cooperation for peace.

The proposals of the Carnegie Commission on Preventing Deadly Conflict in 1997 suggest how the international community might take further steps to protect human rights worldwide in the interest of blocking mass violence. It can do so by strengthening existing international law to set standards aimed at deterring human rights abuses; by stimulating and integrating international efforts to develop an early warning system of human rights violations; and by funding efforts to advance the rule of law, democratization, and national human rights efforts.

Human rights are gaining significance not only as a moral imperative but also as an impetus to forming decent policy. Violation of human rights gives early warning of worse problems to come. Thus, systematic monitoring of human rights abuses can serve as an early warning system for deadly conflict. Preventing human rights abuses can help to prevent deadly conflicts from taking place at all. Interestingly, the major democracies and international organizations (governmental and nongovernmental) are moving in this direction.

Rule of law has become increasingly vivid in our highly armed, interdependent world. It is the basis for just management of relations between individuals and groups; it helps ensure the protection of fundamental human rights, fair political participation, and mutual accommodation of diverse groups as well as equitable socioeconomic opportunities.

In the chapter on democracy, we considered why and how the international community should aid the transition to democracy. A state's internal political system influences its dealings with other states as well as its own people.

Democratically organized states tend not to fight one another. Their habits of negotiation and tolerance of domestic dissent in the context of conflict-resolution institutions lead them to resolve conflicts without resorting to mass violence. Human rights protection is a crucial part of this enterprise. This pervasive outlook and appropriate institutional mechanisms aid peace by moderating relationships between democratic states so as to prevent the onset of serious disputes in the first place. Democratic states create new institutions and processes to meet new circumstances, such as the dispute resolution mechanisms in global economic organizations that had previously been neglected.

National governments must take the lead in establishing and implementing domestic institutions devoted to the promotion and protection of human rights—with whatever help the international community can acceptably provide, encouraging cooperation to the extent possible. National human rights institutions have been evolving all over the world with varying efficiency. They need to set forth a constitutional or legislative text that specifies the institution's composition and mandate for action. The responsibilities of such institutions, in the view of the Carnegie Commission, should be to:

- Submit recommendations, proposals, and reports to the government, parliament, and any other competent body on any matter relating to human rights (including legislative and administrative provisions and any circumstances conducive to violation of human rights);
- Promote conformity of national laws and practices with international human rights standards;
- Encourage ratification and implementation of international standards;
- Contribute to the reporting procedure required under international instruments;
- Assist in formulating and executing human rights teaching and research programs, increasing public awareness of human rights through formal and informal education; and
- Cooperate with the United Nations, regional institutions, and national institutions within the country.

Some national institutions have jurisdiction to act on *individual* complaints of human rights violations. Their functions may therefore include several valuable processes. These include seeking an amicable settlement of the matter through offering conciliation, binding decision, or other cultur-ally acceptable means; informing the complainant of his or her rights and of available means of redress and promoting access to such redress; hearing complaints and referring them to a competent authority; and making recom-mendations to the appropriate authorities, including proposals for amending laws and regulations that obstruct the free exercise of human rights. A new breed of human rights institution is emerging in a variety of countries. The extension of human rights norms, laws, and institutions can in due course make a long-term constructive difference.[1]

PEOPLE POWER AND NONVIOLENT SOCIAL ACTION

"People power" is a term used to characterize events dating back a long time in modern history, perhaps best known through Mahatma Gandhi. A vivid case led to Ferdinand Marcos's fall from power in the Philippines in 1986. The mass use of nonviolent direct action by civilian populations spread throughout the late 1980s and early 1990s. Indeed, the essence of people power is the mass use of nonviolent direct action. Other examples were the revolutions throughout East-Central Europe, the Chinese student uprising of 1989, resistance to the failed Soviet coup in 1991, the South African struggle against apartheid, and in 2011 the Arab Spring revolutions of the Middle East and North Africa. These are mass efforts, largely nonviolent, aimed to overthrow repressive regimes. Some terrible events occur as dictators react violently against their own people, yet there is sometimes remarkable persis-tence in people power resistance to sustained oppression.

In the past, nonviolent action has often been improvised. The tendency in recent years is to plan, organize, and follow disciplined guidelines. Past cases give important clues about ways to make nonviolent mass action more effective. Several aspirations are powerful: freedom, democracy, security, health, and food. Efficiency can be enhanced by careful formulation and well-organized action; the strategy chosen in nonviolent striving makes a difference. Ter-rorism has taken on an increasing importance in recent years. The technical capabilities of terrorists are increasing, and they have developed such deadly skills as suicide bombing. The miniaturization and availability of weapons in the context of crowded, complex societies provide favorable conditions for terrorists. Yet these groups have mostly failed to achieve their grandiose ambitions and have inflicted indiscriminate damage on many people over religious, ethnic, and national differences. This includes their own people. This fact may lead populations away from terrorists and toward the strategic use of nonviolent action in seeking a better life. It is a reasonable estimate that most people would prefer nonviolent pressures for freedom and decency rather than terrorism.

As international cooperation in response to human rights abuses increases in much of the world, there should be an incentive for groups to adopt non-violent action to expose those abuses and gain a serious hearing for their own plight—nationally and internationally. Among the points of leverage are media coverage of oppression, charismatic leaders for human rights such as Desmond Tutu, individual institutions, and the carrots-and-sticks of democratic countries.

Nonviolent action in a democratic spirit may precede, inform, and stimulate the democratizing process. New opportunities have arisen. The 2011 Arab Spring highlights the importance of communications technology in the quest for democracy. Access to cheap, efficient, social communications makes non-violent action more feasible and meaningful to the participants. A variety of techniques permit opportunities for nonviolent democratic initiatives. Given the wide distribution of repressive regimes and their ruthless repressors in many cases, there is no guarantee of success. But there is a better chance than ever before for the vigorous self-assertion of organized, committed groups in search of decent governance, democratic practices, and movement toward equitable socioeconomic development.[2]

Brian Urquhart, one of the first staff members of the UN shortly after its founding and one of the most respected wise men in the world of international conflict, believes that a revolution without violence is possible. In a 2011 analysis, he recognizes from long, firsthand experience that civil resistance usually has not been able to survive deliberate, persistent violent repression, especially in a totalitarian police state. But in some parts of the Arab world, this seems at last to be changing, following the example of Eastern Europe in the time of Gorbachev. There are variations in the methods used by suc-cessful civil resistance movements, and different countries can engage in *peer learning*. The basic rationale is that even repressive rulers require the obedience of their subjects.

Gorbachev's rise to power brought profoundly new ideas about the desir-ability and feasibility of change for freedom. Even a decade before Gorbachev, the 1975 Helsinki agreements gave momentum to this movement when they committed all their signatory governments to respect human rights. Though many observers were skeptical, the movement spread through Europe and showed what could be done.[3] Putin's Russia is, however, sliding back, and international as well as domestic pressures will be needed for years to come.

Peaceful mass action can be a powerful force on behalf of human rights.[4] In East Germany in 1989, street protests became common as citizens, heartened by Mikhail Gorbachev's policy of liberalization, demanded not only the right to move freely across borders but also the achievement of democratic reform on behalf of human rights. The situation was dangerous: East Germany's leader, Erich Honecker, was a hard-liner who favored the traditional Soviet policy: violent repression of rights and dissent. But Protestant clergy were among the leaders of the popular movement. They used their status to ensure that the demonstrations remained peaceful, and their churches became sanctuaries to protect and assemble reform-minded activists—especially a church in Leipzig, where a crowd of nearly 70,000 people gathered in nonviolent protest. Organizers exerted strong social pressure to maintain order, and the security forces backed down from confrontation. Within days, people from all walks of life joined the demonstration and swelled the number of protesters to more than 150,000.[5]

A number of cities throughout East Germany followed Leipzig's peaceful example. Their nonviolent behavior not only removed any plausible excuse for a government crackdown but also gave the protesters and their message considerable moral authority. The outwardly impervious East German regime fell in November 1989. Leadership matters, as we have learned from Gandhi onward. For example, the revered orchestra conductor Kurt Mazur, as well as several distinguished clergymen, not only sustained the demonstrations for liberty but also helped to keep them nonviolent. This is similar to the superb role of Archbishop Desmond Tutu in South Africa as well as the legendary Nelson Mandela. Other Soviet attempts to stifle reform were met by peaceful demonstrations, notably when Czechoslovakia staged its "Velvet Revolution"—another case of nonviolent mass action for democratic change.

Other movements—for example, in the Philippines—confirm the formidable strength of a united and resolute nonviolent population, even though some mass demonstrations, such as the one in Tiananmen Square in China, have been viciously repressed. Such protests build on the nonviolent movements of Mahatma Gandhi and Dr. Martin Luther King Jr., which can be forces not only for democratic change in behalf of human rights but also for the prevention of deadly conflict.[6] Challenging imperial power, racism, or authoritarianism is a dangerous venture. Yet increasingly the people themselves understand in many cases the power of mass, nonviolent protest. They have made as sure as possible that their demonstrations remained peaceful in the face of provocation, and opened the way to negotiation.

In his study *Gandhi and Beyond: Nonviolence for an Age of Terrorism,*[7] distinguished scholar David Cortright of the University of Notre Dame surveys a history of social justice movements. Drawing on the work of Gandhi, King, Dorothy Day, Cesar Chavez, and others, Cortright gives a comprehensive assessment of people power, nonviolent movements. He includes the work of Gene Sharp, Peter Ackerman and Christopher Kruegler, and Saul Alinsky. Cortright identifies elements that contribute to success: the awareness and use of power dynamics; building and maintaining an institutional base; effective use of Internet-based organizing; creative articulation of practical, modest objectives; inspiring fund-raising for these specific purposes; use of media; a large, humanitarian vision; readiness to propose plausible, hopeful options; and perseverance in the long dangerous quest for social justice. We see many of these elements in the 2011 Arab Spring—with remarkable success, yet horrible repressive responses in Syria and elsewhere—and the prospect of a long, hard struggle to establish decent governments. The power of nonviolent aspiration for human rights is great and increasing, thanks in part to new communication technology, but it takes immense courage and persistence. The international community must learn how to help, especially in the long phase after initial liberation.

Prevention is not simply smoothing over rough spots in intergroup or international relations—it requires creating a durable basis for peaceful conditions of living together.[8] Governments that abuse the rights of their own citizens are not likely to respect the rights of their weaker neighbors. In the long run, human rights abuses and the atrocities that typically follow them must be eliminated by promoting democracy, equitable market economies, and the strong civil institutions that protect human rights.

Democratic nations, working together, must monitor human rights both for their intrinsic value and for their value as early signals portending deadly conflict, up to and including genocide. Indeed, preventing human rights abuses consistently diminishes the risk that deadly conflicts will take place at all.

Recognition of early warning signals is futile without the preparation of a variety of policy options and contingency plans in response to them. Prominent among these responses are the development and implementation worldwide of clear concepts, orderly processes, and effective institutions to promote and protect human rights.

COMMISSIONS ON TRUTH AND RECONCILIATION

The South African Commission on Truth and Reconciliation was created after the freedom of Nelson Mandela under the leadership of Archbishop Tutu as a way of dealing fairly with both immediate sources of deep resentment and the need for long-term reconciliation. This commission established an invaluable precedent for the entire world, and I joined with others who felt that we should bring together in New York an organization that would make the lessons learned from this commission readily available to everyone and adaptable to the circumstances of different countries. Although many people contributed, I pay special tribute to Vincent Mai, a highly progressive and successful businessman. He grew up in South Africa; moved to New York; and continued a lifelong, thoughtful, generous interest in the work toward South African democracy and development. He played a crucial role in putting together an international organization, of which I was one of the original board members along with Ted Sorensen, who had been so important to President Kennedy, and Alex Borrain, who had been Tutu's strong right arm in the truth commission. Together we formed the International Center for Transitional Justice. A most stimulating person in this enterprise, from the point of view of scholarship, was Priscilla Hayner. She has studied and written extensively in the intervening years, integrating experiences of more than forty countries around variations on the theme of human rights commissions. The many innovations arising from the South African experience offer great promise on a worldwide basis.

Both truth commissions and courts have valuable *educational* functions. Each of these has uniquely valuable lessons. The presidentially appointed truth commission in Nigeria illustrates the formidable impact of public hearings. For a full year, the Nigerian public took keen interest in the commission's televised sessions. They were shown during the day, then repeated at night on several channels, and played live on many radio stations. The appearance of many human rights abuses provided a wide understanding of events that had taken place under harsh military rule.

These efforts highlight the value of peer learning. Countries or groups in conflict can learn from others who have successfully come through similar experiences. Indeed, international organizations such as the EU and the UN can efficiently and clearly bring the world's experience to the attention of those caught up in a dangerous situation. This is certainly applicable to emerging human rights abuses.

The newer truth commissions are more likely than their predecessors to hold public hearings; this is important in educating the public on the norms of government behavior and on their own (and others') rights. They tend to have stronger powers of investigation, use increasingly inventive approaches to investigation, and cover a longer period of time. Strong public involvement in these commissions is evident in the fact that political leaders have felt compelled to appear voluntarily before them, even when the commission had no power to force them to do so, and even when they themselves had been accused of abuses. The growth of truth commissions shows an increased appreciation of the value of a holistic approach to reestablishing justice in a society after a history of atrocities or governmental repression and abuse. Both judicial and nonjudicial initiatives should be used to meet the many needs of a transitional society, and it is best to plan and design these multiple initiatives—truth-seeking programs, targeted prosecutions, reparations, legal reforms, and reconciliation programs—to complement and strengthen each other. The balance of punishment and reconciliation in these societies is a delicate one. Revenge motives are strong, yet the people must find ways to live together in an atmosphere of truth.

BUILDING DEMOCRACY IN SOUTH AFRICA

In 1997, midway through Nelson Mandela's presidency, the Carnegie Commission on Preventing Deadly Conflict sponsored a two-day seminar in Cape Town,[9] at which South Africans who had participated in their country's transition to democracy were invited to reflect on past progress and future prospects and to examine how South Africa succeeded in avoiding genocide or civil war.

The seminar concentrated on three broad goals that every country struggling to build a sustainable democracy must meet: (1) a government generally recognized as accountable, competent, and fair; (2) broad-based economic well-being; and (3) social equity and opportunities. How and in what order each goal is achieved will depend on the country's history, culture, and resources, as well as international cooperation to assist socioeconomic development. For us, this was an unforgettable experience.

In the political domain, three elements—extraordinary leadership, the new constitution drafted by distinguished, indeed exemplary, South African lawyers deeply committed to democracy, and the work of the Truth and Reconciliation Commission—clarify how South Africa answered the threat of mass violence and built the foundations of sustainable democracy.

TRANSFORMATIVE EXPERIENCES: ESTABLISHING HUMAN RIGHTS AFTER WORLD WAR II AND THE HOLOCAUST

Professor Louis Henkin of Columbia University, who has carefully studied the *human rights movement* from its beginnings more than half a century ago, illustrates its remarkable growth, influence, and efficacy in a magisterial essay.[10]

International concern about the condition of human rights everywhere began early in World War II. The human rights movement's normative and institutional foundations were established during the decades after the war, with the extraordinarily determined leadership of Eleanor Roosevelt, and the movement continues to the present day. These norms and institutions had furthered the human rights of billions of people by the end of the twentieth century. The universality of human rights became an ideology, one of the most important of the twenty-first century.

Owing to the remarkable leadership, ingenuity, and perseverance of Roosevelt, this principle of human rights received global recognition when the General Assembly of the United Nations approved the Universal Declaration of Human Rights on December 10, 1948. Roosevelt integrated intellectual, moral, and political skills in this creative enterprise. President Franklin Delano Roosevelt's "Four Freedoms" message to Congress on January 6, 1941, is an authentic historical landmark. Speaking before the United States entered the war, President Roosevelt said: "In the future days, which we seek to make secure, we look forward to a world founded upon four essential human freedoms": freedom of *speech*, freedom of *religion*, freedom from *want*, and freedom from *fear*. Shortly thereafter, Franklin Roosevelt and Winston Churchill expressed in the Atlantic Charter a strong reinforcement of these human rights requirements. Thus, they gave a prompt impetus to the core concept of *universal human rights*: that every human being has legitimate, recognized claims to specific freedoms and benefits *by virtue of being human*. They are not gifts owing to grace, love, charity, or compassion but rights that society has a moral, political, and legal obligation to respect and ensure.

This powerful human rights concept grows out of earlier notions of "natural rights" in the writings of Enlightenment thinkers. This ideology has suffered numerous setbacks over the years. In France, for example, the Reign of Terror swept it away, and it was not restored until after World War II. The United States essentially maintained the ideology of rights proclaimed in its Declaration of Independence—with the degrading exception of slavery. The US Constitution at the time of its writing guaranteed some individual rights, further elaborated in its first ten amendments, the Bill of Rights. Even so, slavery was maintained under the US Constitution for three-quarters of a century, whereas racial equality and the equal protection of the laws were not established in writing until the Fourteenth Amendment was passed in 1868. Truly universal suffrage was only achieved through the civil rights movement of the 1960s and is now at risk again with recent challenges to the Voting Rights Act of 1964. Thus, the United States, for all its democratic ideals, continues to confront many obstacles in reaching a comprehensive implementation of human rights. This is a lesson of worldwide significance: the achievement of human rights requires *ceaseless vigilance* and ongoing struggle.

FROM CONSTITUTIONAL RIGHTS TO INTERNATIONAL HUMAN RIGHTS

Henkin puts the post–World War II human rights movement in global perspective by observing that the "international human rights movement" is in reality a movement that affirms an international responsibility to promote, define, and safeguard national human rights within national boundaries. It aims at setting internationally accepted standards of human rights that all nations should meet, supported by legally binding commitments to respect those standards. The movement has generated international institutions that encourage and oversee the compliance of individual nations with these norms.[11]

In the dangerous years before World War II, the concept of "sovereignty" permitted autocrats and tyrants to treat their own people as they wished without serious question from outside. In the name of self-determination, they felt free to abuse their own citizens as they saw fit. In this view, what Hitler did to Jews and other "unwanted" groups was his own business. Movement from the perception of human rights as a purely domestic issue to a serious international concern began early in World War II. All of the nations at war with Germany adopted the Atlantic Charter as their statement of war aims. Even though cynics saw it only as a weapon in psychological warfare, many people in the midst of the war's anguish took it seriously.

The United Nations Charter, one of the most important treaties of the century, specified promotion of respect for human rights as one of the purposes of the new United Nations. This was the first appearance of the phrase "human rights" in an important international treaty. It committed all signatories to vigorous action in support of "universal respect for, and observance of, human rights and fundamental freedoms for all without distinction as to race, sex, language, or religion."[12]

This led to the Nuremberg war crimes trials and, beyond, to the Convention on the Prevention and Punishment of the Crime of Genocide, the first international human rights treaty of the new world order. From Nuremberg one can see a direct line, with long delays and formidable obstacles (principally related to the Cold War), to the international tribunals established by the UN Security Council in the 1990s. The path from the postwar treaties led during a half century to international commissions and committees and courts, to the UN High Commissioner for Human Rights, to a permanent International Criminal Court, and finally to the growing network of nongovernmental human rights organizations—such as Human Rights Watch and Amnesty International—all striving to induce compliance with international human rights standards throughout the world. Central to this history is the Universal Declaration of Human Rights so inspired by Eleanor Roosevelt and her international collaborators in 1948 and beyond. The Universal Declaration of Human Rights is now widely considered one of the most important international instruments of the twentieth century, on a par with the United Nations Charter. Here are its great accomplishments:[13] It helped transform the obsolete concept of "natural rights" into a prevailing political ideology, based on a universally attractive notion of *human dignity*. It made the vague term "human rights" specific in defining fundamental rights. It universalized human rights by making their acceptance the heart of constitutionalism for all countries It further internationalized human rights by redefining as an international concern matters that had once been the sole province of each sovereign nation. From this has flowed a structure of international norms and institutions, becoming a major source of international law on human rights. Nevertheless, as we note in the chapter on the UN, the implementation of the charter has been a continuing struggle.

Over nearly two decades, negotiations led to two international covenants, one on civil and political rights and the other on economic, social, and cultural rights. Many nations also supported further rights promoted by the United Nations, including the Genocide Convention, Elimination of All Forms of Racial Discrimination, Elimination of All Forms of Discrimination against Women, the Convention against Torture, and the Rights of the Child. Although the implementation of these agreements is very difficult and uneven around the globe, they establish unprecedented norms that can in due course have a strong effect on human behavior. It would be impossible to overemphasize the inspiring, intellectual, and moral contributions of Eleanor Roosevelt to the establishment of universal human rights, not only in the postwar period but also in the precursor of planning an evaluation during the years of the war itself and indeed in prewar foresight.

The second half of the twentieth century reflected these agreements in the end of colonialism and the emergence of independent states, the end of communism and fascism, and the establishment of democracy as the leading aspiration of the twenty-first century.

Some states have grouped into important *regional systems* for the protection of human rights. In Europe and in the Americas, regional organizations have developed strong human rights codes comparable to the Universal Declaration and the International Covenant on Civil and Political Rights, as well as institutions for enforcing them, such as national commissions and international courts that have had considerable success. Most notable is the experience of Europe, and so we now turn to its accomplishments.

THE POWER OF HUMAN RIGHTS IN EUROPE

Shirley Williams, a great democratic leader in the United Kingdom and throughout Europe, has written a definitive account of European progress in human rights.[14] She points to the same Europe that contemptuously crushed human rights in the period of World War II (and earlier in colonialism) as the architect, less than a half century later, of the world's strongest institutional system for protecting them.[15]

The Nuremberg trials, which began in February 1946, established the precedent that even rulers of sovereign states could be held responsible for acts condemned as criminal by international law. This was a step in the direction of legally binding cooperation in enforcement.

In the immediate postwar years, Western Europe's dismal economic situation made it seem susceptible to communism, a vivid threat to human rights. An economically strong Germany was an essential part of an economically strong Europe. But Germany's neighbors were profoundly distrustful after the Nazis. Alleviating their fears required continuing American involvement in European security, first through the Marshall Plan and then through the North Atlantic Treaty of 1949, which created NATO. Intense efforts were made to move Germany toward democratic institutions and the rule of law within a closely integrated Europe. To general surprise, Germany's constitutional court became a stalwart protector of human rights and stimulated the progress of human rights law throughout Europe by insisting that before the Federal Republic transferred its authority to the European Community, basic human rights had to be guaranteed under the protection of fully developed democratic institutions. This was evidently a bitter lesson of World War II and the Holocaust. How many catastrophes do we need around the globe to learn such lessons and put them into practice of decency?

The Council of Europe was another essential actor in securing a democratic Western Europe. With the European Court of Human Rights at its heart, it engaged all Western Europe in a unified community dedicated to maintaining human rights.[16] Williams gives an institutional and historical overview of Europe's mechanisms for human rights promotion and protection, starting with efforts of the Council of Europe in maintaining and protecting human rights through the 1950 European Convention for the Protection of Human Rights and Fundamental Freedoms. There followed an evolution of human rights, from the 1957 Treaty of Rome, which established the European Economic Community, to the 1997 European Union Treaty of Amsterdam.[17]

Thus, Europe has developed two independent legal entities that deal with human rights. The European Court of Human Rights in Strasbourg is attached to the Council of Europe, and the European Court of Justice in Luxembourg is associated with the European Union. While independent, these institutions influence each other. Taken together, they constitute a powerful bulwark for human rights.

The postwar years saw an outburst of creative thinking and institution building for human rights, democracy, economic cooperation, and nonviolent conflict resolution. Europe had learned deeply bitter lessons. The vital European Convention on Human Rights is still the core of the Council of Europe. It is a simple document, deeply influenced by the United Nations' 1948 Universal Declaration of Human Rights, but more binding. To become a member of the respected Council of Europe, a state must commit to upholding this convention. Each of the council's forty-plus member states appoints one judge to the court and agrees to accept its judgments. The European Court of Human Rights and the Inter-American Court of Human Rights are the only international courts in the world that accept individual petitions against violations of human rights by the governments of member states.

After the disintegration of the Soviet Union, the Eastern and Central European states asked to join the Council of Europe. The European Court of Human Rights became a full-time body in permanent session, composed of one judge nominated by each member state, with jurisdiction over the whole of Europe. Its institutions have substantially strengthened human rights and the promotion of democracy throughout Europe. This has been facilitated by educational programs for the countries of Central and Eastern Europe in transition to pluralistic democracy. They have included training of legal professionals and judicial institution building in most of these countries.

The Council of Europe was therefore in a favorable position to help the emerging democracies at the end of the Cold War. It had decades of experience in building democratic institutions with an independent judicial system and a deep commitment to norms and practices of human rights. Membership in its community of established democracies has had a potent attraction that offers instant status and carries little baggage. Because decisions of its Court of Human Rights have equal authority over every member state, and every member state has the right to name one judge to the court, old and new members enjoy the same rank. Almost every state within the boundaries of Europe, from Turkey to Russia, has ratified the Convention for the Protection of Human Rights.[18] Ceaseless efforts at implementation are required.

The European Court of Justice, the highest court in the European Community, is another bulwark of human rights. Its main responsibility is the interpretation of the treaties that established the EC and the EU. The court quickly established two principles that have served as powerful weapons, allowed it to broaden its authority, and made a vital contribution to the continuing success of the European Community. The first, the principle of direct effect, makes EC law directly binding on member states, not indirectly through their national governments. The second, the principle of the supremacy of EC law, gives community law precedence over national law, including national constitutional law. However, this precedence is restricted to those areas over which the EC has jurisdiction. It is truly remarkable how much a basically economic charter could contribute to advancing the human rights spelled out in other international agreements.[19]

International human rights norms are now an integral part of European morality and policies. The EU learned from the tragic situations in Bosnia, Rwanda, and Kosovo and is assuming a global role as a promoter of human rights and significant source of financial aid for countries building democratic institutions. The EU, working closely with the Organization for Security and Co-operation in Europe (OSCE) and the Council of Europe, has supported programs of education on human and minority rights that extend far beyond the borders of Europe.

Europe has learned from a century of extensive human rights violations (colonial opposition, wars, genocides) that new norms, laws, and institutions must be firmly established; the benefits of international cooperation recognized; and a helping hand extended to peoples seeking freedom, human dignity, and nonviolent intergroup relations. The European experience offers an authentic basis for hope in all lands and provides a model for other regions to emulate, each in its own way, but consistent in adhering to basic human rights. Here again, perennial vigilance will be required because the potential benefits for *all humanity* are at stake.

INTERNATIONAL COURTS PERTINENT
TO MASS VIOLENCE

The International Criminal Court (ICC) is relatively new and is struggling to establish itself. National courts have primary jurisdiction over cases involving genocide, war crimes, and crimes against humanity, but they are required to cede power to the ICC if they prove unable or unwilling to carry out a particular prosecution. The purpose of the ICC is not to supplant but to supplement national courts. One of its principal goals is prevention of a crisis by strengthening domestic officials and groups who support the rule of law. To get national courts to try their own war criminals and perpetrators of crimes against humanity and genocide, it offers incentives that range from supporting domestic groups that advocate trials to alerting recalcitrant domestic courts (and the criminal elites who intimidate them) that the international community is monitoring their actions.[20]

International tribunals are useful in particular circumstances:[21] when the national government is unable or unwilling to prosecute; when there is a question of conflict of interest because the national government is (or is perceived to be) in control of, complicit with, or sympathetic to the alleged criminals brought to trial; or when the gravity of the crime gives the international or even the whole human community a substantial interest in the case.

There are achievements of tribunals in Rwanda, South Africa, and the former Yugoslavia that reflect the moral value of these international courts. The tribunals have widely publicized the *norms of international humanitarian law*. Their procedures and decisions have begun a new international jurisprudence that can have a beneficial influence on national law as well. They have started to move international humanitarian law from a state-centered approach toward a human rights–oriented approach.[22] The UN Security Council created the tribunals to notify abusers that they will not have impunity in the future. So far, so good. But the implementation is difficult as perpetrators are often protected at home. Strong pressure from the international community is needed.

In today's increasingly globalized world, major problems tend to be no longer simply domestic but rather domestic aspects of international problems. As national regulators, judges, and legislators encounter their foreign counterparts, they create horizontal networks that foster practical cooperation. International learning, whether by governments, academic scholars, or NGOs, can be helpful.

The Rome Statute that established an international criminal court foresaw direct working relationships between national and international tribunals. These relationships have already had significant unforeseen consequences, most notably when interactions between the European Court of Justice and domestic EU member-state courts triggered the establishment and operation of a comprehensive EU legal system.

When recommending the European Union's excellent work in this field as a stimulating model for other regions, one must take into account its distinctive advantages. EU member states have a shared history, area, and culture, as well as common political and economic beliefs, all conducive to cooperative networks. These networks, realizing the dreadful pain of earlier experience, also share a considerable trust in each other, underpinned by the awareness that they will be partners for a long time.[23] Other regional organizations will in due course be able to build similar strengths—but not quickly or easily. *The importance of enduring relationships* cannot be overemphasized—among nations as well as among individuals and families.

Following the Nuremberg trials, decades passed before national and international bodies began negotiations about establishing a permanent international court to punish war crimes, crimes against humanity, and genocide. One side in the negotiations, which included international law groups and human rights NGOs, argued that an international court should be given primary jurisdiction over such crimes. The other side, which included the United States, some other states, and some national law groups, argued for "complementarity"—granting primary jurisdiction to national courts but giving the ICC "complementary" jurisdiction if the national courts were unwilling or unable to act.[24]

After much debate, the Rome Statute was adopted in 1999 and signed by 160 countries. It established a complementary jurisdictional structure, according to which the ICC may take jurisdiction of a case *only* after the ICC prosecutor judges a member state unable or unwilling to tackle it; the prosecutor's decision is subject to review by an ICC panel. It will probably take years of litigation to establish precisely what "unable or unwilling" actually means in this context. The ICC's relationship with national courts around the world is likely to make it a stronger and more effective institution. The relationship may well become a mutually beneficial full partnership, in which ICC decisions help national courts in handling newly emerging subjects in international criminal law.[25] Indeed, this may facilitate a new model of states in which national government officials interact substantively with one another, share best practices, and agree on cooperative solutions to joint problems.

HUMAN RIGHTS: PATHWAY TO INTERNATIONAL COOPERATION FOR PREVENTING MASS VIOLENCE

There is a strong link between virulent human rights abuses and the instigation of deadly conflict—war or genocide or both. Conversely, reliable safeguards for human rights go a long way to prevent mass violence.[26] When, in the post–World War II period, Eleanor Roosevelt and her valiant international collaborators set in motion the human rights movement, very few "sophisticated" observers expected a pervasive worldwide movement for human rights to follow. Yet that is what happened, in response to a deeply felt human need for decency. Human rights have increasingly transcended the boundaries of individual countries and become a legitimate domain of politics and human relations, not only for nation-states, but also for international and regional organizations, both governmental and nongovernmental.

The growth and strength of human rights beliefs, norms, processes, and institutions have largely been a surprise throughout the world. One remarkable achievement of the human rights movement that occurred in a Cold War context has become known as the Helsinki Process. It began in 1973—at the instigation of the then Soviet Union—with the establishment of the Conference on Security and Cooperation in Europe (CSCE). The Soviet leadership wanted to secure an agreement that would in essence legitimize its hegemony in Eastern Europe. To get this, they had to agree to human rights provisions that ultimately contributed to the dissolution of the Soviet empire, exposing its grand illusions of social justice that had earlier seemed so attractive in many countries.

The first major agreement was the Helsinki Final Act, signed by CSCE heads of state in 1975. In this document, for the first time, respect for human rights and fundamental freedoms was recognized as a basic principle for regulating relations between states. As usual, there was much ambivalence about this step—on both sides of the Iron Curtain. But over time it had a contagious effect, especially as courageous dissidents fought for its implementation. Governmental leadership also became important, as exemplified most vividly by presidents Ford, Carter, Reagan, and Gorbachev.

The Helsinki Process fulfilled its promise as it moved beyond anti-Soviet rhetoric to principles and practices for the protection of human rights throughout Europe, east and west. A variety of vigorous, democratic, converging nongovernmental organizations arose in the post-Helsinki context. This movement became a constructive part of the new European system for human rights and democracy. Thus, the Helsinki Process was a significant part of the worldwide movement toward an international regime for human rights and democracy.

THE PERSPECTIVE OF A PRESIDENTIAL HUMAN RIGHTS LEADER

President Jimmy Carter points out that one of the sources of rising human rights awareness after World War II was the decolonization movement in

Asia and Africa, accompanied by economic and political development.[27] These campaigns for independence and equal rights had a cross-pollinating character: Gandhi profoundly influenced Dr. King's thought, and he in turn inspired Nelson Mandela, Desmond Tutu, and Tibet's Dalai Lama.[28]

Technological advances accelerated the demand for fundamental rights: first radio and film, then television, and today the Internet give a clear picture of the advantages of a free life. Improvements in medicine and public health have provided better nutrition, sanitation, and basic health care, and with this the energy and hope to strive for basic rights. NGOs, such as the Carter Center, have helped developing nations to take advantage of these opportunities.

President Carter writes that he was inspired by Harry Truman's and Lyndon Johnson's dedication to civil rights and outlines the steps his own administration took to promote human rights (although he is too restrained to point out that he was the first president to make that issue an explicit high priority in foreign policy).[29] He argues against shortsightedly using US support of human rights only as a propaganda weapon and stresses the importance of urging our sometimes autocratic allies to move toward higher standards.[30]

The United States, and other influential nations as well, can exert strong pressure for constructive change and give hope to the oppressed by supporting treaties and institutions that endorse the *universal* nature of human rights and encourage their enforcement. They must also take action, using their material and technical resources, to reduce poverty and disproportionate economic inequity in less fortunate states. This will be done best by encouraging and cooperating with both governmental and nongovernmental organizations, as outlined in our chapter on development.

CAN INSTITUTIONS OF INTERNATIONAL JUSTICE HELP TO PREVENT MASS VIOLENCE?

Such institutions make it less likely that mass murderers can act with impunity behind the shield of sovereignty, and have an important role in public education by developing and communicating compelling norms of decent human relations at all levels: intranational, intergroup, and international. They probably influence for the better those populations susceptible to hateful demagogues. Still, they are no panacea. Would a fanatic such as Hitler be inhibited by the threat of an international criminal court at the end of his road? Probably not. But early conditions would be less conducive to his virulent, destructive prejudices and actions, and the inhibiting influences on his less fanatic supporters might well make a difference. Opposition to tyranny takes many paths, especially democratic rule of law, nationally and internationally. As in all prevention of mass violence, the necessary metric for efficacy is decades or generations. But surely the time has come to provide multiple obstacles to mass murder and build a cumulative record of increasing knowledge and skill to prevent atrocious behavior in whatever ugly form it may take. People and societies have a decent, pragmatic, problem-solving aspect that may yet build concepts, processes, and institutions that fulfill the promise of our common humanity.

SEVEN

— ⸎ —

WEAPONS AGAINST PEACE

Overcoming History's Most Dangerous Armaments

> *Napoleon supposedly once said to his men before they went to battle—he pointed to a bayonet and said—"Men, you can do anything with your bayonet except sit on it." He wanted them to use it. I felt just about the opposite about nuclear weapons: the only thing you can do with a nuclear weapon is sit on them because it's too horrible to think about even the use of those weapons.*
> —**Senator Sam Nunn**, *former chair of the Armed Services Committee, US Senate, from Eric Hamburg/Rick English documentary* Preventing Genocide, *2009, Stanford University Library*

MOVING TOWARD ELIMINATION OF NUCLEAR WEAPONS

A remarkable meeting between American president Ronald Reagan and the Soviet leader Mikhail Gorbachev occurred at Reykjavik, Iceland, in 1986. At that summit, still in the midst of the Cold War, Gorbachev and Reagan faced the danger of a nuclear conflict directly. They agreed on the revolutionary goal of eliminating all nuclear weapons. Their effort was a profoundly significant and serious one, but they were unable to complete the deal. The

110

seriousness in the discussions between Reagan and Gorbachev is evident in the official transcript of their anguished final negotiating session, an extra one not originally scheduled for their meeting. Both leaders had become nuclear abolitionists—a position for which the world was not yet ready. Problems of domestic politics interfered in both countries.

During the first decade of the twenty-first century, a group of eminent physicists, arms control experts, and diplomats took up the Reagan-Gorbachev challenge and have been exploring how a world free of nuclear weapons can become technically and politically plausible. They build on recent negotiations relying on cooperative transparency, reliable information exchange, and on-site challenge inspections to ensure the control of nuclear weapons and their delivery vehicles. Their focus is on a condition of no assembled nuclear weapons, limiting weapon components and delivery vehicles to declared facilities that are open to inspection.[1] In moving toward zero nuclear weapons, difficult as that is politically, they are concerned with end-state variations, whether requiring control of all nuclear explosive materials or only of nuclear weapon components—that is, construct new steps toward a state in which there would be no functional nuclear weapons in the world. They propose very serious measures to make the end state stable, desirable, and feasible in itself, no matter how or when it might be reached.

They provide examples of the ability to establish that a nuclear weapons program has been successfully dismantled. In the twenty years since the original Nunn-Lugar Cooperative Threat Reduction Program, this has become the most successful and comprehensive effort to restrict the spread of weapons of mass destruction. It has deactivated more than 7,600 strategic nuclear warheads in the former Soviet Union. Senator Lugar points out that this is a number larger than the arsenals of France, Britain, and China combined. Moreover, the program has destroyed more than 2,300 nuclear-capable missiles and nearly 700 missile launchers. In addition, 820,000 rounds of chemical munitions have been destroyed, and more than 2,247 metric tons of chemical weapons have been neutralized. These results, though not yet complete, suggest the potential effectiveness of our response to some of the world's most crucial problems, including energy supplies, abundant food production, dealing with water scarcity, combating virulent diseases, coping with drastic climate change, and restricting proliferation of weapons of mass destruction.[2]

A global consensus and commitment will have to be established to further drastically reduce the nuclear danger. Recent expressions of support from international leaders—both scientific and political—have been of growing importance. But a much broader and more intense engagement of the public at large is needed. This will depend on a strong, well-known, highly respected international commitment of experts who have examined the end-state options in moving toward a nuclear-free world and who explain broadly and clearly to a worldwide, thoughtful audience the immense nuclear danger—past, present, and future—and the options for diminishing it. The public must be brought into an understanding that will enable them to act and advocate from an educated perspective.

As global nuclear arsenals are reduced to very small numbers, the world will have to confront very difficult challenges. Sidney Drell, a prominent physicist and arms control expert at Stanford University, working together with George Shultz, William Perry, Sam Nunn, and Henry Kissinger plus a number of highly respected scholars and scientists, has played a leading role in examining ways of greatly reducing the nuclear danger, preferably leading eventually to zero nuclear weapons. Drell and James Goodby, an eminent diplomat, put forward key reasons to examine these challenges now. A serious commitment to moving in this direction requires the best possible understanding of potential dangers as the numbers of weapons decline from hundreds all the way to *zero—the end state*. A persuasive case for worldwide commitments to zero nuclear weapons must be based on the best possible analyses of feasibility and risk and a clear understanding of what zero means in practice, because knowledge of nuclear weapons cannot be globally erased.[3]

Drell and Goodby describe useful techniques: satellites; standardized data exchanges; on-site inspections on a scheduled basis, but also challenge inspections that are unexpected; monitoring from multiple perspectives—tags and seals, sensors, and detection devices; remote viewing as conducted already by the International Atomic Energy Agency; and human intelligence. Thus, concerns about slipping out of agreements can be minimized by careful, systematic techniques applied consistently over time.[4] The current concern about Iran illustrates this problem.

This work is realistic in constructing steps through which the end state might ultimately be reached. It includes major, important efforts by the United States and Russia (still the largest bomb-holders) to reduce their operationally deployed nuclear weapons of all types to a much lower range than the current one, amounting to a few hundred. This still represents a gigantic destructive capacity but is much better than anything we have had in decades. Other nuclear powers, notably France, the United Kingdom, China, India, Pakistan, and Israel, have shown some understanding of these issues and would need to grasp the very practical fact that they would be better off at lower levels than those they have now. There are various paths to such reductions, each of which offers some reassurance to the participating states, and these various options need to be considered carefully by all of them. One possibility is that each nuclear nation could reduce its warheads to zero while retaining the capacity to reconstitute some or all of them within agreed ground rules of numbers, procedures, and duration.

The creative and courageous proposals of Drell and Goodby's work necessarily involve both strategic and tactical (short-range and readily movable) nuclear weapons. Recent years have seen a drastic spread of technology attractive to suicidal terrorist organizations and highly violence-prone entities. This changes the outlook on nuclear deterrence. Rather than continuing to deploy nuclear weapons for "hair trigger" launch, allowing only a few minutes for an utterly fateful, catastrophic decision, it is essential to move toward a situation in which nations are months away from being able to take such a disastrous action. Moreover, every effort must be made to extend the Cooperative Nuclear Threat Reduction Program, known as Nunn-Lugar, around the world. Governments and populations need to see that it is in their self-interest to do so. Apathy in this regard is exceedingly dangerous for the whole world.

These two experienced leaders emphasize tactical weapons because of their suitability for terrorists and leaders in panic. Russia retains a large stockpile of tactical nuclear weapons, estimated at about 2,000, and many of these are deployed in Europe. Russia, too, has a vital interest in the security of tactical nuclear weapons—its own and those of others. A dialogue among the United States, NATO, and Russia focused on accountability, transparency, reductions, and elimination should be a high priority and should not await formal agreements. Steps to increase warning and decision time for political and military leaders should be central to this dialogue, so that no nation fears a short-warning conventional attack or perceives the need to deter or defend against such an attack with tactical nuclear arms. Progress including action on these issues can be made separately, as long as all issues are being seriously addressed in parallel and within a common framework. Military-to-military discussions mandated by political leaders are essential.[5]

Changes in leadership in each of these countries (e.g., the return of Putin in the Russian presidency) are likely to complicate these tasks, yet there are powerful reasons of self-interest that may be clarified across boundaries.

PIONEERING INITIATIVES IN COOPERATIVE THREAT REDUCTION

The breakthrough work on cooperative threat reduction illustrates improbable initiatives that can in fact be accomplished. The original Nunn-Lugar proposal for cooperative threat reduction was opposed by a bevy of senior senators, who saw it as helping the enemy. Nunn then looked for a better way to persuade. Shortly after the failed coup to overthrow Gorbachev, we felt that a nuclear Soviet Union might be descending into chaos. I organized a briefing in Nunn's Senate office in which Ashton Carter described a study he had recently completed for Carnegie, titled "Soviet Nuclear Fission: Control of the Nuclear Arsenal in the Disintegrating Soviet Union." Its effect was strong in clarifying the nuclear danger in a time of chaos. Nunn and Lugar proposed the program as an amendment to the defense budget rather than foreign aid, thus making it more acceptable. When they proposed it to a group of senior senators, there was strong opposition. Remarkably, the senators changed their positions when the study with its dangerous facts was presented to them, and the proposal passed, setting in motion years of progress described elsewhere in this book.

To keep the arms control momentum going, Nunn led a Senate delegation to Russia and Ukraine in March 1992. Perry, Carter, and I accompanied the group. All were concerned with what was happening with nuclear weapons in Russia and Ukraine, both of which were in a state of turmoil. On the long flight home, we drafted a more expansive plan for a cooperative threat-reduction program. Congress approved the bill, the Freedom Support Act, in the summer of 1992. It provided another $400 million for a variety of steps, including the safeguarding and dismantlement of nuclear, chemical, and biological weapons, as well as the establishment of science and technology centers to keep weapons scientists and engineers engaged.

William Perry has played a highly constructive role in reducing the nuclear danger and in formulating a doctrine of preventive defense. It was a privilege to work with him in developing a preventive orientation, which he established as secretary of defense, and in the years since then in collaboration with

Ashton Carter in the Stanford-Harvard Preventive Defense Program. The latter has conducted many useful studies, meetings, and defense doctrines. Carter is now one of the highest officials in the Department of Defense and still oriented to prevention.

Perry was attending a Carnegie-sponsored Aspen Institute meeting when Les Aspin, Clinton's initial choice to be secretary of defense, asked him to serve as deputy secretary. His first reaction was to decline, but he spent many hours with Nunn and me considering the possibilities. We favored his doing it, and he came around to our viewpoint. As punishment for our persuasion, we spoke at his swearing-in, and it was apparent from the start that his role as a high defense official would be exceedingly valuable, not least in minimizing the dangers of nuclear war.

In the formulation following Reykjavik, nuclear deterrence would still exist, thereby providing some reassurance for states that feel vulnerable, but the deterrence would be latent or virtual. It is essential to bear in mind that there is no final escape from the catastrophic consequences of nuclear conflict if it were to occur. But there could be much more time to reconsider panicky orientations and devise alternatives that are not apocalyptic.

We must reiterate that during the perilous years of the Cold War, a group of distinguished collaborators in the scientific and policy communities urged leaders of the superpowers to develop rules of mutual accommodation: avoid direct superpower confrontation; avoid nuclear threats; respect the vital interests of the adversary; avoid expounding grandiose interests; avoid dehumanization or humiliation of the adversary; keep in mind the common humanity of the adversary, especially in times of stress; and take advantage of favorable conditions to widen contacts across adversarial boundaries to the extent possible. These remain useful guidelines for future conflicts throughout the world.

MOVING TOWARD THE NUCLEAR END STATE

In the end state, a line must be drawn between permissible agreed-upon activities and those that must be explicitly restrained or prohibited altogether. The length of time would vary—for example, an appropriate time for a former nuclear weapons state that had dismantled its entire nuclear arsenal but retained the facilities, spare components, and technical expertise to support a declining nuclear stockpile during the reduction process. A longer period would be reasonable for a country that had no nuclear weapons infrastructure at all.

Advances toward the end state will require several actions:

1. Limiting national nuclear forces for all nations that have nuclear arms, including warheads and delivery systems, tactical and strategic, both in deployed and nondeployed circumstances;
2. Strengthening the Nuclear Non-Proliferation Treaty;
3. Creating a fissile material cutoff treaty to prevent production of more nuclear material, and requiring that existing nuclear supplies be made unsuitable as weapons;
4. Universally accepting the Comprehensive Test Ban Treaty; and
5. Establishing an international control regime of the highest quality for the complete fuel cycle for civil nuclear power—especially in light of the 2011 Japanese nuclear disaster.

Once the number of US- and Russian-deployed strategic warheads approaches levels close to 1,000, negotiations on reducing nuclear forces will have to include other nuclear-capable nations. Even sooner, other states will have to be involved intellectually, technically, and politically because a world without nuclear weapons is only feasible as a deeply international enterprise. The nuclear danger exists everywhere. It is destructive in the extreme, and this provides *motivation for all humanity to invest in its own survival.*

HOW TO KNOW WHAT IS HAPPENING

More transparency will be required than is now considered acceptable politically, including direct access to nuclear test sites and information exchanges on R&D programs, nuclear experiments, fissile material production, and the stockpiling of fissile materials. The scientific community has shown that it is possible to increase transparency and mutual trust by organizing programs involving scientific collaboration in interlaboratory exchanges. This must go beyond short inspection visits. One important precedent is the way the United States has worked cooperatively with Russia in the Nunn-Lugar program on the construction of facilities for secure, consistently monitored storage of dismantled nuclear warheads.

Given the almost unimaginative destructive power of even a few nuclear weapons, it is vital to solidify cooperative efforts that provide protection against cheating during the final stages of drawdown. This will call for research on systems for detecting and tracking nuclear components, as well as shared early warning systems and defenses against all forms of nuclear attack.

Nuclear disarmament, important as it is, could not end international disputes and military conflict. Intense diplomatic efforts to resolve emerging regional crises at an early stage, establish norms for limiting conventional force levels, and strengthen multiple prevention mechanisms will be essential to make sustainable a world free of nuclear weapons. This will require broad international cooperation beyond present levels—based on the understanding that such cooperation is of mutual benefit to all.

Drell and Goodby have drawn together much careful analytical work—physical, political, and psychological—to make this approach sustainable in the end state. They summarize as follows. Before eliminating all their nuclear weapons, the nations involved would need to be confident of the following:

1. Permissible activities that are part of a responsive nuclear infrastructure could be monitored and verified, even after reaching zero;
2. Warheads scheduled for elimination could be dismantled under conditions that would ensure their actual dismantling, with the nuclear components placed in secure and monitored storage pending final disposition;
3. Procedures for challenge inspections to search for concealed warheads had been established and satisfactorily exercised;
4. Delivery vehicles scheduled for elimination had been verifiably destroyed, and procedures were in place to confirm that dual-use systems were not armed with nuclear warheads;
5. Cooperative defense systems against nuclear attack had been deployed by the nations that wished to participate in joint defense; and
6. Compliance mechanisms had been established to enforce nuclear agreements.

To minimize the risks of breakout from agreed constraints, the nations involved will need to agree on answers to three important questions: (1) What are the necessary elements of an adequate nuclear infrastructure, that is, one with a capacity for limited and timely reconstitution of a deterrent should that become necessary? (2) What activities, facilities, or weapons-related items should be prohibited? (3) What can be done to ensure early and reliable warning of a breakout attempt? Expert personnel with the requisite skills and adequate circumstances are the most important components of a responsive infrastructure. Given the necessary resources, the experts can be relied on to respond quickly and accurately to unanticipated problems or changes in requirements. Without such talent and consistent dedication, no amount of resources will be adequate. Preparation for prevention of disaster crucially requires highly competent, trustworthy, interdisciplinary, and international cooperation in this great mission.

The establishment of interdisciplinary, international *centers of excellence for prevention* will be increasingly important. Some serious people who want to reduce the nuclear danger are afraid to do so because the knowledge, and sometimes the motivation, of destruction exists. Yet the intellect to constrain the weapons and their delivery systems also exists, as well as motivation for survival. Thus it should be possible to implement the concepts of this chapter.

DIPLOMACY, POLITICS, AND PSYCHOLOGY

Ambassador Chester A. Crocker envisions a prospective world order that vastly reduces the role of nuclear weapons and emphasizes the importance of the geopolitical context in which reductions take place, thus requiring in-depth, sustained diplomatic efforts. Such efforts would direct attention to neglected areas of decent international relations, a major advantage of the elimination enterprise.

Approaching the end state, and after reaching it, crucial questions are: Would instabilities among the nuclear weapons states arise? If so, what are they, and how can they be overcome? Would drastic nuclear reductions become a temptation for aggression against one of the current nuclear weapons states by a nonnuclear weapon state? How do conventional forces fit into the picture? What would be the possible effects on alliances? What would be the possible effects on international organizations?

Thus, more than ever before, we see a readiness and competence to ask the hard questions that must be answered for safety. The unique strength of the United States in nuclear weapons and delivery systems has elicited fear and envy in some governments and peoples. They might think that the United States is urging nuclear disarmament on others to gain total domination for itself. It is necessary to buffer such attitudes constructively and consistently.

The resurgence of analytical work on behavioral and political obstacles gives a realistic basis to do what is necessary.

Crocker's analysis suggests that the United States must either strengthen the international institutions in which it participates or create new ones. Some experts in this field who have a worldwide view recommend establishment of a new, overarching framework that constitutes a comprehensive forum to resolve the basic issues and ongoing tensions in a manifestly open and fair way. Whatever one's view of the feasibility of eliminating nuclear weapons, the world needs *unparalleled cooperation* in moving toward effective verification and keeping the deadliest weapons of all time out of dangerous hands. All of this involves far greater public understanding of the continuing nuclear danger as well as viable paths toward its reduction. The same is true of the entire problem of preventing mass violence.

Ingenious possibilities arise that offer a basis for hope. For example, Drell and Christopher Stubbs, a Harvard physicist, recently reexamined a technical possibility to improve the situation. For more than half a century, the Open Skies Treaty has had the agreed capacity for short-notice, unrestricted territorial access to verification from aircraft. This gives atmospheric collection options that cannot be done from satellites. A renewed engagement in Open Skies, to update its technology to modern standards, can be achieved with modest investments from the United States Departments of State and Defense in cooperation with other countries. This can lay an important foundation for the technical verification challenges ahead, based on an existing and successful international cooperative agreement that involves the kind of international cooperation that will be essential for drastic redirection of the nuclear danger. "The fact that the Open Skies collection platforms are aircraft provides technical verification opportunities that simply are not possible from satellites, for example airborne collection of trace gas and particulate samples. These data are important in searching for covert weapons of mass destruction development programs, and the fact that Open Skies allows for full, unrestricted, territorial access is an important feature."[6] Such observation could very well offer authentic reassurance to an apprehensive public.

ADDRESSING OTHER DANGERS

We have necessarily reiterated that "small arms" and "light weapons" now cover the world. This collective euphemism includes highly lethal machine guns, mortars, automatic rifles, and rocket launchers as well as dirty bombs. Only modest efforts have been made to get a handle on this problem, yet international interest is growing. We have seen that highly lethal weapons—whether or not they technically qualify as weapons of mass destruction—have an intoxicating effect on political demagogues, religious fanatics, and ethnic haters. There is a recent and exceedingly dangerous movement toward proliferation of nuclear weapons in the context of fanatical leadership (e.g., North Korea, Iran). There is now serious consideration of this problem in some academic institutions and human rights organizations, in the United States and other democratic governments such as the Scandinavian countries, as well as the UN and the EU. The problem is not beyond human capacity.

We have reached a point in human history in which all populations, states, and regions are vulnerable to large-scale casualties from well-organized, fanatical haters, religious and political ideologues, repressive states, or deeply troubled individuals. The threat is one that already involves many countries, and in principle could involve *all*. This should urgently stimulate the building of internationally cooperative efforts to overcome the very dangerous problems of terrorism and other highly lethal conflicts. As a practical matter, these problems simply cannot be overcome without a high degree of international cooperation around the world. There are many aspects of human relations having deep satisfaction in joint accomplishment.

The worldwide danger includes the possibility of mass atrocities motivated by religious and/or political and/or ethnic hatreds. It is difficult to contemplate any stronger stimulus for the international community to come together in common cause and in urgent cooperation for survival. Humanity must come to realize that these are not useful weapons of war but rather instruments of *mass suicide*. Surely this is not what we humans want or seek. Thus, the unique intellectual capacities long central to human adaptation must be brought to bear on this existential crisis.

PROMOTING SAFE AND PEACEFUL GROWTH OF NUCLEAR ENERGY: CAN IT BE DONE?

"Promoting Safe, Secure, and Peaceful Growth of Nuclear Energy"—a joint study of Harvard's Belfer Center for Science and International Affairs (headed by Graham Allison), a pioneer in preventing nuclear danger, and the Kurchatov Institute (headed by Evgeniy Velikhov, who played a major role in coping with Chernobyl)—spells out some steps the two countries could take to meet their common objectives. The report is part of a broader effort, the US-Russia Initiative to Prevent Nuclear Terrorism, which the Belfer Center launched in 2010. The report's central premise is that enhanced nuclear security—including measures to protect nuclear facilities and prevent the spread of nuclear materials and weapons—is not only important for the well-being of the world's citizens, but also essential to the future of nuclear energy—which has major potential advantages over traditional fuels yet also serious danger.

That future has been darkened since the joint study was published by the 2011 nuclear crisis in Japan. Still, this dreadful event leaves the fact that economies the world over confront the immense burden of finding ample energy sources that can be used with minimal environmental harm and whose supplies are not easily disrupted or subject to dramatic price increases. This is an exceedingly difficult, high-risk task.

The greatest danger is the fact that the traditional fossil fuels providing 80 percent of the world's energy are also the main contributors to global warming and climate change, owing to the carbon dioxide given off during their combustion. Carbon-free nuclear power plants could be a big part of satisfying the world's growing energy requirements while reducing our dependence on fossil fuels. Yet a large question remains about dispersing the waste safely. There has been a major decline in the construction of large power plants since the height of nuclear expansion in the 1970s—influenced by the severe accidents of Three Mile Island and Chernobyl, and now reinforced by the Japanese experience.

This Belfer study recommends coping with the problem by the construction of smaller (and intrinsically less hazardous), factory-built reactors of a standardized design that could be exported throughout the world with the leading nuclear powers overseeing the design of these reactors and helping with their installation and operation.

Study codirector Matthew Bunn recommends bolstering security at nuclear plants "because in an age of terrorism, the probability of a big radioactive release from an accident may be less than the probability of someone deliberately trying to make that happen."[7]

ORGANIZING THE VITAL TASKS

Joan Rohlfing, president and CEO of the Nuclear Threat Initiative, in collaboration with former senator Sam Nunn, incisively states vital needs and opportunities[8] in creating the norms, systems, practices, and legal arrangements for regulating nuclear weapons, materials, and technology globally. This includes a universal declaration of materials and weapons inventories by all states that have them; creation, acceptance, and transparent implementation of best practices to achieve security; universal acceptance of monitoring for all facilities with weapons and weapons-usable materials; eliminating weapons stockpiles over time and reducing civil stocks of weapons-usable materials to the barest minimum to support legitimate peaceful uses; shared international management of fuel-cycle facilities and stringent restraints on individual states' possession of such facilities; and a clear way to punish violations.

For all such progress, we need a global understanding of the immense dangers of nuclear weapons, materials, and technologies. We need a much more ambitious global dialogue about risks and dangers, and much more vigorous political and diplomatic engagement to persuade international partners to accept the need to limit and regulate access to materials and technologies of mass destruction. Overall, the dangers of nuclear materials are so great that, even with the potential of clean energy, a global cooperative effort of the highest technical and political quality will be required if this avenue is to be pursued.

BIOSECURITY AND PREVENTING
THE MISUSE OF SCIENCE

The National Research Council of the National Academies, United States, summarized in 2011 the vital issues in this field. The life sciences now have profound and pervasive significance for health, prosperity, security, energy, and environmental safety from single cells to global cycles. The life sciences community is in a ferment of inquiry and innovation in research and development, making unprecedented advances. Yet these opportunities also have great responsibilities—especially in the practice of biosecurity and biopreparedness. This means advancing the life sciences for legitimate purposes while minimizing the risks that some materials, knowledge, and technologies could also be used for great harm. Soon after the 9/11 terrorist attacks on the World Trade Center towers and the Pentagon, letters containing lethal anthrax powder were sent through the mail to New York City; Washington, DC; and other locations. Those letters, which resulted in five deaths and put thousands of people at risk, exemplify serious misuse of biology. Globalization has expanded such vulnerabilities. The scientific and public health communities have seriously addressed this problem only in recent years. Constructive proposals and initiatives are coming into view.

As scientific research evolves, so does its biosecurity context. Policy, governance, and oversight frameworks that affect research in the life sciences are also in ferment. Life scientists, the security community, policymakers, and the public need to be educated about the risks and ways to cope with the dangers preventively. Research institutions, scientific journals, universities, professional societies, governments, and international organizations such as the World Health Organization and the National Academies must tackle these problems.

The National Research Council report of 2011 summarizes crucial considerations:

- Synthesis of infectious poliovirus. Researchers sought to resolve the unusual nature of poliovirus, which behaves as both a chemical and a "living" entity. They succeeded in re-creating the virus through chemical synthesis. Some critics assert that the publication of their methods provided a recipe for terrorists by showing how one could create any virus from chemical reagents purchasable on the open market. The researchers acknowledged this potential but noted that a threat of bioterrorism arises only if mass vaccinations against polio end.
- Development of "stealth" viruses that could evade the human immune system. These viruses are being developed to serve as molecular means for introducing curative genes into patients with inherited diseases. However, the research has raised questions about whether they could potentially be induced to express dangerous proteins, such as toxins.
- A method for the construction of fusion toxins derived from two distinct nontoxic chemical predecessors. This technique was originally investigated for the purpose of killing cancer cells, but it might be redirected to develop novel toxins that could target the normal cells of almost any tissue when introduced into a human host.
- Genetic engineering of the tobacco plant to produce subunits of cholera toxin. Because tobacco is easy to engineer, it is a likely candidate for producing plant-based vaccines. The technique could be used to produce large quantities of cholera toxin cheaply and relatively easily, paving the way for fast and efficient vaccine production.

- Development of new technologies for delivering drugs by aerosol spray in individual doses. This development, intended to improve the ease of use and rate of compliance among diabetic users of insulin, could be adapted to allow aerosol sprays to cover wider areas in an attack.[9]

All this makes it clear that strong insights, guidelines, and procedures for biopreparedness must be advanced on an interdisciplinary, internationally cooperative basis—accompanied by public education on the dangers and the necessity for serious, sustained prevention efforts.

One model is provided by the 1975 Asilomar conference, which became a powerful example of the scientific community's ability to lead the way in developing new technologies responsibly. The focus of the 1975 conference was recombinant DNA, then a novel technology of unexplored potential and unknown risks. These discussions mobilized excellent scientists and guidelines in 1976 by the National Institutes of Health to prevent the unintended creation of harmful organisms in work with recombinant DNA. The influence of this experience has inspired responsible conduct in practical preventive measures in the scientific community that continue to be intrinsically valuable and useful for other problems to the present time. The important step is to keep in mind the potential danger of biological terrorism and to achieve prevention by totally responsible scientific procedures and practical cooperation with the security community.

TAKING PREVENTION TO THE SOURCE

The ubiquitous presence of exceedingly dangerous weapons is enabled by their irresponsible provision by major nations. At the extreme of lethality, biological, chemical, and above all nuclear weapons have almost unimaginable killing power. Highly lethal weapons have an intoxicating effect on political demagogues, religious fanatics, and ethnic haters. There is a renewed and exceedingly dangerous movement toward proliferation of nuclear weapons in the context of fanatical leadership. It is essential that serious consideration of this problem be given in academic institutions, "umbrella" scientific organizations (national and international), human rights organizations, democratic governments, the UN, the EU, and other regional organizations.

We have reached a point in human history in which *all* populations, states, and regions are vulnerable to large-scale casualties from well-organized, fanatical haters; religious and political ideologues; repressive states; or deeply troubled individuals. The threat is one that already involves many countries, and, in principle, could involve all. This should stimulate the building of internationally cooperative efforts to overcome the very dangerous terrorism problem. As a practical matter, the problem simply cannot be overcome without a high degree of international cooperation.

The cheapest and most effective defense is to securely control weapons and fissile materials *everywhere they are stored*. Much progress has been made, but a lot more is needed. The worldwide danger includes the possibility of mass atrocities motivated by religious, political, or ethnic hatreds. Thus, in the first two decades of the twenty-first century, a new ferment of ideas, innovations, deep concern, and long-term vision is coming to life in ways that offer promise of seriously, creatively, and globally addressing the dreadful risks of wildly irresponsible weaponry. There is so much yet to be done that we have no basis for complacency, but at least there is an authentic basis for hope in the long run in the approaches outlined in this chapter. This is a pillar of immense significance.

PART II

WHO CAN DO WHAT FOR PEACE?

EIGHT

❦

THE UNITED STATES AND
OTHER DEMOCRACIES

Worldwide concern to avoid the recurrence of an eminently preventable and highly contagious disaster cries out for establishment of *strong focal units* within major democracies and international institutions that will assemble from around the world the knowledge and skill of many professions, disciplines, and nations. They can develop and make public ways to recognize emerging intergroup tensions that are likely to lead to violent abuses. Action must not wait until it can be determined whether a particular threat of impending violence will lead to genocide or to some other mass atrocity. Action is essential to prevent the lesser atrocity, not only because it *is* an atrocity (and that in itself is a sufficient reason) but also because unresolved bitterness in a society, left to fester, can reemerge and grow into war or genocide, destruction on a vast and hideous scale. Thus, it is necessary for strong democracies and humane organizations to reach out proactively to nations in trouble and help them to avoid descent down the slippery slope to violence. The international community needs to have information ready at hand about practical measures for prevention that follow the public health model—an approach that uses empirical research to develop and apply a wide array of strategies, tools, and practices for preventing violent outbreaks of all kinds.

Such prevention involves identifying an ailing nation's specific problem(s) and employing evidence-based responses toward resolving them. Some measures, such as early, skillful, and respectful preventive diplomacy, can quickly show beneficial results, just as expert care of a sprained ankle results in rapid healing and prevents an injury from getting worse. Fundamental measures, especially helping a troubled nation build a democratic, equitable, and socioeconomic structure, take longer to apply and even longer to show results. However, the effects are likely to be lasting and pervasive, just as promoting a healthy lifestyle and environment can achieve better health for a society. The extraordinary intellectual, technical, and moral resources of the United States make a strong case for this country's active participation, along with other democracies.

THE UNITED STATES AND ATROCITY PREVENTION: NEXT STEPS

On August 4, 2011, the White House announced that President Obama would direct new steps to prevent mass atrocities. He directed a comprehensive review to strengthen the United States' ability to prevent mass atrocities. The president's directive creates an important new tool in this effort, establishing a standing interagency Atrocities Prevention Board (APB) with the authority to develop prevention strategies and to ensure that concerns are elevated for senior decisionmaking. Thus, the United States is better able to work with its allies and partners responsive to early warning signs and prevent potential atrocities. Obama issued a proclamation that, for the first time, explicitly bars entry into the United States of persons who organize or participate in war crimes, crimes against humanity, and serious violations of human rights.

The president ordered the creation of the board within 120 days so as to coordinate a *whole-of-government approach* to engaging "early, proactively, and decisively." He is committed to early prevention and proactive help.

The president rejects the idea that, in the face of mass atrocity, our options are "limited to either sending in the military or standing by and doing nothing." He instructs his administration to undertake an inventory of the full range of economic, diplomatic, and other tools available to US policymakers; to develop the appropriate governmental organization to try to ensure early and less costly preventive action; to improve the collection and processing of predictors of mass atrocity; to provide a channel for dissent to be raised during a crisis; and to appropriately train and prepare American diplomats, armed services, development professionals, and others.

The directive recognizes that preventing mass atrocities is a responsibility that all nations share. Often, other countries are better positioned than the United States to respond to particular crises or potential atrocities. The directive calls for a strategy for engaging key regional allies and partners so that they can help to prevent crimes against humanity.

If effectively implemented, with the full strength of the United States involved, this organization could make an intrinsically valuable contribution to the policies and practices of prevention. This is particularly true if the emphasis on international cooperation is consistently followed so that resources can be shared: intellectual, technical, and financial. About half a year after the president's directive, a particularly active group in the State Department, stimulated by Secretary Hillary Clinton (who has a long interest in this subject), moved toward implementation. Other departments are also seeking useful measures.

A COMPREHENSIVE STRATEGY AND NEW TOOLS TO PREVENT AND RESPOND TO ATROCITIES

On April 23, 2012, President Obama issued a major statement on implementation of policies to help in preventing mass atrocities:

> Preventing mass atrocities and genocide is a core national security interest and a core moral responsibility of the United States. Our security is affected when masses of civilians are slaughtered, refugees flow across borders, and murderers wreak havoc on regional stability and livelihoods. America's reputation suffers, and our ability to bring about change is constrained, when we are perceived as idle in the face of mass atrocities and genocide. Unfortunately, history has taught us that our pursuit of a world where states do not systematically slaughter civilians will not come to fruition without concerted and coordinated effort. (Presidential Study Directive 10, August 4, 2011)

President Obama has made the prevention of atrocities a key focus of his administration's foreign policy. The Obama administration has taken actions to protect civilians and hold perpetrators of atrocities accountable.

- Participating in international efforts to bring pressure to bear on the abusive Muammar Gadhafi and Bashar al-Assad regimes through the formation of a group of friends, the imposition of extensive sanctions, support for the opposition, and support for efforts to bring perpetrators of atrocities to justice;
- Leadership in securing the passage of UN Security Council Resolutions 1970 and 1973, which authorized—in an unprecedented combination of measures—referral of the situation in Libya to the International Criminal Court, an arms embargo, a no-fly zone, comprehensive sanctions against the Gadhafi regime that preserved Libya's wealth for its people, and a mandate for the protection of civilians and civilian-populated areas under threat of attack;
- Leadership of a successful international military effort to protect civilians in Libya;
- Stimulating an international effort to ensure a peaceful and orderly referendum on the independence of South Sudan;
- Supporting regional efforts to counter the Lord's Resistance Army and apprehend Joseph Kony, including sending military advisers to Central Africa;
- Working with regional and international partners—including UN peacekeepers on the ground—to help protect civilians and bring about the end of a violent electoral standoff in Côte d'Ivoire;
- Helping with the creation of commissions of inquiry to investigate alleged gross violations of human rights (in Côte d'Ivoire, Kyrgyzstan, Libya, and Syria);
- Engaging intensively to support the capture of priority figures wanted by international tribunals (including Goran Hadzic and Ratko Mladic);
- Leading efforts to combat sexual and gender-based violence (SGBV) through creating the U.S. National Action Plan on Women, Peace, and Security; launching innovative pilot programs to prevent such violence and expand access to justice for victims in Kenya, Haiti, and the Democratic Republic of Congo; and supporting the appointment of a dedicated special representative position on SGBV in the UN Secretariat. This initiative in the US government will be headed by a proven leader in this field, Melanne Verveer, with strong backing from the secretary of state.

To counter atrocities more effectively, the US government must prioritize this effort, strengthen and expand the tools available, and establish effective organization. A sequence of actions was taken in 2010—the first-ever White House position dedicated to preventing and addressing war crimes and atrocities. In August 2011, a presidential study directive declared the prevention of mass atrocities and genocide to be a core national security interest and core moral responsibility of the United States, ordering the creation of the APB and directing the National Security Advisor to lead a comprehensive review to assess the US government's anti-atrocity capabilities and to recommend reforms. The administration has directed a range of steps to strengthen the US government's ability to foresee, prevent, and respond to impending mass atrocities.

The APB will help the US government identify and address atrocity threats and oversee institutional changes. Because strong organization and a whole-of-government approach are needed to counter atrocities effectively, the APB will include representatives of the Departments of State, Defense, Treasury, Justice, and Homeland Security; the Joint Staff; the US Agency for International Development (USAID); the US Mission to the United Nations; the Office of the Director of National Intelligence; the Central Intelligence Agency; and the Office of the Vice President—all of whom are at the assistant secretary level or higher and have been appointed by name by their respective principals. The APB will meet at least monthly to oversee the development and implementation of atrocity prevention and response policy, and additionally on an ad hoc basis to deal with urgent situations as they arise. The chair of the APB will be the NSS senior director for Multilateral Affairs and Human Rights. The deputies will meet at least twice a year, the principals once a year, to review the work of the APB. The chair will report on this work annually in a memorandum to the president. After six months of operations, the chair (in consultation with the board) will prepare a draft executive order for consideration by the president that will publicly clarify the structure, functions, and priorities of the board and plan further measures for strengthening atrocity prevention.

The intelligence community will collect and analyze information that allows anticipation and understanding and prepares to counter atrocity threats. The APB will monitor the National Intelligence Council's preparation of the first-ever National Intelligence Estimate on the global risk of mass atrocities and genocide.

For congressional reporting, the APB will also work with the director of national intelligence to include information about mass atrocity threats in the annual threat assessment testimony before Congress. The intelligence community will work internally and with foreign partners to increase the overall collection, analysis, and sharing of information relating to atrocity threats and situations. Diplomats will encourage more robust multilateral efforts to prevent and respond to atrocities. This will require deeper and broader support among bilateral partners as well as international and regional organizations.

The United States will show diplomatic initiative and engage with countries and other stakeholders around the world to expand and deepen international commitment and capacity to prevent atrocities. It will also update training programs for UN peacekeepers to focus on enhanced techniques for civilian protection, including prevention of SGBV.

The United States will work with the United Nations to strengthen UN capacity for conflict prevention and crisis management, including preventive diplomacy and mediation, especially when UN missions encounter escalating atrocity threats. The United States will also work with its partners to build the capacity of regionally based organizations to prevent and respond to atrocities.

President Obama signed an executive order in August 2011 that authorizes sanctions and visa bans against those who commit or facilitate grave human rights abuses via information technology related to Syrian and Iranian regime brutality. This novel sanctions tool is pertinent not only to oppressive governments but also to the companies that enable them with technology they use for oppression and the "digital guns for hire" who create or operate systems used to monitor, track, and target citizens for killing, torture, or other grave abuses. Relevant departments will use the president's visa ban on human rights abusers to deny perpetrators of serious violations of human rights entry to the United States.

The Department of State and USAID will increase the ability of the United States government to provide specialized expertise in civilian protection on a rapid response basis. Also, departments and agencies will compile "lessons-learned" reports (of the sort already performed by the US Armed Forces) to record key innovations, areas of success, and issues requiring future work. USAID will, together with cofunder Humanity United, issue a "Tech Challenge for Atrocity Prevention" that will invite ideas and award grants for ways of strengthening the US government's capacity for early warning, prevention, and response with respect to mass atrocities. USAID will also issue a "Grand Challenge for Development" that will provide major investments and leverage those investments with global partners to bring to scale innovative tools, policy initiatives, and advocacy efforts that will strengthen efforts to prevent mass atrocities.

The Department of the Treasury will position itself to quickly use its financial tools to block the flow of money to abusive regimes and will explore with international partners additional financial measures for prevention. The military and civilian workforce will become better equipped to prevent and respond to atrocities. The Department of Defense (DOD) will further develop operational principles and planning techniques specifically tailored to atrocity prevention. The Joint Staff has prepared an appendix on mass atrocity response operations to be included in its *Joint Publication on Peace Operations*—the training and knowledge to succeed in atrocity-prevention missions. Geographic combatant commands will incorporate mass atrocity prevention and response as a priority in their planning and activities. The DOD will routinely organize exercises incorporating mass atrocity prevention and response scenarios to test operational concepts. The faculty from the service academies met at the US Holocaust Memorial Museum in May 2012 to discuss how to incorporate mass atrocity and genocide prevention into their curricula.

All departments and agencies government-wide that have a role in atrocity prevention and responses have been directed to begin to develop curricula and programs to train military and civilian personnel in civilian protection and atrocity prevention. These departments and agencies have also been directed to create performance incentives for work contributing to atrocity prevention.

The United States will hold accountable perpetrators of mass atrocities and genocide. The Departments of Justice, Homeland Security, and State will develop proposals that strengthen the US government's ability to prosecute perpetrators of atrocities found in the United States and permit the more effective use of immigration laws and immigration fraud penalties to hold accountable perpetrators of mass atrocities. Also, the US government will support national, hybrid, and international mechanisms (including, among other things, commissions of inquiry, fact-finding missions, and tribunals) that seek to hold accountable perpetrators of atrocities consistent with the requirements of US law. These departments will develop options for assisting with witness protection measures and providing technical assistance in connection with foreign and international prosecutions. The Obama administration will work with Congress to expand the Department of State's authority to make reward payments for information that leads to the arrest of foreign nationals indicted for war crimes; crimes against humanity; or genocide by international, hybrid, or mixed criminal tribunals.

Key decisionmakers will receive early warning and hear dissenting views. To ensure that information about potential or ongoing atrocities reaches key decisionmakers in a timely way, departments and agencies will be required to have "alert channels" that will allow individuals to share relevant, unreported information about mass atrocities with the APB—including analysis or reporting that a superior may have blocked from being disseminated—without adverse professional consequences. Comparable procedures within the National Security staff will ensure that information about atrocity threats and situations reaches the president. Here as elsewhere (e.g., the UN and EU), the balance between previolent and postviolent situations will require careful attention.

PROACTIVE HELP IN PREVENTING MASS VIOLENCE: THE UNITED STATES, COOPERATING DEMOCRACIES, AND NONGOVERNMENTAL ORGANIZATIONS AND SECTORS

The relevant considerations on this topic go beyond the government. For both substantive and symbolic reasons, the United States needs to tell the world that, strong though it is, it is not seeking hatred, domination, or harm. On the contrary, the United States genuinely seeks peace and prosperity for its citizens and others—not only through goodwill and exhortation, but through specific concepts, techniques, policies, and practices that will greatly improve human relations and strengthen mechanisms for *constructive measures of cooperation*. Thus, a basic organizing principle for American foreign policy is the prevention of mass violence. This certainly does not mean pacifism, let alone weakness or surrender. Rather, it means the conjunction of hard and smart power to fulfill national aspirations in ways that implement the great, eternal values of the US Declaration of Independence and US Constitution, manifesting this authentic land of opportunity, ingenuity for the common good, and enduring democracy. These are ideals that were later carried into the basic documents of the United Nations and have worldwide influence.

We must reiterate that war now has destructive capabilities almost beyond imagination, and mass atrocities are recurring. No part of the world is so remote and no group so small that it cannot inflict great damage on people everywhere. From both disastrous cases and successful ones, specific guidelines emerge for the international community for promoting decent intergroup relations, democracy instead of oppression, equitable socioeconomic development, and creation of mechanisms for prompt, nonviolent problem-solving in dangerous situations—not waiting for the explosive last moment.

Effective prevention of deadly conflict requires a high degree of cooperation among national governments, intergovernmental organizations, nongovernmental organizations, and the pivotal institutions of civil society. Let us look at the roles they can play—through improved *multilevel cooperation*—in mobilizing effective leadership to promote prevention of mass violence and encourage public commitment to support it. We must use the most recent evidence on building education for peace, gaining cooperative access to troubled countries for authentic joint efforts to improve intergroup relations. We must strengthen preventive diplomacy and foster equitable democratic socioeconomic development over time—starting as early as possible with a warning of tensions. The twentieth century, bloodiest of all in history, taught humanity extremely expensive lessons. We must examine them to find how that hard-won knowledge can be used to build a better future.

THE VALUE OF AMERICAN NGOs FOR THE US GOVERNMENT AND FOR WORLD PEACE

US NGOs are increasing their attention to prevention. An important example of work in this area is a recent report from the highly respected Council on Foreign Relations (CFR). The CFR published a report in 2011 titled "Partners in Preventive Action: The United States and International Institutions." This is a function of the Center for Preventive Action of the CFR, which has grown increasingly significant over the past two decades. It began in conjunction with the Carnegie Commission on Preventing Deadly Conflict, and for five years there was substantial cooperation and complementarity between these two initiatives. The 2011 CFR report provides an overview of global organizations that can usefully work with the United States in the understanding and practice of prevention. There is likely to be increasing significance of such cooperation and broadening of the scope of participation.[1]

Reducing violent conflict around the world is not a task that the United States can or should take on alone; the challenges to international peace are too far-reaching. Large-scale deadly conflicts have diminished—interstate war is currently rare, and civil wars have declined since the mid-1990s. Yet there is no assurance that this trend will continue. The twenty-first century poses many dangers: friction between rising and established powers, the spread of deadly technologies not only among nations but by terrorist groups, economic and social pressures aggravated by demographic trends, resource scarcities, and climate change. All these are risk factors for violent conflict. The whole world is vulnerable to these threats, especially in view of the intricacies of globalization. Preventing deadly conflict is a *shared imperative*.

International preventive action can be pursued through informal ad hoc arrangements or formal multilateral organizations such as the United Nations, various regional bodies, and international financial institutions. Though many Americans are uninformed or skeptical about the value of international organizations, they provide advantages over unilateral efforts. Every US administration since the founding of the United Nations has recognized such benefits and used international organizations to promote peace to the extent possible.

The CFR study emphasizes several critical attributes of international organizations. They offer opportunities for implementing international rules and practices that influence state behavior and make the international environment more orderly. The United States has been able from the start of the UN and other international organizations to shape international norms that embody democratic values and humanitarian goals. International organizations' endorsements provide an important source of legitimacy to diplomatic efforts initiated or supported by the United States and other democracies. This backing is especially useful when prevention opportunities involve participating in the internal affairs of another country. Securing a multilateral organization's approval can facilitate assistance from the organization's member states and can help in sustaining domestic support.

The CFR analysis recommends improving the ability of the leading international institutions to carry out violence prevention, thus providing more effective partners for the United States and other democracies. This involves detailed understanding of the strengths and weaknesses of the leading multilateral groupings and how they help prevent violent conflict. We deal with this as a pervasive theme elsewhere in this book.

The CFR describes measures taken to minimize potential sources of instability and conflict before they arise; efforts to reduce the impact of specific threats and to diminish the negative impact of major demographic, economic, and environmental change then can be foreseen. The CFR seeks to promote conditions conducive to peace, such as encouraging equitable economic development, good governance, the rule of law, respect for human rights, rules on the use of force, military and economic cooperation, security guarantees, confidence-building measures, and effective arbitration. Crisis-prevention initiatives can draw upon a variety of diplomatic, military, economic, and legal measures to minimize potential triggers of a crisis. These wisely involve cooperative initiatives as in preference to coercive measures, though both may be necessary. Early interventions to prevent crises have traditionally been difficult, but there is a promising trend toward quiet diplomacy—and *early, ongoing conflict resolution*. These initiatives have been effective in several areas: electoral processes and political transitions, ethnic/religious frictions, boundary/territorial disputes, and resource/food scarcities.

This farsighted assessment of the potential strategies and current utility of international organizations to American foreign policy would not have been a likely conclusion of a major CFR report a decade or two ago. It is now helpful to the US government and other democracies in reducing the risks of mass violence.

INTERNATIONAL CENTERS FOR THE PREVENTION OF MASS VIOLENCE CREATE HISTORIC PRECEDENTS, NEW OPPORTUNITIES

Such centers of excellence can draw together many of the promising developments and farsighted constructive policies described in this book. The UN and the EU are focusing on genocide but go beyond, to reinforce the pillars of prevention of mass violence more broadly. Together with the US APB and an international coalition of democracies, a broad-based network intensely focused on preventing mass violence could:

1. Create a critical mass of knowledge and skill by assembling a permanent core of professional staff drawn from many disciplines and countries.

2. Collect and constantly update reliable information from all sources about circumstances in troubled countries or regions that would predispose them to violence.
3. Then link them to a full array of constructive responsive options, based on its reservoir of knowledge and skill in prevention.
4. Foster a network of cooperating *regional* organizations over time. Established democracies have special responsibilities on these critical issues, both within and outside international organizations.
5. Urge cooperating states and organizations to make their development aid, trade agreements, investment transactions, and other incentives conditional on the recipient's commitment to promote education for early and ongoing conflict resolution, overcoming prejudice, and preventing mass violence, in order to change norms away from violent pseudo-solutions.
6. *Foster cooperative networks* of like-minded institutions of civil society—especially scientific and scholarly communities, educational and religious organizations, businesses, the media, and NGOs oriented to promoting democracy, human rights, intergroup tolerance, and equitable development.

COMMUNITY OF ESTABLISHED DEMOCRACIES

The community of established democracies must get organized, especially with the United States stimulating active and cooperative participation. That can be done only if the democracies are able to relate to others on a basis of mutual respect and genuine collaboration. It means sustained help in building political and economic institutions of democracy. It can be done in a way that is sensitive to cultural traditions and regional circumstances.

Not only is a neo-imperialist approach contrary to the fair-minded attitudes of the American people and other democracies; it backfires because we badly need international cooperation for our own prosperity and for coping with terrorists. By behaving in a bellicose way, depreciatory of most others, we arouse antagonism, increase the pool of terrorists, and jeopardize vital friendships that have functional significance.

Democratic values are not consistent with selfish, greedy, bullying behavior. To whom much is given, much is expected. The established (and mostly affluent) democracies must not use power only for self-interest, narrowly defined. They must, for our sake and for theirs, help to make the world better. We have benefited from our democracy, humanity, opportunity, and decency. However, these precious assets can be rapidly eroded by shortsighted policies and hostile attitudes—internally and externally—that are not worthy of democratic traditions. These policies actually endanger our security by undermining vital cooperation, and they damage our economy. No one can go it alone in a dangerous and highly interdependent world. We cannot arrogantly push everyone around without paying a very high price. The United States must emphasize appreciation of common humanity exemplified in the great leadership of earlier presidents and democratic traditions.

As a practical matter, international cooperation is essential to be sure that the pooling of strengths can provide adequate financial, technical, and human resources to help the process of socioeconomic development over decades, working toward a responsibly regulated market economy and fully open democratic society.

The international democracies can build capacity for nonviolent conflict resolution in economic matters and in relations between ethnic, religious, and political groups. This is feasible when most people in a society feel that they have decent life chances; are not oppressed; have their basic needs met for child and adolescent development; and live in a social environment conducive to hope, physical security, and a reliable standard of living. Then there is greater likelihood for understanding and using concepts and techniques of conflict resolution, respecting laws and institutions intended to achieve fair resolution of conflict without violence. Successful foreign policy requires not only military strength but also judicious use of that strength along with economic, political, social, and psychological assets that hold allies and build friendships for cooperative efforts to shape a better world.

Fortunately, the democracies have a great resource to draw upon as they develop steps toward equitable socioeconomic development—the world's experience over half a century. One crucial lesson we can learn from these democratizing efforts is that unilateral efforts almost always fail. There are many reasons why going it alone is a poor strategy. Multilateral efforts allow nations to share the human and financial costs of these huge undertakings. They can learn so much from each other and heighten morale. Let us not forget the decades of effort we put into building NATO, the UN, and the EU—and the value of these relationships for many countries. We must reach out respectfully to our friends and overcome differences insofar as possible. Multilateral efforts invite the aid of nongovernmental and intergovernmental regional organizations experienced in nation building. It typically takes about a decade of turbulence to get a new democracy established, and another decade to consolidate its assets—namely, the knowledge, skill, norms, and institutions required to implement its own democratic processes. No outside army can be expected to occupy a developing nation for this lengthy period of time, nor can any one nation alone be expected to provide the financial, technical, and human resources to carry through this long, hard process. So we must pool strengths, share burdens, and divide labor.

For many of the world's people, democracy is not just a new political system; it is also a new way of life. Citizens of oppressive regimes operate in a closed, stifling environment, without the experience of publicly sharing opinions on political matters or learning the arts of compromise and mutual accommodation among ethnic, religious, and political groups. All this takes time, solid advice, and security on the ground. Friends of transitioning nations must help newly free citizens to realize the full benefits of the democratic way of life and ways of decently taking advantage of their unprecedented opportunities. America in collaboration with the international community of democracies can help to create a new context for national order, rule of law, and hope for a new political and economic future.

ORGANIZING FOR THE PREVENTION OF MASS ATROCITIES

As we have noted, focal points associated with major democracies can provide an extremely valuable reservoir of knowledge and skills, as well as a home base for mobilization of many different institutions and organizations that can make good use of this information. Such centers can stimulate worldwide cooperative efforts in the next few decades to greatly reduce the occurrence of mass atrocities. They would stimulate new ideas, new research, new education, and new modes of cooperation among diverse entities that can contribute to prevention. Thus, I have concentrated much effort since 2004 on institutional innovations that have been pursued by remarkable leaders such as Kofi Annan at the UN and Javier Solana at the EU. Their experience is applicable to the US government. Of course, leaders change, sometimes for

⟨⟨⟨⟩⟩⟩

First, we are putting new emphasis on prevention, and second, we are seeking to expand the range of partners contributing to this cause because no one country can be effective alone. Let me start with prevention. You want to stop atrocities before they start. How do you know what to look for?

Well, genocides and mass atrocities don't just happen spontaneously. They are always planned. Genocides are preceded by organized, targeted propaganda campaigns carried out by those in power.

It's like stacking dry firewood before striking the match. Then there is a moment of ignition. The permission to hate becomes permission to kill. . . .

There are responsibilities for this effort now across our government from the intelligence community to the Defense Department to the Treasury to the State Department. And at the center of our work is our core asset, our diplomats and development experts.

We are making sure that our officers serving in at-risk countries are trained to understand the warning signs, to provide accurate assessments of emerging crises, to take the first mitigating steps. That might mean engaging governments and their supporters. It might mean talking to local media about growing violence. It might mean supporting those who are countering propaganda.

We are enhancing our civilian surge capacity. We already have personnel trained to analyze conflicts and defuse potentially violent situations. Now we will be using those personnel to focus on atrocity prevention.

We're deploying new tools through our National Action Plan on Women, Peace, and Security because women are often the first to know when their communities are in danger, and they are often the first to suffer. So we're working with women at-risk in areas where they are to make sure there are early warning systems responsive to sexual and gender based violence. . . . But one thing must be noted: all nations have some influence and leverage that they can put to use if they are so engaged and focused. Even if nearly every country in the world takes a stand, we have seen recently how one nation or a small group of nations' obstruction can derail our efforts. . . .

But we are struggling with some of the deepest and most difficult impulses of human beings to protect themselves, to obtain power, to dehumanize others in order to enhance their own position and standing. And we have to do everything we can to keep pushing forward humanity's moral response and effective efforts. . . .

If one were to look at the great sweep of history, one has to believe that we can together overcome these challenges, that there will slowly but inexorably be progress. And at the root of that must be our resolve, and that resolve must never fail so that we can say and mean it, "never again."

—**Hillary Clinton**, *Secretary of State, "Remarks at the US Holocaust Memorial Museum Forward-Looking Symposium on Genocide Prevention," Washington, DC, July 24, 2012* better, sometimes for worse. But basic values endure. The central function now is to assemble a dependable core professional staff with a critical mass of knowledge and skill drawn from scientists, scholars, diplomats, lawyers, political and military leaders, and specialists in the fields of conflict resolution and violence prevention. Such prevention centers can recognize in advance trends in hatred and incipient violence, atrocity outbreaks, and growing human rights abuses—for example, atrocity-prone or atrocity-susceptible behavior. Such centers are now developing in several regional organizations and major democracies. The current US initiative is consistent with this trend and can provide an important stimulant.

Secretary of State Hillary Rodham Clinton reinforced this approach and the new US priorities in an address at the US Holocaust Museum in July 2012. Secretary Clinton and her superb colleague, Melanne Verveer, have worked with President Obama and his staff to reinforce the importance of women in peace and security since women have suffered so much and yet have so much to offer in constructive ways. This is highlighted in a Presidential Executive Order (13595) issued in December 2011.

INSTITUTING A NATIONAL ACTION PLAN ON WOMEN, PEACE, AND SECURITY

Section 1. Policy. (a) The United States recognizes that promoting women's participation in conflict prevention, management, and resolution, as well as in post-conflict relief and recovery, advances peace, national security, economic and social development, and international cooperation.

(b) The United States recognizes the responsibility of all nations to protect their populations from genocide, war crimes, ethnic cleansing, and crimes against humanity, including when implemented by means of sexual violence. The United States further recognizes that sexual violence, when used or commissioned as a tactic of war or as a part of a widespread or systematic attack against civilians, can exacerbate and prolong armed conflict and impede the restoration of peace and security.

. . .

Sec. 2. National Action Plan. A National Action Plan shall be created pursuant to the process outlined in Presidential Policy Directive 1 and shall identify and develop activities and initiatives in the following areas:

(a) *National integration and institutionalization.* Through interagency coordination, policy development, enhanced professional training and education, and evaluation, the United States Government will institutionalize a gender-responsive approach to its diplomatic, development, and defense-related work in conflict-affected environments.

(b) *Participation in peace processes and decisionmaking.* The United States Government will improve the prospects for inclusive, just, and sustainable peace by promoting and strengthening women's rights and effective leadership and substantive participation in peace processes, conflict prevention, peacebuilding, transitional processes, and decisionmaking institutions in conflict-affected environments.

(c) *Protection from violence.* The United States Government will strengthen its efforts to prevent—and protect women and children from—harm, exploitation, discrimination, and abuse, including sexual and gender-based violence and trafficking in persons, and to hold perpetrators accountable in conflict-affected environments.

(d) *Conflict prevention.* The United States Government will promote women's roles in conflict prevention, improve conflict early-warning and response systems through the integration of gender perspectives, and invest in women and girls' health, education, and economic opportunity to create conditions for stable societies and lasting peace.

(e) *Access to relief and recovery.* The United States Government will respond to the distinct needs of women and children in conflict-affected disasters and crises, including by providing safe, equitable access to humanitarian assistance.

. . .

The Secretary of State, the Secretary of Defense, and the Administrator of the United States Agency for International Development shall each:

(i) designate one or more officers, as appropriate, as responsible for coordinating and implementing the National Action Plan. . . . (President Barack Obama, December 19, 2011)

Overall, there is a vigorous, forward-looking upsurge of American effort to build a strong prevention agenda in cooperation with other democracies and international organizations. Such efforts are novel and subject to the fluctuations of domestic policies. But the trend is clear and encouraging.

NINE

THE UNITED NATIONS

Dag Hammarskjöld was the pioneer in the work of preventing violence early in the UN's history. His successors gradually came to use their position of secretary-general to promote prevention. After the Cold War—which was a major obstacle to any UN role—and near the end of his term of office, Secretary-General Boutros Boutros-Ghali issued three major studies in the 1990s on the UN's historical core values that could guide its work in the first decades of the twenty-first century: *Agenda for Peace*, *Agenda for Development*, and *Agenda for Democratization*.[1] Then Secretary-General Kofi Annan undertook groundbreaking, farsighted work with a number of studies that offered suggestions for improving the UN, including self-criticism of high integrity. Among them were Lakhtar Brahmini's report on peacekeeping; a report on preventing armed conflict at the outset of the twenty-first century; a series of major speeches by Annan on human rights, democracy, and creating a culture of prevention (published by the Carnegie Commission on Preventing Deadly Conflict); detailed analyses of the genocidal tragedies of Rwanda and Srebenica in the former Yugoslavia; and reports on the responsibility to protect the human rights of one's own citizens as well as one's neighbors, putting *human* security on a par with national security. His 2006 report on prevention of armed conflict[2] updates his landmark report on this subject in 2001. We had the privilege of working with both Boutros-Ghali and Annan on these moves toward prevention.

In the Carnegie Commission publication of his speeches and reports,[3] Secretary-General Annan considers how an international *culture of prevention* can be built over time and underscores the vital role the UN has to play in its formation. For the long term, he emphasizes human security as an essential ingredient of national security. This sort of security requires a society based on fairness, with good government that is transparent, is nondiscriminatory, and allows equal access to economic opportunity. With his integrative mind, Annan linked security policy with development, poverty eradication, protection of our common environment, and the spread of human rights and democracy.

Annan advocates not only early preventive diplomacy in "hot spots" but also the fostering of democratic socioeconomic development as the best infrastructure for enduring peace. The UN has a network of well-trained, professional, dedicated staff and representatives in almost every country in the world. Many of them can help in early warning and formulation of conflict resolution without mass violence.

Thus, the secretary-general can stimulate the UN system to bring serious problems to the attention of the international community and can use its moral standing and extensive tool kit to help disputing parties work toward resolution. But all this, however important, is late in the day. *Early* involvement, as we have seen, is both *preferable and feasible*.

The legitimacy of outside assistance is an important determinant of its success. The UN, a universal organization whose charter expresses the highest ideals, has considerable legitimacy throughout the world. Early, respectful, cooperative engagement can do much to foster decent intergroup relations and diminish the risk of mass violence. A serious defect in the UN's history has been to wait until violence is not only under way but often far advanced. There has been a neglect of early conflict resolution and previolence cooperative assistance.

SPECIAL REPRESENTATIVES

One proven way in which the UN can employ the resources of experienced diplomats is in the capacity of special representatives of the secretary-general. The secretary-general needs an international panel of conflict-resolution experts—as exemplified by Lakhtar Brahmini and our late collaborator Cyrus Vance—with the extensive experience, intellect, integrity, and distinction that would give them world recognition as suitable envoys for violence-prevention missions. These experts, in turn, need support staff with thorough knowledge of different regions of the world—something the UN could be in a good position to supply, though historically it has not. The special representatives of the secretary-general and senior staff collaborators should combine expertise in both the principles and techniques of conflict resolution with in-depth knowledge of a particular region, including the main historical and cultural factors bearing on a specific conflict. Connie Peck's studies[4] on strengthening the knowledge base for preventive diplomacy and the practical leadership of the secretary-general in this vital field are illuminating here.

In a study for the Carnegie Commission,[5] Peck developed a highly promising practical model, growing out of UN experience and research: regional centers for sustainable peace, established under the auspices of the UN, or regional organizations, or both. This UN/regional approach emphasizes regional promotion of capable democratic government, coupled with preventive diplomacy—early, and then ongoing as may be necessary. The structure she proposes would draw on broad international expertise to determine the most successful conflict-prevention instruments and adapt them to local needs and circumstances. These centers represent a promising way to pool the strengths of the UN, intergovernmental regional organizations (such as the EU), nongovernmental organizations, and a variety of regional analytical centers in a comprehensive preventive system. The work of Francis Deng during the span 2007 to 2012 is one illustration of the UN's potential for leadership in this direction on a collaborative basis.

EDUCATIONAL ROLE OF THE UN IN VIOLENCE PREVENTION

The UN can be a powerful force in worldwide public education aimed at countering intergroup violence. Because the UN has responsibility for helping in conflict resolution, it can work to create a world constituency for prevention—though it has not yet done so to the extent that the founders had foreseen. The policy community in much of the world is not deeply familiar with the principles and techniques of conflict resolution. The UN can help in the education of both policymakers and the general public.

The UN can support and reward leaders committed to conflict resolution, build educational opportunities worldwide, and provide useful early information about growing dangers. Contending parties throughout the world can be educated about the nature and consequences of ethnocentric hostility: the action/reaction cycles of violence; the buildup of revenge motives; and the proliferation, escalation, and addiction to hatred and killing that emerge from intergroup animosity.

In cooperation with universities and research institutes, the UN can sponsor *world leadership seminars* that include new heads of state and foreign, defense, and development ministers. These seminars could clarify how the UN and other organizations can help states avoid violent conflict and deal nonviolently with problems of intense nationalism, ethnocentrism, prejudice, and hatred.

TOOLS FOR VIOLENCE PREVENTION AVAILABLE TO THE UN SECURITY COUNCIL

Elizabeth Cousens outlines some resources available to the UN Security Council for preventing violence.[6] Because the UN Charter gave the Security Council a central role, and because its performance in that role has often been very disappointing, the focus must be on what it can do better than in the past. Agenda-setting and fact-finding missions, diplomatic initiatives, economic sanctions, peace operations, and peace enforcement are instruments the council can deploy to prevent outbreak or escalation of mass violence.

The council can publicize a potential conflict to attract diplomatic and public attention and to mobilize resources. Throughout the 1990s, the Security Council increasingly engaged in highly visible diplomacy through greater interaction with the media, encounters with key NGOs, and frequent field missions.

The council has potentially valuable diplomatic tools. First, it can mobilize broad support for diplomatic efforts of the UN or other organizations, as when it authorizes fact-finding missions and investigations to support mediation efforts through special representatives, the secretary-general him- or herself, regional organizations, or the recently developed and promising UN unit that supports mediation. Second, the Security Council can send its own members on fact-finding missions to improve its deliberations by reporting the situation on the ground and also to raise the visibility of the problem by taking a problem-solving interest and communicating directly with conflicting parties.

The council can send troops or observers to a potential conflict zone to prevent conflict. This may involve preventive deployment to separate adversaries and otherwise buffer aggression—allowing space for negotiation. The scope and efficiency of this approach have been increasing in recent years but have a long way to go—witness Syria 2012.

The Security Council can conduct arms embargoes, disarmament efforts, and specifically targeted sanctions to contain wrongdoers. Arms embargoes can have a de-escalating effect in ongoing conflicts. Imposed at the end of a conflict, embargoes can form part of a stabilization strategy to prevent recurrent conflict. Economic and other sanctions, though primarily used to contain an existing conflict, can also be part of a preventive effort. Studies that examine sanctions and their efficacy stress the importance of carefully targeting these instruments on perpetrators to avoid collateral damage and perverse effects. In general, coercive tools have been very difficult to organize, chiefly because of disagreement among council members and reluctance of member states to provide necessary resources: in the massive slaughter of Syrians by the Syrian government in 2011 and 2012, Russia and China vetoed sanctions.

THE ROLE OF UN AGENCIES IN PREVENTION

A common misunderstanding about the UN is that it consists essentially of the secretary-general, the Security Council (hobbled by the absolute veto power given to the five powers left standing at the end of World War II), and the disorderly (and often harsh) General Assembly. Both the council and the assembly have constructive capacities, but they are hampered by authoritarian, dictatorial, and hegemonic member states. Yet the UN has many agencies that clearly do much good in the world, not least in the area of prevention. For example, the World Health Organization has acted rapidly and effectively to stave off a catastrophic worldwide epidemic of SARS, and earlier (culminating in 1980) to eradicate smallpox. UNICEF probably does more for the education, health, and well-being of children in poor countries than any other entity in the world. The World Food Program has been highly effective in providing sustenance to victims of disaster. The UN High Commissioner for Refugees has vast and useful experience in coping with refugee problems: in the 1990s, Sadako Ogata set valuable precedents and provided immense humanitarian services. The UN High Commissioner for Human Rights has a nearly worldwide staff. UNESCO conducts Holocaust education programs.

The World Bank and the United Nations Development Program have done valuable work in socioeconomic development, so important in building competent, democratic, and ultimately prosperous nations. In the past decade they have become more democratically oriented, they focus more on people and less on monuments, they foster cooperation of public and private sectors in building market economies, they cooperate more with each other, they have major resources, they cover the world, and they now pay serious attention to preventing deadly conflict beyond previous experience. All this provides powerful incentives, skills, and hope to move poor countries away from poverty, corruption, tyranny, repression, epidemic diseases, and breeding grounds for terrorism.

The United Nations Environment Program (UNEP) is valuable. Environmental resource issues often lie at the heart of conflicts that hold the potential for mass violence.[7] Existing tensions can be deepened by deliberate manipulation of resource shortages for hostile purposes (for example, using food or water as a weapon). Competition between or within nations for natural resources such as water increases the potential for conflict. *Climate change* is beginning (sooner than expected) to have serious effects that could precipitate violence. Environmental degradation and resource depletion have a role in promoting conflict that is bound to increase in areas characterized by poor governance, rapid population growth, severe poverty, and widespread stressful experiences.

Finally, the UN Institute for Training and Research (UNITAR), a small gem in the crown of the UN, conducts excellent training and research all over the world on subjects of great practical importance for the international community, such as climate change. Connie Peck's work there has made outstanding contributions to the understanding and practice of preventive diplomacy.

These few examples of valuable and effective UN agencies illustrate that it is not just a windy debating society but a global network of competence, skills, and dedicated people making the world better than it was before. To work effectively, it needs farsighted, constructive participation of the international community, in particular the established democracies. Its assets can be helpful in the prevention of deadly conflict. A vital challenge is to consider how effective components of the United Nations might be extended in order to strengthen their roles in preventing mass violence—for example, educating at all levels on early, decent intergroup relations; reaching just resolutions; and fostering healthy development throughout the world.

STRENGTHENING THE UN FOR THE
PREVENTION OF MASS VIOLENCE

The tasks of prevention require international pooling of strengths, sharing of burdens, and division of labor. Without a commonly accepted international system of violence prevention, many different efforts toward prevention are made in a groping, uncoordinated way. More widely accepted and regularized arrangements are necessary, and the UN can be helpful in working them out—though these arrangements cannot be limited to the UN.

For the Carnegie Commission on Preventing Deadly Conflict, I had the opportunity to bring together Graham Allison of Harvard and Hisashi Owada (formerly Japan's ambassador to the UN, now on the International Court of Justice) and persuade them to formulate practical ways in which the community of established democracies could foster effective and cost-effective prevention—acting partly through the UN and partly outside it—but always in the spirit of the UN Charter, which so strongly reflects the basic principles of democracy.[8]

In exploring ways the United States could be effective at the UN, a CFR[9] task force comes to a similar conclusion. First, it recommends that the United States strengthen its relationship with the European Union. The two bodies, representing the world's leading democracies, can make a powerful team, and they should support each other to the maximum extent—both within the UN and outside it. The EU has been receptive to this approach. Because the world is so highly interdependent, international cooperation is essential for almost every constructive purpose—for example, the safety of food and medicine.

The CFR suggests that the established democracies institutionalize a "democracy caucus" at the UN as a forum for building cooperation on issues of human rights and democracy. It could also unite to block nondemocratic nations from membership on UN bodies that focus on democratic development and firmly support the work of the UNDP in strengthening legislatures, fair electoral processes, and other elements of democratic governance, as well as in developing free and independent media. The report suggests that the United States and the UN should spell out explicitly how essential the promotion of human rights, democracy, development, and poverty eradication is to a long-term strategy to overcome mass violence.

The UN is learning from the European experience: the OSCE, Council of Europe, and especially the European Union, for which democracy, protection

of human rights, the rule of law, and a market economy are the basic requirements for membership. These cooperative European institutions have had a
strong influence on Eastern European countries emerging from authoritarian
regimes—and, in the process, moving toward peaceful conflict resolution
as well as economic benefits. Periodic reassessment and negotiations are essential. So far, the EU has worked its way out of difficult situations and will
probably do so again even in the face of financial problems.

WORKING TOGETHER TO MAXIMIZE
LEVERAGE FOR PREVENTION

A group of friends of the secretary-general (seriously interested and fair-
minded member states) can form to provide a useful source of help. The
presence of a preventive mission itself may be a source of influence on political
leaders, their constituents, and the population at large. The better their training, the deeper their commitment, and the more substantial their experience,
the more likely they are to be effective. All too often, these favorable conditions are not met. Yet there is a trend toward learning from these experiences.

Two main incentives are *economic support* and *legitimacy*.[10] A study of actual attempts at conflict resolution confirms that positive incentives offering
the parties a promising future are more likely to be effective than negative
pressures.[11]

Cooperation between the UN and regional organizations (RO) can help
struggling nations achieve progressive reforms. An important report on UN/
RO relations for violence prevention was prepared in 2006 under the excellent
leadership of Finland's Tapio Kanninen and was strongly endorsed by Annan.

All concerned are helped by clear, well-documented, practical information
about best practices in all forms of violence prevention, including *worldwide
mediation capacity* and substantial *economic incentives for peace*. The UN has
become increasingly helpful in making that useful toolbox available to many
players in the international community, especially regional organizations.
Special attention is now paid to mediation, particularly in early preventive
diplomacy. Indeed, almost every RO is now engaged in such activity—a
drastic change.

The recent Mediation Support Unit of the UN Department of Political
Affairs is compiling the UN's experience in a variety of conflicts all over

the world. One of the most encouraging developments in preventing deadly conflict is the prospect of a worldwide cadre of mediation professionals acting under the auspices of the UN and/or regional organizations.

MILITARY FUNCTIONS

The UN has historically been ill-prepared for military functions. Yet it cannot be credible and effective in fostering global peace unless it has competent military capability—not for fighting wars, but for separating adversaries to make space for mediation, and for protecting groups at high risk while settlement efforts proceed.

Sir Brian Urquhart, a great UN pioneer, suggests a highly trained UN volunteer military force of approximately 5,000 soldiers that the Security Council could use for rapid deployment to trouble spots. This force, unlike peacekeeping forces, would be trained both in combat and in negotiation, with the mandate to use force if necessary to stabilize circumstances at an early stage in low-level but dangerous conflicts, especially those involving irregular militias and similar groups. Such a force could be deployed in the early days of an impending crisis to get the situation quickly under control and prepare the way for preventive diplomacy that would address the immediate precipitating causes of the conflict. Then a longer-term process could begin to resolve the fundamental causes. Political objections to this by UN member states have been fierce, and there is little prospect for near-term movement in this direction.

Professor Joshua Goldstein, a distinguished political scientist, has pointed out recent evidence for accomplishments in "winning the war on war." Not only have the number and size of wars decreased in recent years, but there has been a change in military emphasis—primarily to protect civilian organizations and to help build peaceful societies. They are not only fighters but can be diplomats and educators. Of course, one nuclear attack could change this picture grotesquely.

Goldstein takes an optimistic view of the UN's peacekeepers—perhaps more than most observers. Yet he sees the improvements and above all the future potential. It reminds us of the decades since Hammarskjöld's pioneering efforts to build the power and prestige of the secretary-general's capacity for prevention.

The Cold War intervened and diminished the promise of the UN, but the basic idea did not die. Forty years later, Kofi Annan, influenced by the

Carnegie Commission on Preventing Deadly Conflict, sought to move the United Nations from a culture of reaction to a culture of prevention. He proposed making prevention the centerpiece of UN action in the twenty-first century.

The Carnegie Commission on Preventing Deadly Conflict concluded that of the $200 billion spent in the 1990s intervening in Bosnia, Somalia, Rwanda, Haiti, Cambodia, El Salvador, and the Persian Gulf, about two-thirds could have been saved by taking a preventive approach. In addition to the money, so many lives could have been saved. Early warning systems linked with informed response preparation make early prevention possible.

Goldstein also emphasizes the emergence of the Organization for Security and Co-operation in Europe (OSCE), which created a high commissioner for national minorities and emerged as a potent force for preventive diplomacy in the Baltic countries and Russia as the Cold War was precariously winding down.

Goldstein closes with the basic concept of one world, one humanity. Despite the resistance of sovereignty against humanitarianism, the people of the world, and not just their governments, are increasingly assertive on freedom, opportunity, and even democracy.

Professor Paul Kennedy, a distinguished historian at Yale who has a masterful grasp of the UN, expresses respect for the symbolism and growing efficacy of UN peacekeepers. He notes, as we do, other promising elements in the UN despite many obstacles. Thus, the UN and other international organizations can embody high ideals of humanity and learn how to implement these ideals in the decades ahead, despite formidable obstacles.

STRIVING TO OVERCOME UN LIMITATIONS

Essential to fulfilling the promise of the UN is to recognize its limitations and seek ways to overcome them. Former UN secretary-general Annan has addressed some disadvantages the UN faces in developing a preventive system. His frank recognition has long-term value for improving this universal organization.

1. With limited resources and a massive agenda, the secretary-general and the Security Council are overburdened and are forced to focus on crisis situations rather than preventive strategies.

2. Although its charter allows the UN to respond to threats or breaches of peace within or among states, it has trouble dealing with conflicts involving nonofficial bodies and internal disputes, and so far has had major problems with very early prevention.

3. The UN is hindered in its security efforts by the threat of a veto in the Security Council. The Permanent Five (United States, United Kingdom, France, Russia, and China) have been slow to grasp the significance of prevention. Democratic, humane, and compassionate initiatives are likely to be blocked by Russia and China (with the veto if necessary) and nonpermanent rotating members usually include some dictatorships.

4. The high stakes surrounding the UN's involvement in a conflict sometimes make states apprehensive about bringing their conflict to it. The Security Council may be inflexible or partisan, or pass resolutions that cannot be implemented, as it did in the former Yugoslavia.

5. The UN struggles to be organizationally efficient but has the image of being wasteful and is hampered in administrative reform by a variety of member states, especially autocratic ones.

Still, the desirability of violence prevention in both internal and external conflicts has become broadly accepted. Moreover, there have been important though rare innovations, such as preventive deployments, and increasing sophistication in use of established techniques, such as special representatives and direct diplomacy through Security Council missions. The council needs to be better informed about the necessity and feasibility of prevention. Annan launched this process by convening the first-ever weekend retreat of the Security Council, asking David Hamburg to reflect on the findings of the Carnegie Commission. The Security Council needs continuing education on prevention to enhance the contribution of the Permanent Five and to inform nonpermanent rotating council members.

Survey research for many years has shown majority support in the United States for the UN as an institution that can be beneficial to the whole world, as the Roosevelts had envisioned. Most agree on the UN's value in technical areas of global significance, such as civil aviation, weather forecasting, public health, and food safety standards. So too there is agreement that UN agencies should take the lead in international responses to humanitarian emergencies.

In the aftermath of World War II and the Holocaust, the peaceful resolution of political issues was the UN's original reason for being. Its effectiveness in maintaining peace is the criterion most used to rate its performance. The UN's role in peace and security has greatly expanded since the end of the Cold War. Formerly, its role on the ground was limited to sending lightly armed peacekeepers to monitor hostile parties—trying to keep peace where there was no peace to keep, and then being blamed by the perennial cynics. Today, UN peacekeeping troops enforce peace settlements and sometimes hold war-driven societies together until the rival parties learn to live together. Once the secretary-general only offered "good offices" as an impartial mediator between belligerents. Now UN special representatives might construct a transitional government in a war-torn country or even act as head of an interim international administration.

The UN today monitors elections and sets the standard for electoral fairness and legitimacy, working with the Carter Center, the EU, and increasingly a world network of monitors. Weapons inspectors earned respect for their accuracy in Iraq, thus strengthening the global authority of impartial UN arms verification.[12]

Secretary-General Annan considered the lack of progress in reforming the Security Council one of the 2005 summit's two biggest failures, the other being the lack of progress on nuclear nonproliferation and disarmament. This most dangerous of all problems was completely neglected in the 2005 summit outcome document. For the foreseeable future, we must look elsewhere for ways to address this immense problem, and our chapter on weaponry (see Chapter 7) suggests promising ways to do so.

RECENT WINDOWS INTO THE UN'S WORK ON PREVENTION

It was my privilege to play an advisory role at the United Nations with three secretaries-general, Boutros Boutros-Ghali, Kofi Annan, and Ban Ki-moon. Examples of our work at the UN include facilitating links between the global scientific community and the UN (1996–2001); establishing an international policy framework and network on "Health as a Bridge for Peace" based out of the World Health Organization (1997–2006); serving as adviser to the UN High Commissioner for Refugees (Sadako Ogata) (1997–2001); serving on the Board of Trustees for the UN Institute for Training and Research (1998–2009); and, at Annan's request, creating a strong network of advisers to launch the University for Peace (UPEACE) (2000–2001). I was able to facilitate the appointment of the special adviser to the secretary-general on the prevention of genocide (2004–present); to help establish an advisory committee to the secretary-general on the prevention of genocide, which I chaired (2005–2010); and to strengthen the Office of the Special Adviser on the Prevention of Genocide (2006–2012).

These years of helping to build a prevention agenda for the UN involved cooperation with several of the key colleagues of the secretaries-general, among them (in alphabetical order) Mark Malloch Brown, Michael Doyle, Ibrahim Gambari, Angela Kane, Tapio Kanninen, Elizabeth Lindenmeyer, Edward Mortimer, Robert Orr, Gillian Sorensen, Maurice Strong, John Ruggie, Danilo Türk, and Nita Yawanaraja. We worked in different capacities toward a sustainable prevention agenda.

This work was reflected in several major reports. The Carnegie Commission on Preventing Deadly Conflict was completed in 1997. Annan promptly responded positively to the commission's opportunities, and the final report of the commission was presented at the United Nations by him to a large session in early 1998. We also played a role in the drafting, launching, and implementing of Annan's landmark report on the "Prevention of Armed Conflict" (PAC Report, 2001) and the related call by the secretary-general for responses by UN departments and agencies in 2002.

A singular accomplishment was the creation in 2004 of the UN's unique unit on prevention of genocide, first headed by Juan Mendez and then by Special Adviser Francis Deng (2007–2012). Nearing completion of a distinguished and groundbreaking five-year period, Deng gave an overview of his experience that points the way to future directions of prevention, examining the challenge of preventing genocide and mass atrocities. His was truly a unique experience that earned respect throughout the world. As leader of the UN's first strong genocide-prevention unit in the history of the organization, he built a framework for cooperation of member states, regional organizations, nongovernmental organizations, and important elements of civil society.

He points out that most countries facing the challenge of protecting populations within their national borders were divided to some extent, even sometimes experiencing a crisis of national identity. Such a crisis sharply divides populations into in-groups and out-groups, and often the national governments fails to protect the out-groups, not building norms and institutions for mutual accommodation. If the out-groups are depreciated or even persecuted, they are likely to turn for help to the outside world, especially regional organizations or the United Nations.

Under these conditions, national authorities are likely to claim sovereignty as a barricade against even the most benign external involvement. Therefore, there are now increasing efforts to reformulate sovereignty in a positive light with the UN and other organizations offering help. Sovereign nations earn respect and opportunities by decent behavior, akin to other similar countries.

Deng's unit earned great respect throughout the world by sharing information available to the UN from many countries in every part of the world. For example, it highlighted international standards for protecting and assisting populations in need. Deng and his staff communicated with government officials, human rights organizations, and many others who have reason to be concerned about intergroup conflicts, both within countries and across national boundaries. Their functions were fundamentally educational, helping many leaders and concerned citizens to see that genocide is an extreme form of identity conflict in which there are predisposing factors of gross inequality, discrimination, exclusion, and even dehumanization. Therefore, the most effective form of prevention is constructive management of diversity, especially because almost every country is more diverse than we generally recognize. The UN unit headed by Deng clarified ways of promoting equality, including all groups in the making of decisions that affect their lives, respecting basic human rights, and in due course observing democratic values and practices. This approach has increasingly been understood and well received by individual governments; regional organizations; and influential nongovernmental organizations concerned with human rights, democracy, education, and research.

Deng's unit collected and analyzed information of practical value in early warning and provided clarification to many elements of the UN, including the secretary-general and the Security Council. It issued statements on situations of risk, not attempting unrealistic precision about what would happen or when, but highlighting susceptibility to hatred and violence. This unit undertook a major program of *capacity-building*: training seminars and workshops on prevention of genocide and other mass atrocities. These have been increasingly in demand, for example by UN staff members. In just two years, from 2009 to 2011, almost 800 people in thirteen countries were involved in substantial training.

Thus, the program collaborated with partners inside and outside the UN and is in the process of generating a network of informed people dedicated to prevention, influencing policies and practices throughout the UN system. The collaborative activities with regional organizations have become increasingly important, drawing on resources that are particularly useful in helping their neighbors, especially in light of the legitimacy and complementarity they bring to a situation. They have mutual interests in avoiding mass murder. Altogether this pioneering work can help the international community to understand and cope with the risks leading to mass atrocities.

HOPEFUL SIGNS FOR THE LONG TERM

Supported by five governments, the *Human Security Report* is the most comprehensive annual survey of trends in mass violence. Its central thrust involves the linkage of democracy, development, and human rights—with a focus on individuals and their dignity. Recent reports indicate that several forms of political violence have declined worldwide since the early 1990s. After nearly five decades of inexorable increase, the number of genocides declined somewhat after the Cold War (here the time interval is so short that the result is ambiguous). Data also suggest that wars are becoming not only less frequent, but also less deadly. (Yet there have been conspicuous exceptions, as in Syria and Congo.) Analyzing the causes of the improvement in global security since the early 1990s, the report argues that the UN played a critically important role in spearheading an upsurge of international conflict prevention, peacekeeping, and peacebuilding activities. Although these are promising observations, they could be utterly transformed by one nuclear attack. So caution is necessary.

The *Human Security Report* points out that in the long run, equitable economic development, increased constructive state capacity, and the spread of inclusive democracy play a vital role in reducing the risk of political violence. The UN and the EU, among others, are fostering such beneficial changes. Still, the report warns against complacency. Although wars and war deaths are down, it reports some sixty armed conflicts in progress. Gross abuses of human rights, widespread war crimes, and ever deadlier acts of terrorism are still widely prevalent. The danger of nuclear weapons is immense, and so too is biological terrorism. Creative, sustained efforts, informed by research and implemented by institutional innovations, can do much to prevent the worst disasters.

Kofi Annan set two important precedents at once by appointing a special adviser for prevention of genocide. It was the first time any prevention professional had been appointed at such a high level, reporting directly to the secretary-general. Moreover, it was the first time that a unit focusing specifically on genocide prevention had ever been created at the UN. In 2006, Annan strengthened this effort by appointing a distinguished, worldwide committee to advise him on ways of strengthening genocide prevention in the future, with particular attention to the special adviser. It was my privilege to chair this committee, and I offer my perspective on the UN's potential here.

The UN's growing preventive orientation has begun to emphasize *primary* prevention, yet most of its efforts are directed toward *post*-conflict situations. The UN has potential to survey the world's experience; to seek to extract the most promising actions; and to make them available to groups in distress, nation-states, regional organizations, and nongovernmental organizations. Over time, the UN can develop a comprehensive program of prevention, a set of principles and practices for long-term prevention of genocide and war. Steps can be taken to identify areas at serious risk of genocide and other mass violence and offer help from the international community to the troubled country or region.

The world's heads of state met in an extraordinary summit at the UN headquarters in New York in 2005. Their Outcome Document of September 15, 2005, endorsed the UN's efforts to prevent genocide. The terms of the endorsement were general.

Secretary-General Annan's successor, Ban Ki-moon, has supported these concepts. The first director of the full-fledged effort has been a distinguished world leader, Francis Deng. As he rotates out after five years, much will depend on the quality of his successor. These are always works in progress.

TEN

---⸺∽⸺---

THE EUROPEAN UNION AND OTHER REGIONAL ORGANIZATIONS

For twenty years, Javier Solana has held high leadership positions in NATO and then in the EU. His security knowledge and diplomatic skill proved especially valuable. He emphasizes that to prevent mass violence, it is vital to have the cooperation of the European Union and the United States. He believes much was learned in this respect in Bosnia, Kosovo, and Macedonia. Recently, the outreach of these organizations to the African Union (AU) has been promising. He believes the AU is making rapid progress from a low baseline and is increasingly contributing to prevention of mass violence in Africa. In due course, this can provide lessons for other regions, especially those constrained by poverty and earnestly striving for improvement.

The formidable resources of the established democracies give them great potential to form groups that can recognize early warnings of emerging conflict and respond promptly with preventive and sustainable actions. A focus on prevention has emerged in the EU since 2001.

States wisely reluctant to act alone but unable to achieve strong international consensus can establish a "friends group," "contact group," or other ad hoc cooperative international coalitions. Even a few countries working together can substantially increase their sources of information, their range of policy options, and the checks and balances of multiple inputs. They are unlikely to rush prematurely into military action and are more likely to use other instruments effectively.

As emphasized in Chapter 8, particularly significant in this context is the growing community of established democracies. By and large, they are stable and sturdy, technically advanced, relatively affluent in spite of the current recession, and demonstrably able to work together effectively in many situations. Some excellent examples of their successful cooperation are the EU and its ultimate parent, the Marshall Plan; NATO; the G8 and now G20; the Organization for Economic Cooperation and Development; and the Organization for Security and Co-operation in Europe (OSCE). Yet, on occasion, the established democracies have failed badly: their apathy in the early years of Yugoslavia's ruin, especially their inaction during the early years of the conflict in Bosnia; their total failure in dealing with the Rwandan genocide; and then for years their prolonged dithering over catastrophe in Sudan. The question is how they can become more effective on a consistent basis in dealing with violence-prone states or groups, and in particular, how they can develop regular and clear-cut mechanisms of prevention.

There is much promise in an ever-closer cooperation among established democracies—*the enlarging group of nations that share humane values, effective mechanisms for coping with conflict, and formidable resources for preventing mass violence.* In the face of foreseeable atrocities, they can act effectively in different groups all over the world, whether or not the UN is able to act, functioning within the spirit of the UN Charter but not limited by its political and procedural constraints in the face of great danger. This would provide a flexible system of action for peace and justice. It would amount to an extensive voluntary coalition, arranged in different configurations for different situations, according to the requirements and opportunities of a particular conflict—yet familiar with and adapted to cooperation.

The EU is the clearest example of a set of established democracies sharing basic humane and peaceful values, able to act effectively, and morally committed to the prevention of mass atrocities. In the decades ahead, more countries will emerge as fully fledged democracies and concomitantly develop technical, economic, and moral strength. This set of nations has the opportunity within sight to upgrade and regularize their cooperation in preventing violence. They can provide a focal point for coalescence on a particular problem of exceptional gravity.

Preventive actions need not be military. By preference, they should involve political, psychological, social, and economic measures—applied early in an emerging conflict. In all cases, the democracies involved in a preventive action should consult widely and transparently on a systematic basis so that other governments and nongovernmental organizations can be kept aware of the considerations leading to a particular decision and can participate if appropriate. The mode of operation should be democratic in spirit across all national boundaries. Over time, this would make the principles embodied in the day-to-day work of the democracies familiar and attractive throughout the world.

THE EUROPEAN UNION AND PREVENTION OF MASS VIOLENCE

The work of the EU in the field of conflict prevention and prevention of genocide is reflected in its 2004 annual report. Cooperation with the UN is emphasized, as are EU support and assistance in the development of regional organizations such as the African Union. With the adoption of the European Security Strategy, the capability of the EU to prevent violent conflicts and potential genocide can increase considerably.

The EU formulated a set of aspirations for prevention of violent conflict based on principles:

> The belief that the international community has a political and moral responsibility to avoid the human suffering and the destruction of resources caused by violent conflicts. The European Union is in its own experience a successful example of violence prevention based on democratic values and respect for human rights, justice and solidarity, widely shared prosperity and sustainable development.
>
> Conflict prevention depends on cooperation to facilitate peaceful solutions to disputes and insofar as possible helping with the basic causes of conflicts. This view is both within and beyond its international relations. EU actions are undertaken in keeping with the principles and purposes of the UN Charter. The main responsibility for conflict prevention rests with the parties concerned; assistance to local and regional capacity building respects local ownership and responsibility.

The mutual support and concentration of expertise in prevention of mass violence provided by an EU-based International Center for Prevention of

Genocide could make a crucial difference. The center could elicit cooperation to pool strengths, share burdens, and divide labor in the tasks of genocide prevention. It could affiliate with other institutions for particular tasks, for example, an EU core linked to the UN, NATO, AU, and OSCE. It could stimulate the international community in many ways to understand mass violence, to recognize early signs of trouble in violence-prone societies, and to provide response options/contingency plans for preventive action.

Such an ongoing service would stimulate new ideas, new research, new education, and new modes of cooperation among diverse entities that can contribute to prevention of mass violence, thus providing hope for effective action. The remarkable, ongoing progress of the EU in preventing deadly conflict during the past decade shows that, for all the difficulties, opportunities can be seized in this field. The EU has been working on such a center with excellent professional skills, but the severe recession and associated political stresses have slowed the pace of progress. Still, determination remains and ingenuity is evident. The EU is unprecedented as a family of democratic European countries working together for peace and prosperity. It arose in reaction to the horrors of World War II and the Holocaust. European statespeople together with American leaders had the vision to see the beauty of cooperation, first at the economic and then at the political level, and now at the level of human relations in the broadest sense.

In its early years, cooperation among EU countries focused on trade, but now the EU also deals with such subjects as citizens' rights; ensuring freedom, security, and justice; job creation; regional development; environmental protection; and making globalization work equitably.

The economically powerful EU (though temporarily restrained by the worldwide recession of the early twenty-first century) is a strikingly successful example of how close cooperation and understanding among nations that waged massive wars against one another within living memory can lead to reconciliation that is the basis for peace and prosperity. As the most prominent representative body in one of the most highly developed and influential areas of the globe, the EU is well placed to play a major role in preventing violent conflict. It can use not only its civilian and military crisis management capabilities, but also the diplomatic instruments of its members. It can also wield trade policy instruments, cooperation agreements, development assistance, economic cooperation, and social and environmental policies as mechanisms and incentives to ensure peace. What the EU is currently seeking to achieve is extensive coordination of these different capabilities with an explicit focus on prevention. This is an innovative approach to international affairs. Only a few years after prevention was established as a priority in the EU, there is evidence of progress and long-term commitment. The EU prevention activities address root causes of conflict, such as poverty, lack of good governance and respect for human rights, as well as competition for scarce natural resources. None of this is easy, but there is a fundamental commitment to humane values. One intrinsic asset of EU experience is the ability to overcome internal strains through negotiation, as is the case in the financial sphere in 2012.

THE CENTRALITY OF EUROPE IN FOSTERING INTERNATIONAL COOPERATION FOR DEMOCRATIC DEVELOPMENT AND PREVENTION OF MASS VIOLENCE

Timothy Garton Ash, a distinguished observer of Europe, makes the case for strong cooperation among the established democracies, especially the Transatlantic Alliance, in coping constructively with global problems and minimizing the risk of mass violence. He contrasts the "rich north" and "poor south." In the developing countries of the Southern Hemisphere, the horrors of severe malnutrition, disease, and poor governance are becoming more widely understood in recent years. The gap between rich and poor is greater than ever, even in the United States. This is a global problem of profound significance, with moral, political, economic, and health dimensions—all potential areas that could lead to violence.

Ash makes the case that, despite burgeoning world population, there is enough food to feed the world. The central problem with both food and water is equitable distribution, and this in turn rests on substantial democratic cooperation. Amartya Sen has done great work on this approach. Indeed, these problems, as well as the impending global energy crisis and the consequences of global climate changes, all require an unprecedented level of technical, intellectual, and international cooperation on the solid moral basis of our common humanity.

Because Europeans not in the EU have been so strongly attracted to joining it, they have accepted its intrusive yet highly desirable criteria for membership: *free elections, the rule of law, free markets,* and *respect for individual and minority rights.* These concepts are dealt with in our chapter on democracy, and they are crucial for the global outlook of the EU. Both in principle and in practice it is better that people find their own path to freedom, in their own countries, in their own time, and, wherever possible, peacefully. But should we help those people as they fight freedom's battle? Most emphatically we should, by every nonviolent means at our disposal.

Ash recommends ways to foster the basic aims of the EU as its functions expand. Governments and companies should link trade and investment to respect for human rights. They should press parliaments to support foundations that work for democracy in restricted countries. They should support nongovernmental organizations that work for freedom in other countries. Important is use of the Internet, international broadcasting, and scholarships for foreign students to expose restricted peoples to the benefits of a free society. These are difficult processes. Bureaucratic obstacles, vague political commitments, and recently the severe recession have been impediments to realizing the EU's ambitions of becoming a major global actor in conflict prevention. This requires improving the EU's early warning system and organizing well-informed units to respond effectively to such warning in the mode of centers of excellence for prevention described elsewhere in this book.

The EU has the capacity for early and ongoing conflict prevention—helping to build internal capacity in vulnerable countries. One asset is its provision of development aid; another is delegations worldwide. Thus, the EU can help many conflict-prone, fragile countries and regions where intergroup tensions can be recognized and understood early. Sometimes, the EU's low political profile lends itself to violence prevention in sensitive situations, offsetting the obsolete colonial stereotypes by empathetic attitudes, early diplomacy, and cooperative economic actions. The profound transformation of Europe from World War II and the Holocaust to humanitarian prevention of violence gives it well-earned credibility.

The EU has advanced in prevention of mass violence during the past decade, with strong preventive values and actions, but the emphasis on early prevention is still in need of strengthening, as it is almost everywhere in the world. Effective cooperation across twenty-seven democracies is highly desirable and essentially unique in its potential, but difficult to achieve fully. During the decade of Solana's leadership, the direction of movement was highly positive.

EARLY WARNING AND WELL-PREPARED
CONTINGENCY PLANS: CRUCIAL LINKS
IN PREVENTING MASS VIOLENCE

Informed decisionmaking on early action is impossible without early warning. Little more than a decade ago, the EU had no system dedicated to early detection of emerging violent conflict. Since then, new mechanisms have been developed, which do not yet operate to their full potential. To build effective partnerships for violence prevention, the EU has built "desk-to-desk" dialogues between EU and UN officials. It has similarly enhanced cooperation with other international organizations on peace and security matters, especially with the AU and the Economic Community of West African States (ECOWAS). Thus, capacity-building for crisis preparedness of partners is crucial in the long run, including the AU, the Arab League, and civil society actors. The EU has created the African Peace Facility (APF), which mainly funds African military peacekeeping operations, but this is late in the day. A stronger focus on capacity-building of the African institutions for preconflict activities would be valuable. One or more centers of excellence must integrate violence-relevant information and stimulate operational units of the EU region constructively, strengthening EU programs that encourage, train, and support civil society and democratic political parties in various countries over the long term. Building on its own experience, the EU can promote regional integration all over the world, helping regional associations build their own capacity.

Increasingly, the EU emphasizes early prevention by recognizing emerging indications of intergroup hostility. It is complementing this approach by developing a strong capacity for crisis management. The need to link the two is now generally recognized and in essentially the same categories formulated by the Carnegie Commission on Preventing Deadly Conflict and later adopted by the UN: "structural prevention" (long-term) and "operational prevention" (near-term impending crisis). The later in the day, the harder it is to see plausible solutions.

In line with its belief in multilateralism, the EU wants to work with other partners to promote this combined approach. It has increased cooperation with the UN and the AU. It has sought collaboration with NATO. With the advent of the Obama administration, inter-democracy cooperation has been further strengthened. Both conflict prevention—which is far cheaper than dealing with conflict after it erupts—and continued engagement in reconstruction after a conflict has been suppressed are necessary tasks for joint multilateral action. The moral basis for this approach is clear and compelling.

CONFLICT PREVENTION AND NGOs

The EU has fostered NGOs that have played an important role in helping governments to make systemic changes and in contributing their own skills in policy and implementation. Their roles have been as many and varied as their organizations—think tanks/research institutions/policy forums (such as Centres for Strategic Studies, Councils on Foreign Relations, Institutes of International Affairs, and large foundations such as the Carnegie Corporation); watchdog operations (such as Amnesty International and Human Rights Watch); on-the-ground organizations that engage in mediation, build capacity, and inspire confidence in democracy (such as the Carter Center and Open Society Institute); and humanitarian relief organizations (such as Doctors without Borders or CARE).

The European Institute of Peace (EIP) is an independent organization with close links to the EU that engages in mediation and dialogue and provides best practices in these early prevention measures. It illustrates the emerging scope of activities in the field. The primary mission of the EIP is to help the EU in its growing ability to prevent violent conflicts. As an independent organization with close ties to the EU, the EIP can engage in dialogue and mediation where the EU has interests but cannot act today. The institute can also, by working closely with other key actors, identify best practices in mediation and dialogue, focusing on EU priority areas. This work can be in direct support of mediation efforts of the EU, the UN, and other organizations—and pave the way for systematic, preventive diplomacy. It can make contributions to the general lessons learned, with the aim of increasing professionalization in this field.

One product of a greatly enhanced focus on prevention is a substantial amount of research-based analysis of what generates conflict. A whole literature now exists on economic causes of war, both within and between states, and the roles of greed and grievance in fostering and sustaining violence. The focus is on structural prevention—building institutional structures and processes (military, political, legal, economic, and social) that can resolve without violence the stresses that arise between individuals and groups. A focus on conflict prevention since the early 1990s, stimulated in part by the Carnegie Commission on Preventing Deadly Conflict, has not only increased our understanding of the causes of conflicts but also suggested a repertoire of measures to deal with them.

Corruption, human rights abuse, natural resources profiteering, and absence of rule of law are dangerous signs of fragile or nonfunctioning state institutions and bad governance. Early action to identify such distortions and intergroup tensions can lead to development activity that deals with root causes of state fragility and violent conflict, promoting measures with incentives that provide every member of society, regardless of background, with access to adequate food, clean water, health care, and education and fostering opportunity and ingenuity in all sectors of society. Development cooperation can also play an important preventive role by becoming involved in security systems of developing countries through stable and effective partnerships, rather than waiting for a crisis. This cooperation should have military forces firmly under the control of civilian authority. These are the directions in which the EU is moving.

Working in relation to fragile, failing, or repressive states is very difficult, but such states cannot be abandoned. Europe must look for a variety of earlier *entry points* to support governance reform, institutional capacity-building, and the delivery of basic social services. Respect for basic human rights, democratic principles, and the rule of law constitutes the essence of partnership agreements that are natural to the EU. These fundamental efforts must not be destroyed by economic recession or revival of nationalism, as in Hungary during 2011. The EU has overcome so many obstacles that it cannot be deterred by the inevitable fluctuations of economic and political stress. Serious, sustained dialogue with recalcitrant leaders is important, highlighting how much leaders benefit in their own right and in respect of their own people by going beyond greed and corruption. Earning respect in world citizenship is also an incentive.

THE EU AS A LEADER IN CONFLICT PREVENTION

Overall, the EU has made remarkable progress in the years of leadership of Solana in developing an effective approach to preventing violent conflict through building partnerships for prevention with other actors, as well as strengthening its own capabilities. It is integrating preventive instruments effectively; developing capabilities; and, most important, taking a very active and informed approach to conflict-related issues. The European Security Strategy placed prevention at the center of EU efforts to address both violent conflict (long a priority of the EU) and other security threats. This provides an exceptionally suitable basis for leadership in the prevention of mass violence in the long term.

ELEVEN

NORTH ATLANTIC
TREATY ORGANIZATION

The North Atlantic Treaty Organization (NATO) was created in the aftermath of World War II as the Soviet Union became alienated from its former wartime allies; occupied most of Eastern and Central Europe; and, under the brutal leadership of Joseph Stalin, defiantly faced Western Europe as well as the United States.

In response, the Western allies formed a close alliance that became an exceedingly powerful military force, bridging the North Atlantic between Western Europe and North America. As the decades passed, its functions broadened to include a modicum of diplomatic, educational, and scientific functions. With the end of the Cold War, at the outset of the 1990s, it broadened its activities considerably, creating relationships with additional countries, expanding diplomatic and *civil-military* functions, and considering "out-of-area" tasks—for example, a catalyst for regional organizations beyond Europe in conflict resolution.

In 1994, to enhance security and stability throughout Europe and to strengthen ties with countries emerging from the former Soviet Union, the member countries of the North Atlantic Treaty Alliance invited the emerging democratic states in Eastern Europe to join them by creating the Partnership for Peace—a sort of first cousin.[1] This Partnership for Peace program expanded and intensified political and military cooperation throughout Europe, thereby diminishing threats to peace and promoting the commitment to democratic principles that are essential to the alliance. In joining the partnership, these states subscribed to the preservation of democratic societies, freedom from coercion and intimidation, maintenance of the principles of international law, and civilian control of the military.[2] In endorsing these values, they were emphasizing their desire for NATO membership—which most of them achieved. Thus, beyond military functions, NATO can help others in peaceful enterprises.

They reaffirmed their commitment to fulfill in good faith the obligations of the Charter of the United Nations and the principles of the Universal Declaration of Human Rights—specifically, to refrain from the threat or use of force against the territorial integrity or political independence of any state, to respect existing borders, and to settle disputes by peaceful means. They also reaffirmed their commitment to the Helsinki Final Act (human rights) and all subsequent OSCE documents, to the fulfillment of the commitments they have undertaken in human rights and arms control. These were years of remarkable transformation in East/West relations and indeed in European history. Thus, the Soviet propaganda about the imminent menace of NATO was badly distorted and in any case has nothing to do with its potential today.

The Euro-Atlantic Partnership Council (EAPC) was formed in 1997 to enhance the efforts of the Partnership for Peace in both an expanded political dimension of partnership and practical cooperation. It observed carefully and complemented the activities of the OSCE, the European Union, and the Council of Europe[3]—valuable interinstitutional cooperation. The EAPC maintained important principles for the success of cooperation between allies and partners: inclusiveness, providing opportunities for political consultation and practical cooperation to all allies and partners equally, and distinctive roles so that partners could decide for themselves the level and areas of their cooperation with NATO.

In late 2002, NATO undertook a comprehensive review of all of these newer activities.[4] It reaffirmed its strategic concept of outreach and openness, preserving peace, promoting democracy, contributing to prosperity, and fostering genuine partnership among all democratic Euro-Atlantic countries. The commitment aimed to enhance the security of all, to exclude none, and to overcome disagreements that could lead to violent conflict. These ties proved very attractive to the countries of East-Central Europe and served a "magnet" function similar to that of the European Union. *Both fostered the transition to democracy* and eventually their countries' entry into NATO.

A BROADER APPROACH TO SECURITY
IN THE NATO "FAMILY"

Allies have welcomed requests by partners for political consultations with the alliance, individually or in smaller groups, on issues of special political and security importance to them. Consultations led to more systematic political and psychological relationships. Allies consulted with partners to develop further cooperation in civil emergency planning to protect the civilian population from weapons of mass destruction, terrorist attacks, technological accidents, and natural disasters. This included work on ways to promote interoperability between relevant national capabilities. In the years ahead, this is likely to include ways of coping with the impending dangers of mass atrocity.

Thus, allies and partners developed a broader approach to security in their political consultations and other discussions. They sought complementarity with other international organizations in their response to security challenges, including but not limited to weapons of mass destruction and terrorism. Thus, cooperation with the EU and the UN became feasible and desirable. Military constitutions meshed with civilian ones.

Recognizing that the struggle against terrorism requires collaborative efforts of the international community, member states of the EAPC endorsed a Partnership Action Plan against Terrorism.[5] To this end, they explored ways to facilitate the exchange of operational information about terrorists and their networks. The plan emphasized increased cooperation at national, subregional, regional, and international levels to strengthen the global response to terrorism This is a plan that can extend to prevention of mass atrocities. NATO can intensify consultations and information sharing on terrorism, and also on threats of genocide as a matter of vital priority in light of democratic principles, international law, and sheer human decency.

BUILDING PEACE IN CRISIS REGIONS:
THE ROLE OF NATO

The wars of Yugoslavia's dissolution, and especially the Bosnian War, caught the international community largely unprepared. Initially, the UN was the principal institution attempting to broker an end to hostilities, keep the peace in regions where a cease-fire had been agreed upon, and alleviate the suffering of noncombatants. Over the years, NATO became involved in support of the UN through various air- and sea-based support operations—enforcing economic sanctions, an arms embargo, and a no-flight zone—and by providing the United Nations with detailed military contingency planning of safe areas and the implementation of a peace plan.[6]

These measures helped to contain the conflict and save lives, but in the end proved inadequate to bring an end to the war. The turning point in the Bosnian War came, significantly, when NATO took the lead, launching a two-week air campaign against Bosnian Serb forces in the summer of 1995. This paved the way for the Dayton Agreement, the peace accord ending the Bosnian War that came into force on December 20, 1995, under which a 60,000-strong NATO-led Implementation Force (IFOR) took military responsibility for the peace process.

The deployment of IFOR, which included soldiers from both NATO and non-NATO countries, was the alliance's first military engagement on land and points the way toward making NATO an increasingly effective instrument for military and political crisis management of the most constructive sort. This helped forge closer links between the peacekeeping force and its civilian counterparts in developing a doctrine for civil-military cooperation. The experience stimulated work on *earlier* intervention, using NATO resources *before* mass violence.

Yugoslavia was NATO's first venture into genocide-prone territory. Although the prevention of mass violence prior to the necessity for military action is certainly preferable, there are times when military strength is essential—either in the background to strengthen diplomatic efforts or in the foreground as in Yugoslavia.

Military victory was the first step on a long road toward building a durable, multiethnic society free from the threat of renewed conflict. In addition to helping preserve a secure environment, NATO actively helped refugees and displaced persons return to their homes, sought out and arrested individuals indicted for war crimes, and helped to reform the domestic military structures in such a way as to prevent a return to violence—all tasks that require a long-term commitment. NATO's first three peace-support operations took place in Europe, yet the need for long-term peacebuilding is *global*.

In order to be effective when deploying far from alliance territory, NATO militaries must invest in power-projection capabilities. To meet this challenge, the alliance adopted a series of measures aimed at ensuring that NATO is equipped for the full spectrum of modern military missions. It involves the creation of a NATO Response Force, which will give the alliance the capacity to move a robust force quickly to deter or respond to attack. Such a force could be very helpful in a *genocide-prone situation* by keeping the would-be perpetrators away from their likely victims and providing space for diplomacy—coercive if necessary to prevent mass killing.

EU/NATO COOPERATION

An effective working relationship between the European Union and NATO is critical to successful early prevention, later crisis management, and the prevention of mass violence in general. A breakthrough came in 2002 with the adoption of the strong EU-NATO declaration on security cooperation. Since then, the EU and NATO have negotiated a series of documents on cooperation in crisis management, known by insiders as the "Berlin-Plus" package, which made it possible for the EU to take over from NATO responsibility for peacekeeping in the former Yugoslav Republic of Macedonia in April 2003.

The "Berlin-Plus" arrangements seek to avoid unnecessary duplication of resources and comprise four elements. These are assured EU access to NATO operational planning; the availability to the EU of NATO capabilities and common assets; NATO European command options for EU-led operations, developing the European role of NATO's Deputy Supreme Allied Commander; and adaptation of the NATO defense planning system to incorporate the availability of forces for EU operations. The security cooperative orientation reflected in these late actions needs updating toward *early* prevention. The tendency is in this direction.

The whole joint experience in the former Yugoslavia demonstrated *growing cooperation between NATO and the EU.* It all highlights the value of both organizations—separately and together. The potential of the cooperation, not only in military matters but also in economic, political, and civil affairs, is impressive in dealing with dangerous situations—early and late. Thus, the EU and NATO agreed on mutual crisis consultation arrangements that provide for efficient and rapid decisionmaking in both organizations, with their sharing of strategies in the face of growing tensions.

In many current conflicts throughout the world, the basic nature of the state is at the heart of the problem. Thus, the international community finds itself called upon to reform dysfunctional institutions, including the state administration, the legal system, and even the media if they are promoting hatred. In addition to the military aspect, many other activities have become necessary for an effective operation to prevent mass violence. Only a careful, well-planned, and coordinated *combination of civilian and military measures* can create the conditions for long-term peace, based on good governance and democratic socioeconomic development.

These examples show how a cooperative, democratic, broadened NATO can help in the prevention of mass violence. Whereas this book clearly emphasizes ways of preventing disasters that have not reached the crisis of military conflict, and whereas the EU itself has developed military capacity adequate for most early prevention tasks, the availability of powerful, diversified NATO forces would rarely be needed in combat but could be helpful in a background capacity and might sometimes be crucial if strong force is needed (most likely due to international delay in addressing signs of emerging, serious trouble). Thus, cooperative arrangements with NATO involving the EU could be a formidable asset in preventing rotten outcomes. Some "hawks" criticize the EU for not developing more powerful forces. Other statespeople admire the restraint from severe coercion that characterizes the EU. Judicious assessment in each stressful situation is required with the emphasis on peaceful values to the extent possible.

PROSPECTS FOR NATO'S FUTURE

Without formal declaration, NATO has recently been exploring a new and global reason for existence—*helping to preserve peace in dangerous areas throughout the world*. In this new century, it has acted as a peacekeeper in Afghanistan; given training to Iraqi security forces and logistical assistance to the AU mission in Darfur; and contributed to humanitarian relief of tsunami victims in Indonesia, to Hurricane Katrina victims in the United States, and to earthquake victims in Pakistan.

When the collapse of the USSR occurred, uncertainty arose about how best to use the alliance's strength. The United States considered taking advantage of the "peace dividend" by focusing the role of Western military forces on peacebuilding, support of humanitarian relief efforts, and prevention of mass atrocities.[7] After the September 11, 2001, terrorist attacks, NATO allies for the first time volunteered to deploy their forces outside allied territories, under the treaty provision that *an attack on one member state was an attack on all of them*. The United States, reluctant at first, but overextended in Iraq, accepted NATO's offer to deploy peacekeeping forces in Afghanistan, and those forces grew from 5,000 to 15,000 in a few years.

Coping with global problems at their sources requires a global reach. NATO leaders are discussing these problems carefully. High on their agenda is how to strengthen relations with friendly democracies outside the transatlantic area, such as Japan, Australia, South Korea, and New Zealand. The United States and United Kingdom have proposed "global partnerships" to create a network with established democracies outside Europe. It makes sense in a tightly interconnected world to choose new members according to their *democratic values* rather than their regional location. NATO has already cooperated with friendly nations in ad hoc coalitions beyond Europe or North America.

A wider, well-organized membership might well be more effective than ad hoc coalitions because it would create reliable forces that had trained, planned, and exercised together, resulting in the technically cooperative "interoperability" that has allowed NATO to react quickly and competently to crises. NATO can evolve with the times to represent not just the transatlantic community but a *global community of democracies*. A regional organization can help substantially with global security but cannot do all that is necessary. NATO can usefully extend its alliance to democracies worldwide on the basis of their commitment to NATO's founding principles. In so doing, it could facilitate prevention of mass violence over the whole spectrum of emerging dangers. This depends on the most careful consideration of how to integrate military, economic, social, and psychological factors. NATO no longer can be a stereotype of its Cold War functions but rather a new sort of force for peace. Active American participation without domination would provide a crucial benefit. The 2012 US commitment to prevention of mass atrocities may heighten the significance of NATO in decades to come, helping with both military and nonmilitary functions.

NATO is not a new imperialism. Rather, it is a promising model for civil-military relations that bring countries together in cooperation for peace and build a sharing of assets and norms of human decency worldwide.

TWELVE

PROMISING CHANGES IN A
DECADE AND A GENERATION

> *For it isn't enough to talk about peace. One must believe in it. And it isn't enough to believe in it. One must work at it.*
> *—Eleanor Roosevelt, in a broadcast on the work of the United Nations over the Voice of America, November 11, 1951*
>
> *Roosevelt's appointment as US representative to the UN from December 1945 until January 1953 led to her leadership of the Human Rights Commission, which produced the Universal Declaration of Human Rights, one of the most important documents of the twentieth century.*

This book shows that there has been a burst of activity to prevent mass violence in the early years of the twenty-first century that stands in dramatic contrast to the attitudes in the nineteenth and twentieth centuries. This involves very serious problems that have been historically neglected. There is a conjunction of new moral commitments, new ideas, new organizations, and new initiatives for existing institutions. Tools and strategies are being developed beyond prior experience and tried out in highly innovative ways across many nations and sectors. No one can be sure how far and how fast this movement will go; the near-term prognosis is encouraging, and the long-term prognosis has great potential for a healthy humanity. Persistence, ingenuity, and dedication to humane values will be essential and probably feasible. This book offers a compendium of ideas on minimizing mass violence, integrated from worldwide scholarship, experience, and personal leadership. Our strongest wish is that the book will stimulate serious interest and better ideas in the years ahead.

PILLARS OF PREVENTION

At the heart of this work is prevention of mass violence by building *pillars of prevention*; leadership in many sectors is badly needed. These pillars are multipurpose in preventing human suffering related to hatred and violence. Mass atrocities have important shared properties—often-virulent prejudice predisposes to slavery, terrorism, civil war, revolution, or interstate war. Under those conditions, the door is opened to mass violence as the norms and institutions that restrain such behavior are badly eroded. Killing becomes the order of the day, and established targets become exceedingly vulnerable. So it is highly desirable and increasingly feasible for the international community—especially the established democracies worldwide—to take measures that help to put out fires when they are small, yet the danger of conflagration is visible. If not extinguished, these fires may well lead to mass violence of one form or another.

Altogether, the international community no longer has a viable excuse for inaction. The years required to go from the initial jeopardy to full genocide offer an interval for the international community—if it is alert, well informed, morally committed, and organizationally prepared—to take preventive actions: the earlier and more cooperative, the better. To do so, we must clarify the pillars of prevention, make them widely understood, and strengthen institutional/policy/practice paths to their implementation.

These concepts delineate pillars of prevention: education for peace and justice, indeed for survival; *early, proactive* help to countries in trouble with intergroup relations; the development of *equitable socioeconomic democracies*; the *protection and promotion of human rights*; and *constraints on weaponry*. In short, these issues are so important for humanity that they must be clarified on an interdisciplinary and international basis, involving all sectors of society and broad public understanding.

LEADERSHIP FOR WORSE AND BETTER

Leadership matters greatly in overcoming all of our severe problems, and humanity must learn to recognize and cultivate leaders of vision, courage, and humane and democratic policies and to reinforce their commitment to compassionate and nonviolent problem-solving. How to do this should become a substantial part of the international agenda, including formal education, the media, the Internet, discourse of international organizations, and democratic dialogue and analysis. It applies not only to high levels of government but to communities, corporations, universities, and other leading organizations. It surely includes emerging (usually young) leaders whose core values are peaceful. Earlier in this book, we suggested ways in which they can be helped to fulfill their promise.

A major focus of research has been on *malevolent leadership*. The more we can understand about the ideologies, social facilitators, and unrestrained actions of such leaders, the better our opportunity to foresee and prevent future mass murderous episodes. Another focus of research is on the implementation of destructive orders. Who does the killing and why? Progress has been made in this sphere, and much more could be clarified by research on significant organizations and institutions and the interplay of leaders and followers.

Political leaders make war or mass atrocities possible by lighting the fires of hatred, but they do not act alone. They are supported by machinery of the state, the dominant political party; the police forces; paramilitary and military forces; as well as professionals such as lawyers, professors, doctors, and engineers. *This time interval to build the machinery of violence-prone behavior can be used for prevention.* Effective prevention is facilitated by ample warning time. Warning time is typically not weeks or even months but actually years. Mass violence is not like a tsunami that bursts upon humanity with hardly any warning. Early prevention is most effective, and this requires serious attention to these problems, in age-appropriate and context-appropriate ways from childhood to the leadership of many sectors, especially political, military, religious, and business.

Incitement is a hallmark of mass violence. Every modern case of genocide—and most cases of mass violence—have been preceded by a mass media propaganda campaign directed by political leaders. Thus, the cultivation of moderate, pragmatic, *problem-solving*, and *humane* leaders is essential on a worldwide basis. We have suggested incentives at different levels that can strengthen the hand of those who wish to help or at least need help and are willing to accept it.

A determined commitment to *nonviolent conflict reduction* is essential. Altogether, the international community stands warned. Ignorance is no longer a viable excuse for inaction. The years required to go from the initial jeopardy to mass slaughter offer an interval for the international community—if it is alert, well informed, morally committed, and organizationally prepared—to take preventive actions—the *earlier* and more *cooperative*, the better. A range of preventive options derived from multiple disciplines and world experience is crucial and has been largely lacking—yet every year brings new knowledge and relevant experience.

The urgency and gravity of the problems of deadly conflict, currently evident in one way or another on every continent, cry out for a fundamental upgrading of education on matters of conflict resolution—especially mechanisms for early, ongoing mutual accommodation. We need prompt and just ways of dealing with grievances and need to learn how to construct solidly—for the first time in history—an evidence-based picture of how to move forward to a peaceful world. Norms of fair-minded mutual benefit must be built. A useful global bumper sticker would be *"Mutual Aid for Mutual Benefit."*

Toward this difficult but attainable end, the international community (and especially the established democracies) must make every effort to assign and implement a high priority for education in general and four paths of education in particular: (1) education in mathematics, science, and technology so that every country can have the knowledge and skills to participate fruitfully in the modern economy oriented toward widely shared prosperity; (2) education for health so that diseases and injuries that now constitute a huge burden of illness, disability, and death can be prevented in the first place; (3) education for conflict resolution, violence prevention, and construction of a peaceful world through specific tools and strategies that enable diverse peoples to live together amicably; and (4) education that is equally available to girls and boys, women and men, and all ethnic, religious, and political groups.

To help poor countries implement these difficult priorities, education of this sort should be closely linked to problem-solving diplomacy, fostering of mutual respect between groups, developing aid in joint efforts of high integrity, promoting international trade on a fair basis, and directly investing in emerging markets. These actions provide powerful economic and psychological incentives to shape behavior in ways that could have a transforming effect throughout the world. We must clarify superordinate goals and show how highly desired aims (e.g., avoidance of nuclear war) can be achieved only by cooperation. This becomes feasible if we can mobilize the intellectual, technical, and moral strength over sufficient time to bring it about. The needs are urgent and worldwide. The time has come to go beyond well-meaning slogans such as "never again" as well as the glorification of nuclear weapons. Instead, we must formulate well-analyzed attitudes, norms, policies, and practices that bring us together in our *common humanity*. There is need for global understanding of the paradox that advances in technology are both beneficial through education and exceedingly dangerous through the facility of fostering hatred and building weapons.

Pillars of Prevention: A Recap

In summary, these are pillars of enduring value, and leaders of various sectors can do much to bring them to fruition: educating for human survival; helping proactively, including preventive diplomacy; fostering indigenous democracy; building equitable socioeconomic development; promoting and protecting human rights; and restraining highly lethal weapons.

BENEVOLENT LEADERS, PAST AND PRESENT

In 1994, Mikhail S. Gorbachev, in talking with the authors of this book, reflected on a decade of intensive involvement with political leaders all over the world. One of his outstanding conclusions was the large extent to which they see "brute force" as their ultimate validation. His observation, based on abundant experience, highlights a long-standing, historically deadly inclination of leaders of many kinds from many places to interpret their mandate as being strong, tough, aggressive, and even violent. For all too many, this is indeed the essence of leadership.

Gorbachev, in control of a vast nuclear arsenal, not to speak of immense power in conventional, chemical, and biological weapons, was wise enough *not* to interpret his own leadership in terms of brute force. Yet there is no shortage of leaders who do. They will have mass killing powers at their disposal in the twenty-first century. This is true not only of national leaders but also of subnational groups, such as al-Qaeda, a vivid example of horror.

By the same token, this observation highlights the *critical importance of international leadership for effective prevention of deadly conflict.* That is why the Carnegie Commission on Preventing Deadly Conflict emphasizes, "although the prevention of deadly conflict requires many tools and strategies, bold leadership and an active constituency for prevention are essential for these tools and strategies to be effective."

Peace-oriented leaders can help mobilize public understanding and great financial or military resources, build international coalitions, and create a strong constituency for prevention. The Carnegie Commission recommends that *prevention* be on the agenda of every head of state and government meeting and all foreign and defense ministerial gatherings. The international community should champion and reward good governance, especially in countries struggling toward greater democracy, as we see today in the Middle East.

International leaders can call attention to the problem of intergroup violence and tap into latent public inclination toward prevention. They have the scope to explain the need for prevention. They can help build the political will necessary to mount an effective response to complex emergencies and to help people prevent violence before it erupts.

Leaders close to potential conflict can help educate the public about nonviolent ways to settle disputes. Gorbachev effectively addressed nonviolent responses to the breakup of the Soviet Union. He pointed out that modern leaders need to change their outlook; because of the shadow of nuclear weapons, the use of massive force cannot possibly be a first resort—or indeed a useful weapon at all. Instead, a modern leader needs the intellectual and moral authority to persuade rather than to compel.

We strongly reiterate that leadership needed to prevent deadly conflict is not confined to the political sphere. Leaders of other powerful institutions can make a profound difference: for example, religious, business, media, science, and technology. Indeed, they can have a moderating effect on unwise political leaders. Leadership must come to mean *drawing on the best resources—* intellectual, technical, and moral as well as material resources; being thoughtful, well informed, active, creative, and respectful of others in helping to clarify great dangers and ways of coping; and providing a moral and operational basis for dealing constructively with international problems.

There are illuminating examples in the violent twentieth century. Harry S. Truman, George Marshall (a great military leader), and Jean Monnet (a French statesman) looked beyond the devastation of World War II and the underlying hostilities to envision a Europe in which regional cooperation would transcend adversarial boundaries and traditional rivalries. They foresaw that large-scale economic cooperation could facilitate not only postwar recovery but also long-term prosperity and international peace. More than half a century so far confirms their vision. Bringing this vision to fulfillment required creative efforts to educate the public, mobilize key constituencies, and persuade reluctant partners. Maintaining this support required courageous use of scarce political capital.

An *enduring constituency for international cooperation* can be fostered through measures that identify public inclinations toward problem-solving engagement and reinforce these impulses with clear rationales, approaches, and vivid successful examples. It helps to have analogies from familiar contexts of home and community. As we have seen, a useful model is provided by the experience in public health over several decades. A strong constituency for preventing deadly diseases has emerged. This has led to improved rates of immunization, better diet and exercise practices, reduced cigarette smoking, and in turn diminishing the casualties of a variety of diseases. This approach to leadership and public education can be usefully applied to the worldwide problems of conflict. This is no easy task, flying in the face of complacency, wishful thinking, pleasurable habits, and intergroup tensions. Yet good examples are emerging, new ideas are formulated, monitoring is enhanced, and democratic leadership is spreading. The promise of major advances is visible on the horizon.

ENEMIES CAN BECOME FRIENDS

Charles Kupchan, a distinguished scholar who is a senior fellow at the Council on Foreign Affairs, has carefully constructed a book on this vital transformation. In 2010, Kupchan focused, through case studies, on two principal questions in clarifying how enemies become friends. First, through what pathway do states succeed in overcoming their grievances, minimize geopolitical competition, and construct an enduring relationship that eliminates armed conflict? Second, how can we understand zones of stable peace?

If a state is faced with insufficient resources, it may deal with threats by unilateral accommodation to befriend an adversary. If reciprocity follows,

> *The establishment of clear mechanisms for resolving disputes and checking power helps institutionalize the practices of restraint and cooperation.*
> —**Charles Kupchan**, *in* How Enemies Become Friends

it regularizes cooperation and dampens rivalry. Integration of societies can then follow, building personal and institutional linkages among the partner states, then the origin of new narratives of friendship and the emergence of compatible, shared, or common identities.

Negotiation initiates the process of reconciliation, and friendly contact fosters international society; reasonable political discourse and moving beyond narrow identity are helpful. Institutionalized restraint favors accommodation that sets adversaries on the path to peace. It is helpful if political and economic elites seek to advance reconciliation. Perception of mutual benefit helps adversaries become potential partners, and over time this consolidates stable peace.

Transformative experiences are notable in history. For example, Sweden overshadowed Norway in material terms and held a threatening position for a long time, but peace occurred after 1905, in step with Sweden's embrace of liberal democracy and international restraint. Abu Dhabi was by far the largest and wealthiest emirate, but it withheld its power, redistributed its wealth, and ceded political influence to the smaller emirates. This cleared the way for a stable, peaceful union. On the other hand, the Concert of Europe collapsed after the revolutions of 1848 aroused nationalist passions, stimulating Britain and France to capitalize on rather than to avoid opportunities to pursue unilateral advantage. Contrast this with what was achieved after World War II.

For example, the Concert of Europe grouped dissident members, restoring consensus through persuasion coupled with the threat of isolation in case of noncooperation.

The geographical and temporal diversity of Kupchan's case studies exhibits a remarkable similarity in the basics of the power-checking mechanisms that enable zones of stable peace to take shape. The parties embrace decision-making rules to avoid excessive concentration of power. Some examples show how zones of peace are created by cooperative institutions rather than dominant powers. In the long history of the Swiss Confederation, its components struggled to acquire sufficient authority to provide order while preserving the traditional autonomy of the individual cantons. The United States worked to centralize enough for federal institutions to provide effective governance, but not so far as to cause the individual states to fear tyranny and avoid participation in the union. In the emergence of the EU and its periodic reforms, there has been care to balance the power of the Franco-German coalition and the centralized institutions in Brussels with the political powers of national governments.

Kupchan's case studies wipe away the illusion that preponderant power, wielded with relentless resolve, is a key ingredient of order in the international system. The opposite conclusion emerges: excessive threat of power undermines a rules-based order. Strategic restraint fosters and sustains international society, drawing on mutual reassurance and respect, not mutual suspicion and resentment. Giving peace a chance in the international system depends on how powerful states *use* their strength, not just on the distribution of the power.

William Zartman, an extraordinary scholar on negotiations, emphasizes that research on conflict resolution has a long and productive history, especially in social psychology. His perspective offers hope for benefit from future behavioral sciences. The pioneering work of Solomon Asch in the 1950s demonstrated how easily individuals could be swayed to change their views even on objective data to comply with those expressed by others in a group. Stanley Milgram showed that individuals have a strong tendency to conformity when instructed to perform painful acts on others even if this violates their personal moral codes, especially if they are following the instructions of a seemingly legitimate authority. They seek to avoid social rejection. Fear of betrayal is a powerful incentive even for acts of serious damage.

This leads to the familiar, indeed historic, orientation, forcing moderates into extreme positions. There is nothing more damaging than leadership exacerbation of in-group versus out-group differences. Even previously decent

---

The management of fear and repression and the selection of appropriate partners are two crucial elements in reducing identity conflict, either in prevention or as a path to resolution.

    —*I. William Zartman*, in The Slippery Slope to Genocide:
      Reducing Identity Conflicts and Preventing Mass Murder

individuals can come to see themselves as protecting their own at whatever cost to others. Such conformity is rewarded by the in-group. Then a kind of social immunity rejects the virus of negotiation, moderation, or mutual accommodation. This is a pervasive danger of worldwide significance that, as a practical matter, must be offset by the kind of measures outlined in this book that lead ultimately to powerful norms and institutions of decent human relations.

THE SCIENTIFIC COMMUNITY: PROBLEM-SOLVING, PUBLIC UNDERSTANDING, AND PATHWAYS TO PEACE

The eminent, farsighted biologist Alex Keynan, of the Hebrew University, elicited the cooperation of many scientists in various fields who have worked across adversarial boundaries. They clarified the intrinsic value of cooperative efforts to enhance technical and social capabilities and the possibility of helping to move toward conflict resolution in the societies at large. He included from the scientific community, among others, Wolfgang Panofsky, Mahmoud Mahfouz, Jean-Jacques Salomon, and Jesse Ausubel. He summarizes key advantages of scientific cooperation for diminishing mass violence.

Scientists are nearly always able to use their international scientific network to establish effective contacts with other scientists across conflict lines, whenever they personally believe such contact to be of importance. The scientists' wish to cooperate professionally, part of the scientific ethos, often transcends the government's motivation, whatever that may be. This strong wish to cooperate motivates scientists to overcome great obstacles. Contacts between Palestinian and Israeli scientists, scholars, and clinicians occurred when such interactions were still illegal in both communities. Despite the Soviet policy of controlling all scientific cooperation, Russian physicists were able to convince their government that contact with international science was absolutely imperative for their own research effectiveness, and they were able to stay in touch with their Western counterparts in international forums. Contacts between scientists from hostile governments often occur at international conferences, and at the invitation of scientists in a third neutral country such contacts are often fruitful over time.

Cooperation of scientists across conflict lines, even if it has routine scientific components, is consciously seen in a political context and has, as one of its motives, a deliberate attempt to help resolve international conflicts. The science culture includes a strong international dimension, a common language, a need to communicate, and an increasing recognition of the value of cooperation—interdisciplinary and international.

Another objective is educating the public in as many countries as possible as well as the scientific community itself. The Committee on International Security and Arms Control (CISAC) of the US National Academy of Science has seriously worked on arms control principles with the Russians, and also has educated members of the US academy in matters of arms control.

From our own experience over several decades, we see that the scientific community provides understanding, insight, and novel ways of viewing important problems, not least on deadly conflict. Through their institutions and organizations, scientists and educators can strengthen research and education in areas pertinent to violence in the biology and psychology of aggressive behavior; prosocial child development; peaceful intergroup relations; diminishing prejudice and ethnocentrism; the origins of wars, genocide, and mass atrocities; and mutual accommodation and early conflict resolution. Science can generate new knowledge and explore the application of such knowledge to urgent problems in contemporary society. An emerging process is the recognition that education in science and technology is of importance for prosperity, security, and health worldwide. But this is not enough.

What are the actual and potential contributions of the sciences to early conflict resolution and violence prevention? How can these contributions increase substantially in the years ahead? The scientific community has clarified a lot—and can do much more to bring its international and analytical perspectives to bear on a deeper understanding of preventing deadly conflict.

In a world so full of hatred and violence, past and present, human conflict and its resolution are a subject that deserves major research efforts. High standards of inquiry must be applied to this field, involving many sciences often acting in collaborative ways. Crucial world problems, such as those involved in the human propensity to violence, do not come in neat packages. Information and ideas must be pulled together in mutual aid beyond most prior efforts. Insightful and useful approaches have emerged, as we have seen in this book, and better ones are on the horizon.

There is growing determination to face the obstacles: the inherent complexity of the subject matter, old conceptual rigidities such as the hereditary-environment dichotomy, proper ethical limitations of experimental control in human research, ancient prejudices against objective inquiry on human behavior, dogmatic social ideologies, and institutional inertia. In considering human conflict, avoidance and denial tend to substitute for careful scrutiny, authority often substitutes for evidence, and blaming readily substitutes for problem-solving. The capacity for wishful thinking in these matters is enormous, as is the capacity for self-justification. But the problems must be faced because the stakes will probably reach an unprecedented level in the twenty-first century for reasons we have described.

It is one of the greatest challenges for public policy to organize a much broader and deeper effort to understand the nature and sources of human conflict, and above all to develop effective ways of resolving conflict well short of disaster. The scientific community is the closest approximation we now have to a truly international community, sharing certain fundamental interests, values, standards, and curiosities about the nature of matter, life, behavior, and the universe. The shared quest for understanding is one that knows no national boundaries, has no inherent prejudices, has no necessary ethnocentrism, and contains no barriers to the free play of information and ideas. It is drawn together more than ever by recent advances in telecommunications. These attributes of the scientific community have been highlighted recently, especially in renewed efforts to reduce the nuclear danger.

During the decades of the Cold War, the scientific community sought ways to reduce greatly the number of weapons and especially their capacity for a first strike; to decrease the chances of accidental or inadvertent nuclear war; to find safeguards against unauthorized launch and against serious miscalculation; and to improve the relations between the superpowers, partly through cooperative efforts across adversarial boundaries in key fields bearing on the health and safety of humanity. These efforts brought together scientists, scholars, and expert practitioners to clarify the many facets of avoiding nuclear war. To generate options for decreasing the risk, we needed analytical work by people who knew a variety of fields: advanced weaponry and its military uses, the superpowers and other nuclear powers, geopolitical flash points, the broad context of international relations, policy formation and implementation (especially in the nuclear powers), human behavior under stress (especially leadership decisionmaking), negotiation and conflict resolution—and much more. The relevant knowledge and skills cut right across the sciences: physical, biological, behavioral, and social.

In the world of the twenty-first century, it is crucial to understand *incentives and obstacles for cooperation* and *strategies that mobilize useful and effective cooperation*. Lessons of the Cold War—the most dangerous conflict in all of history—can be useful for this purpose. We need to understand how it was possible that five decades passed without a global war. The Cold War experience makes clear that there is a useful role for the scientific and scholarly community in international conflict resolution—often acting through nongovernmental organizations yet usually maintaining open lines of communication with governments. This involves drawing on science for accurate information, sound principles, and well-documented techniques; acting flexibly; exploring novel or neglected paths toward conflict resolution; and building relationships among well-informed people who can make a difference in attitudes and in problem-solving across adversarial boundaries.

Michael Sandel, a distinguished Harvard scholar, points out that democracy requires that citizens share in a common life even though perfect equality is not feasible. People of different backgrounds must encounter one another respectfully in everyday life, and opportunity must be available to all despite obstacles. This is how people learn to negotiate and resolve differences and thus come to care for the common good, overcoming egocentrism and greed as best we can. This process with its many variations has worldwide significance in fostering democracy. This basic concept applies strongly to the scientific community and its various roles in education at every level.

PERSPECTIVES FOR THE FUTURE

The remarkable improvements in the human condition that have occurred during our lifetimes suggest that *prevention of mass violence is also within reach in this century*. We have recognized in this book that our species is a dangerous one, in all likelihood inheriting behavioral inclinations that predispose it to damaging others. Yet we have also seen the evolution of capacities for conflict resolution; for mutual accommodation; and for cooperation beyond prior experience in seeking peace, shared prosperity, and recognition of our common humanity. We reiterate now some great experiences of the past century.

We have seen the end of colonialism and imperialism; unprecedented advances in health and reduction of poverty; the worldwide spread of human rights, including the success of the US civil rights movement; the end of fascist and Communist totalitarianism; the end of the immensely dangerous Cold War; the end of apartheid and the emergence of democracy in South Africa—indeed, the spread of democracy throughout much of the world; and the end of legal slavery. All of these advances have limits and periodic setbacks, but they represent great changes for the better. These are strong expressions of emerging human decency, yet we need constant vigilance to mobilize human capacities for fully learning to live together in personal dignity and shared humanity. We can do a lot to stimulate interest in this great mission, to disseminate ideas of the kind delineated here, and to generate better ideas so that our children and grandchildren will move us into a world of decent human relations at last.

The approach of the present book, drawing upon human intellect, problem-solving ability, fundamental decency, shared aspiration, and common humanity, may yet greatly diminish the risks of mass violence. But the tasks are exceedingly difficult, and there is no basis here for utopia. Rather, it is a long, hard road to better conditions of life and better human relations. Recent scholarship, as reflected in Steven Pinker's work on the long-term historical record and Joshua Goldstein's work on recent developments in the UN as well as his reinforcement of the public health approach, offers an authentic basis for hope, as does every chapter in this book. But we must remember what a few nuclear weapons could do to shatter our aspirations. We must also remember the many slippages from earlier advances and apply our full capacities in the context of our best values to bring this dream to fulfillment. Every chapter in this book strives to clarify the dangers and above all to suggest from research and personal experiences how we can at last learn to live together amicably and fruitfully. As John Lennon put it, "All we are saying is give peace a chance."

A final word from Albert Einstein:
    "Strange is our situation here upon earth. Each of us comes for a short visit, not knowing why, yet sometimes seeming to divine a purpose. From the standpoint of daily life, however, there is one thing we do know: that we are here for the sake of each other, above all, for those upon whose smile and well-being our own happiness depends, and also for the countless unknown souls with whose fate we are connected by a bond of sympathy."

Notes

CHAPTER 2

1. David Hamburg, *Today's Children: Creating a Future for a Generation in Crisis* (New York: Times Books, 1992).

CHAPTER 3

1. William H. Foege, *House on Fire: The Fight to Eradicate Smallpox* (Berkeley: University of California Press, 2011).

2. "DPA Strengthened," *Politically Speaking: Bulletin of the United Nations Department of Political Affairs* 5 (Spring 2009), www.un.org/Depts/dpa/newsletters/DPA%20bulletin_spring09.pdf.

3. Ban Ki-moon, Report to the 62nd Session of the UN General Assembly, United Nations A/62/521, November 2, 2007.

4. Stephen Weiss-Wik, "Enhancing Negotiators' Successfulness: Self-Help Books and Related Empirical Research," *Journal of Conflict Resolution* 27 (December 1983): 706–735; William Ury, *Getting to Peace* (New York: Penguin, 1999).

CHAPTER 4

1. Robert A. Dahl, *On Democracy* (New Haven: Yale University Press, 1998).

2. Ibid., 38, 44–61, 113–114, 145–147.

3. Thomas Carothers, *Aiding Democracy Abroad: The Learning Curve* (Washington, DC: Carnegie Endowment for International Peace, 1999).

4. Sara E. Mendelson and John K. Glenn, *Democracy Assistance and NGO Strategies in Post-Communist Societies*, working paper of the Carnegie Endowment for International Peace, 2000.

5. Timothy D. Sisk, *Power Sharing and International Mediation in Ethnic Conflicts* (Washington, DC: US Institute of Peace, 1996).

6. Larry Diamond, "Universal Democracy?" *Policy Review* (June/July 2003): 5.

7. Dahl, *On Democracy*, 38.

8. Amartya Sen, "Democracy as a Universal Value," in *The Global Divergence of Democracies*, eds. Larry Diamond and Marc F. Plattner (Baltimore: Johns Hopkins University Press, 2001). Cited in Diamond, "Universal Democracy?," 11.

9. Diamond, "Universal Democracy?," 11.

10. Ibid.

11. Ibid., 13.

CHAPTER 5

1. Edward Miguel, "Africa Unleashed: Explaining the Secret of a Belated Boom," in *Emerging Africa: How 17 Countries Are Leading the Way*, ed. Steven Radelet (Washington, DC: Brookings Institution Press, 2010).

2. BCPR, "Overview," June 19, 2008, www.undp.org/cpr/documents/BCPROverview_Jun08.pdf; "About BCPR," *CPR Newsletter* 1, no. 1 (Winter 2005): 1–2.

3. *Bureau for Crisis Prevention and Recovery 2007 Annual Report* (New York: UNDP, 2008), www.undp.org/cpr/AnnualReports/2007/AnnualReport2007_Full_LoRes.pdf.

4. Ibid.

5. Sakiko Fukuda-Parr and Robert Picciotto, "Conflict Prevention and Development Cooperation" (paper prepared for the JICA/UNDP Sponsored Project for Policy Dialogue on Conflict Prevention and Violent Conflict, background paper I, May 28, 2007).

CHAPTER 6

1. Samantha Power and Graham T. Allison, eds., *Realizing Human Rights: Moving from Inspiration to Impact* (New York: St. Martin's Press, 2000).

2. Peter Ackerman and Christopher Kruegler, *Strategic Nonviolent Conflict: The Dynamics of People Power in the Twentieth Century* (Westport, CT: Praeger Publishers, 1994).

3. Brian Urquhart, "Revolution without Violence?" *New York Review of Books*, March 2011.

4. David A. Hamburg, *No More Killing Fields: Preventing Deadly Conflict* (Lanham, MD: Rowman and Littlefield, 2002), 170–172.

5. Mary King, *Mahatma Gandhi and Martin Luther King, Jr.: The Power of Nonviolent Action* (Paris: UNESCO, 1999), 419–420.

6. Stanford Program on International and Cross-Cultural Education, *Preventing Deadly Conflict: Toward a World without War* (Stanford, CA: Stanford University Freeman Spogli Institute for International Studies, 2000), 125–127.

7. David Cortright, *Gandhi and Beyond: Nonviolence for an Age of Terrorism* (Boulder, CO: Paradigm Publishers, 2006).

8. David A. Hamburg, "Human Rights and Warfare: An Ounce of Prevention Is Worth a Pound of Cure," in *Realizing Human Rights: Moving from Inspiration to Impact*, eds. Samantha Power and Graham Allison (New York: St. Martin's Press, 2000), 322.

9. John Stremlau and Helen Zille, "A House No Longer Divided: Progress and Prospects for Democratic Peace in South Africa," A Report to the Carnegie Commission on Preventing Deadly Conflict (New York: Carnegie Corporation of New York, 1997).

10. Louis Henkin, "Human Rights: Ideology and Aspiration, Reality and Prospect," in Power and Allison, *Realizing Human Rights*, 3–37.

11. Ibid., 8

12. Ibid., 9.

13. Ibid., 11.

14. Shirley Williams, "Human Rights in Europe," in Power and Allison, *Realizing Human Rights*, 77–110.

15. Ibid., 77.

16. Ibid., 81–82.

17. Ibid., 78.

18. Ibid., 86.

19. Ibid., 88–89.

20. Henkin, "Human Rights," 26–27.

21. Richard J. Goldstone, "Advancing the Cause of Human Rights: The Need for Justice and Accountability," in Power and Allison, *Realizing Human Rights*, 206–207.

22. Ibid., 208–210.

23. Juan E. Méndez, "The Inter-American System of Protection: Its Contributions to the International Law of Human Rights," in Power and Allison, *Realizing Human Rights*, 134.

24. Makau Mutua, "The Construction of the African Human Rights System: Prospects and Pitfalls," in Power and Allison, *Realizing Human Rights*, 148–149.

25. Ibid., 149–150.

26. Hamburg, "Human Rights and Warfare."

27. Jimmy Carter, "The American Road to a Human Rights Policy," in Power and Allison, *Realizing Human Rights*, 50.

28. Ibid., 51.

29. Ibid., 52.

30. Ibid., 55.

CHAPTER 7

1. S. D. Drell and R. Jeanloz, "Nuclear Deterrence in a World without Nuclear Weapons," in *Deterrence, Its Past and Future*, eds. G. P. Shultz, S. D. Drell, and J. E. Goodby (Stanford, CA: Hoover Press, 2011), 99–129.

2. Richard G. Lugar, "Nunn-Lugar: Science Cooperation Essential for Nonproliferation Efforts," *Science and Diplomacy* 1, no. 1 (March 2012).

3. Sidney D. Drell and James E. Goodby, *A World without Nuclear Weapons: End State Issues* (Stanford: Hoover Institution Press, 2009); Sidney Drell and Christopher Stubbs, "Realizing the Full Potential

of the Open Skies Treaty," *Arms Control Today*, July/August 2011; Richard Falk and David Krieger, *The Path to Zero* (Boulder: Paradigm Publishers, 2012).

4. Philip Taubman, *The Partnership: Five Cold Warriors and Their Quest to Ban the Bomb* (New York: HarperCollins, 2012).

5. Helmut Schmidt and Sam Nunn, "Toward a World without Nukes," *New York Times*, April 13, 2012.

6. Drell and Stubbs, "Realizing the Full Potential."

7. Matthew Bunn, Belfer Center for Science and International Affairs, and Vyachevslav Kuznetsov, "Promoting Safe, Secure and Peaceful Growth of Nuclear Energy: Next Steps for Russia and the United States," 3, no. 3, Project on Managing the Atom and Russian Research Center "Kurchatow Institute," Spring 2011.

8. Joan Rohlfing, "Regulating the Materials of Mass Destruction: The Need for Comprehensive Materials Management Framework," *NTI Bulletin*, October 2010.

9. "Understanding Biosecurity: Protecting Against the Misuse of Science in Today's World" (Washington, DC: National Research Council of the National Academies, National Academy Press, 2010).

CHAPTER 8

1. Paul Stares and Micah Zenko, "Partners in Preventive Action: The United States and International Institutions" (Washington, DC: Council on Foreign Relations Press, September 2011).

CHAPTER 9

1. Boutros Boutros-Ghali, "Agenda for Democratization: Supplement to Reports A/50/332 and A/51/512 on Democratization," December 17, 1996, www.library.yale.edu/un/un3d3.htm; Boutros-Ghali, "An Agenda for Development: Report of the Secretary-General Boutros Boutros-Ghali, A/48/935," May 6, 1994, www.un.org/Docs/SG/agdev.html; Boutros-Ghali, "An Agenda for Peace: Preventive Diplomacy, Peacemaking and Peace-Keeping: Report of the Secretary-General Pursuant to the Statement Adopted by the Summit Meeting of the Security Council on 31 January 1992, A/47/277-S/24111," June 17, 1992, www.un.org/Docs/SG/agpeace.html.

2. Kofi Annan, *Progress Report of the Secretary-General on the Prevention of Armed Conflict*, Sixtieth Session, Agenda Item 12, 06-39322 (E), September 2006.

3. Kofi Annan, *Toward a Culture of Prevention: Statements by the Secretary-General of the United Nations* (New York: Carnegie Commission on Preventing Deadly Conflict, 1999).

4. See Connie Peck, "Special Representatives of the Secretary-General," in *The UN Security Council: From the Cold War to the 21st Century*, ed. David M. Malone (Boulder: Lynne Rienner Publishers, 2004), 325–339.

5. Connie Peck, *Sustainable Peace: The Role of the UN and Regional Organizations in Preventing Conflict*, Carnegie Commission Series (New York: Rowman and Littlefield, 1998).

6. Elizabeth M. Cousens, "Conflict Prevention," in *The UN Security Council from the Cold War to the 21st Century*, ed. David M. Malone (Boulder: Lynne Rienner Publishers, 2004), 108–115.

7. A 1998 study on the subject, more pertinent than ever, is Donald Kennedy et al., *Environmental Quality and Regional Conflict: A Report to the Carnegie Commission on Preventing Deadly Conflict* (New York: Carnegie Corporation of New York, 1998), wwics.si.edu/subsites/ccpdc/pubs/ken/ken.htm.

8. Graham T. Allison and Hisashi Owada, "The Responsibilities of Democracies in Preventing Deadly Conflict: Reflections and Recommendations," paper prepared for Carnegie Commission on Preventing Deadly Conflicts discussion, July 1999.

9. Council on Foreign Relations, *Enhancing U.S. Leadership at the United Nations*, Task Force Report No. 39 (New York: Council on Foreign Relations, 2002).

10. Interview with Jean Arnault, Geneva, November 2001.

11. Melanie Greenberg, John Barton, and Margaret McGuinness, *Words over War: Mediation and Arbitration to Prevent Deadly Conflict* (Lanham, MD: Rowman and Littlefield, 2000), 366; Joshua S. Goldstein, *Winning the War on War: The Untold Story of Peace Increasing around the World* (New York: Dutton, 2010).

12. Greenberg, Barton, and McGuinness, *Words over War*, 433.

CHAPTER 11

1. "Partnership for Peace," invitation document issued by the heads of state and government participating in the Meeting of the North Atlantic Council, Brussels, Belgium, January 10, 1994, www.nato.int/docu/basictxt/b940110a.htm.

2. "Partnership for Peace," framework document issued by the heads of state and government participating in the Meeting of the North Atlantic Council in Brussels, Belgium, January 10, 1994, www.nato.int/docu/basictxt/b940110b.htm.

3. "Basic Document of the Euro-Atlantic Partnership Council," Sintra, Portugal, May 30, 1997, www.nato.int/docu/basictxt/b021121a.htm.

4. "Report on the Comprehensive Review of the Euro-Atlantic Partnership Council and Partnership for Peace," Prague Summit, November 21, 2002, www.nato.int/docu/basictxt/b021122e.htm.

5. "Partnership Action Plan against Terrorism," Prague Summit, November 22, 2002, www.nato.int/basictxt/b021122e.htm.

6. NATO Public Diplomacy Division, "NATO Crisis Management," NATO Briefing, October 2003.

7. Ivo Daalder and James Goldgeier, "Global NATO," *Foreign Affairs* (September/October 2006): 108.

RECOMMENDED READINGS

CHAPTER 1

Allison, Graham, and Philip Zelikow. *Essence of Decision: Explaining the Cuban Missile Crisis*, 2nd ed. New York: Addison Wesley Longman, 1999.

Brown, Archie. *The Gorbachev Factor*. New York: Oxford, 1997.

Carnegie Commission on Preventing Deadly Conflict. *Preventing Deadly Conflict: Final Report*. Washington, DC: Carnegie Commission on Preventing Deadly Conflict, 1997.

Goodall, Jane, and David A. Hamburg. *Chimpanzee Behavior as a Model for the Behavior of Early Man: New Evidence on Possible Origins of Human Behavior*. Vol. 6, *American Handbook of Psychiatry*, edited by David A. Hamburg and H. Brodie. New York: Basic Books, 1975.

Hamburg, David. "An Evolutionary Perspective on Human Aggression." In *The Development and Integration of Behavior: Essays in Honour of Robert Hinde*, edited by Patrick Bateson, 419–457. Cambridge: Cambridge University Press, 1991.

Hamburg, David, Glen Elliott, and Delores Parron, eds. *Health and Behavior: Frontiers of Research in Biobehavioral Sciences*. Washington, DC: National Academy Press, 1982.

Hamburg, David, and Jane Goodall. "Factors Facilitating Development of Aggressive Behavior in Chimpanzees and Humans." In *Determinants and Origins of Aggressive Behavior*, edited by J. de Wit and W. Hartup, 59–85. The Hague: Mouton Publishers, 1974.

Hamburg, David, Beatrix Hamburg, and Jack Barchas. "Anger and Depression in Perspective of Behavioral Biology." In *Emotions—Their Parameters and Measurement*, edited by L. Levi, 235–278. New York: Raven Press, 1975.

Hamburg, David A., and Elizabeth R. McCown, eds. *The Great Apes*. Menlo Park, CA: Benjamin/Cummings, 1997.

Hamburg, David A., and Michelle Trudeau, eds. *Biobehavioral Aspects of Aggression*. New York: Alan R. Liss, 1981.

Hare, Brian, Victoria Wobber, and Richard Wrangham. "The Self-Domestication Hypothesis: Evolution of Bonobo Psychology Is Due to Selection against Aggression." *Animal Behaviour* 83 (2012): 573–585.

Matlock, Jack F., Jr. *Autopsy on an Empire: The American Ambassador's Account of the Collapse of the Soviet Union*. New York: Random House, 1995.

McGrew, William C., Linda F. Marchant, and Toshisada Nishida, eds. *Great Ape Societies*. Cambridge: Cambridge University Press, 1996.

Smuts, Barbara B., Dorothy L. Cheney, Robert M. Seyfarth, Richard W. Wrangham, and Thomas T. Struhsaker, eds. *Primate Societies*. Chicago: University of Chicago Press, 1986.

Wrangham, Richard. "Why Apes and Humans Kill." In *Conflict: The 2005 Darwin College Lecture Series*, edited by Martin Jones and Andy Fabian, 43–62. Cambridge: Cambridge University Press, 2006.

Wrangham, Richard, and Luke Glowacki. "Intergroup Aggression in Chimpanzees and War in Nomadic Hunter-Gatherers: Evaluating the Chimpanzee Model." *Human Nature* 23, no. 1 (March 2012): 5–29.

CHAPTER 2

Aronson, Elliot. *Nobody Left to Hate: Teaching Compassion after Columbine*. New York: W. H. Freeman, 2000.

Bandura, Albert. *Aggression: A Social Learning Analysis*. Englewood Cliffs, NJ: Prentice-Hall, 1973.

Brewer, Marilynn, and Norman Miller. *Intergroup Relations*. Pacific Grove: Brooks/Cole Publishing Company, 1996.

Carnegie Council on Adolescent Development. *Great Transitions: Preparing Adolescents for a New Century* (Concluding Report). New York: Carnegie Corporation of New York, 1995.

Deutsch, Morton, and Peter Coleman, eds. *The Handbook of Conflict Resolution: Theory and Practice*. San Francisco: Jossey-Bass, 2000.

Eshel, Neir. *The Science Inside Learning*. Education and Human Resources Programs. Washington, DC: American Association for the Advancement of Science, 2007.

Hamburg, Beatrix A., Delbert Elliott, and Kirk R. Williams, eds. *Violence in American Schools: A New Perspective*. New York: Cambridge University Press, 1998.

Hamburg, David, ed. *Psychiatry as a Behavioral Science*. Behavioral and Social Sciences Survey Monograph Series. Englewood Cliffs, NJ: Prentice-Hall, 1970.

———. *Today's Children: Creating a Future for a Generation in Crisis*. New York: Times Books/Random House, 1992.

Hamburg, David, and J. Adams. "A Perspective on Coping Behavior: Seeking and Utilizing Information in Major Transitions." *Archives of General Psychiatry* 17 (1967): 277–284.

Hamburg, David, and Beatrix Hamburg. *Learning to Live Together: Preventing Hatred and Violence in Child and Adolescent Development*. New York: Oxford University Press, 2004.

Sherif, Muzafer, and Carolyn Sherif. *Groups in Harmony and Tension: An Integration of Studies on Intergroup Relations*. New York: Octagon, 1966.

Stewart, Vivien. *A World-Class Education: Learning from International Models of Excellence and Innovation*. Alexandria, VA: ASCD Member Books, 2012.

CHAPTER 3

Benesch, Susan. "Inciting Genocide, Pleading Free Speech." *World Policy Journal* 21, no. 2 (Summer 2004): 62–69.

Boutros-Ghali, Boutros. *An Agenda for Peace: Preventive Diplomacy, Peacemaking and Peace-Keeping: Report of the Secretary-General Pursuant to the Statement Adopted by the Summit Meeting of the Security Council on 31 January 1992*, A/47/277-S/24111 (June 17, 1992). www.un.org/Docs/SG/agpeace.html.

Brewer, M. B. "The Psychology of Prejudice: Ingroup Love or Outgroup Hate." *Journal of Social Issues* 55, no. 3 (1999): 429–444.

Brown, Michael, and Richard N. Rosecrance. *The Costs of Conflict: Prevention and Cure in the Global Arena.* Lanham, MD: Rowman and Littlefield, 1999.

Carnegie Commission on Preventing Deadly Conflict. *Perspectives on Preventive Diplomacy, Preventive Defense, and Conflict Resolution: A Report of Two Conferences at Stanford University and the Ditchley Foundation.* New York: Carnegie Corporation of New York, 1999.

Eliasson, Jan, and Peter Wallensteen. "Preventive Diplomacy." In *The Adventure of Peace: Dag Hammarskjöld and the Future of the United Nations,* edited by Anna Mark-Jungkvist and Sten Ask. New York: Palgrave Macmillan, 2006.

Fisher, Roger, and William Ury. *Getting to Yes: Negotiating Agreement without Giving In.* New York: Penguin, 1983.

Greenberg, Melanie C., John H. Barton, and Margaret E. McGuinness. *Words over War: Mediation and Arbitration to Prevent Deadly Conflict.* Carnegie Commission Series. Lanham, MD: Rowman and Littlefield, 2000.

Hamburg, David A. "Conflict Prevention and Health: An Array of Opportunities." In *Anna Lindh Programme on Conflict Prevention,* 2006 ed. Health and Conflict Prevention, edited by Anders Mellbourn, 33–44. Brussels: Madariaga Foundation, 2006.

———. *No More Killing Fields: Preventing Deadly Conflict.* Lanham, MD: Rowman and Littlefield, 2002.

Jentleson, Bruce W., ed. *Opportunities Missed, Opportunities Seized: Preventive Diplomacy in the Post–Cold War World.* Carnegie Commission on Preventing Deadly Conflict Series. Lanham, MD: Rowman and Littlefield, 1999.

Mack, Andrew, ed. *Human Security Report 2005: War and Peace in the 21st Century.* University of British Columbia Human Security Centre. New York: Oxford University Press, 2005. www.humansecurityreport.info.

Packer, John. "The Role and Work of the OSCE High Commissioner on National Minorities as an Instrument of Conflict Prevention." In *Sharing Best Practices on Conflict Prevention: Strengthening UN Capacities for the Prevention of Violent Conflict—The UN, Regional and Subregional Organizations, National and Local Actors—IPA Policy Report,* 10–14. New York: International Peace Academy, 2002.

Rubin, Barnett L. *Blood on the Doorstep: The Politics of Preventive Action.* New York: Century Foundation Press, 2002.

Rubin, Jeffrey Z., Dean G. Pruitt, and Sung Hee Kim. *Social Conflict: Escalation, Stalemate, and Settlement,* 2nd ed. New York: McGraw-Hill, 1994.

Solana, Javier. "The Health Dimension to Security." In *Anna Lindh Programme on Conflict Prevention,* 2006 ed. Health and Conflict Prevention, edited by Anders Mellbourn, 9–14. Brussels: Madariaga Foundation, 2006.

Zartman, I. William, ed. *Preventive Negotiation: Avoiding Conflict Escalation.* Carnegie Commission on Preventing Deadly Conflict Series. Lanham, MD: Rowman and Littlefield, 2000.

Zartman, I. William, Mark Anstey, and Paul Meerts, eds. *The Slippery Slope to Genocide: Reducing Identity Conflicts and Preventing Mass Murder.* New York: Oxford University Press, 2012.

CHAPTER 4

Ackerman, Peter, and Christopher Krueger. *Strategic Nonviolent Conflict: The Dynamics of People Power in the Twentieth Century.* Westport, CT: Praeger, 1994.

Cortright, David. *Gandhi and Beyond: Nonviolence for an Age of Terrorism.* Boulder, CO: Paradigm Publishers, 2006.

Dahl, Robert A. *On Democracy.* New Haven: Yale University Press, 1998.

Diamond, Larry. *Developing Democracy: Toward Consolidation.* Baltimore: Johns Hopkins University Press, 2005.

———. *The Spirit of Democracy: The Struggle to Build Free Societies throughout the World.* New York: Times Books, 2008.

International IDEA. *Ten Years of Supporting Democracy Worldwide.* Stockholm: International Institute for Democracy and Electoral Assistance, 2005. www.id.int/publications/anniversary/upload/inlay_senttoprint_30May05.pdf.

King, Mary. *Mahatma Gandhi and Martin Luther King, Jr.: The Power of Nonviolent Action.* Paris: UNESCO, 1999.

Krugman, Paul. *End This Depression Now!* New York: W. W. Norton, 2012.

Mandela, Nelson. *Long Walk to Freedom: The Autobiography of Nelson Mandela.* Boston: Little, Brown, 1994.

Roberts, Adam, and Timothy Garton Ash. *Civil Resistance and Power Politics: The Experience of Non-Violent Action from Gandhi to the Present.* New York: Oxford University Press, 2009.

Sen, Amartya. "Democracy as a Universal Value." In *The Global Divergence of Democracies,* edited by Larry Diamond and Marc F. Plattner, 3–18. Baltimore: Johns Hopkins University Press, 2001.

Sisk, Timothy D. *Power Sharing and International Mediation in Ethnic Conflicts.* Washington, DC: United States Institute of Peace Press, 1996.

Snyder, Jack. *From Voting to Violence: Democratization and Nationalist Conflict.* New York: W. W. Norton, 2000.

Stern, Fritz. *Dreams and Delusions: National Socialism in the Drama of the German Past.* New York: Vintage, 1987.

Ury, William L. *Getting to Peace.* New York: Penguin, 1999.

Weitz, Eric D. *Weimar Germany: Promise and Tragedy.* Princeton: Princeton University Press, 2007.

CHAPTER 5

Collier, Paul. *The Bottom Billion: Why the Poorest Countries Are Failing and What Can Be Done about It.* New York: Oxford University Press, 2007.

Commonwealth Commission on Respect and Understanding. *Civil Paths to Peace: Report of the Commonwealth Commission on Respect and Understanding.* London: Commonwealth Secretariat, 2007.

Haq, Mahbub ul. *Reflections on Human Development.* New York: Oxford University Press, 1995.

InterAcademy Council Report, Study Panel on Agricultural Productivity in Africa, Speciosa Kazibwe, Rudy Rabbinge, and M. S. Swaninathan, cochairs. *Realizing the Promise and Potential of African Agriculture.* Amsterdam: Inter Academy Council, 2004. www.interacademycouncil.net/CMS/Reports.aspx.

InterAcademy Council Report, Study Panel on Promoting Worldwide Science and Technology, Jacob Palis and Ismail Serageldin, cochairs. *Inventing a Better Future: A Strategy for Building Worldwide Capacities in Science and Technology.* Amsterdam: InterAcademy Council, 2005. www.interacademycouncil.net/CMS/Reports.aspx.

Kennedy, Donald, et al. *Environmental Quality and Regional Conflict: A Report to the Carnegie Commission on Preventing Deadly Conflict.* New York: Carnegie Corporation of New York, 1998. http://wwics.si.edu/subsites/ccpdc/pubs/ken/ken.htm.

Lancaster, Carol. *Foreign Aid: Diplomacy, Development, Domestic Politics.* Chicago: University of Chicago Press, 2007.

Michel, Louis. "Development Cooperation as a European Tool of Conflict Prevention." In *Development, Security and Conflict Prevention: Anna Lindh Programme on Conflict Prevention,* 2005 ed., edited by Anders Mellbourn, 59–75. Hedemora, Sweden: Gidlunds Förlag, 2005.

Nichols, Rodney W. "Linking Science and Technology with Global Economic Development: A U.S. Perspective." COSTED Occasional Paper no. 5. Committee on Science and Technology in Developing Countries, September 1999.

Raymond, Susan U. *Science-Based Economic Development: Case Studies Around the World.* New York: New York Academy of Sciences, 1996.

Sachs, Jeffrey D. *The End of Poverty: Economic Possibilities for Our Time.* New York: Penguin Press, 2005.

Sen, Amartya. *Development and Freedom.* New York: Knopf, 1999.

———. *The Idea of Justice.* Cambridge, MA: Belknap/Harvard University Press, 2009.

————. *Identity and Violence: The Illusion of Destiny.* New York: W. W. Norton, 2006.

Stiglitz, Joseph. *Making Globalization Work.* New York: W. W. Norton, 2006.

————. *The Price of Inequality: How Today's Divided Society Endangers Our Future.* New York: W. W. Norton, 2010.

UN Development Programme. *Human Development Report 2005, International Cooperation at a Crossroads: Aid, Trade and Security in an Unequal World.* Washington, DC: UNDP, 2005.

World Bank. *World Development Report.* Conflict, Security and Development. Overview by President Robert Zoellick. Washington, DC: World Bank, 2011.

CHAPTER 6

Allen, John. *Desmond Tutu: The Rainbow People of God: The Making of a Peaceful Revolution.* Foreword by Nelson Mandela. New York: Doubleday, 1994.

Carter, Jimmy. "The American Road to a Foreign Rights Policy." In Power and Allison, *Realizing Human Rights*, 49–61.

Hamburg, David A. "Human Rights and Warfare: An Ounce of Prevention Is Worth a Pound of Cure." In Power and Allison, *Realizing Human Rights*, chapter 15.

Hayner, Priscilla B. *Unspeakable Truths: Transitional Justice and the Challenge of Truth Commissions,* 2nd ed. New York: Routledge, 2011.

Henkin, Louis. "Human Rights: Ideology and Aspiration, Reality and Prospect." In Power and Allison, *Realizing Human Rights*, 3–37.

Human Security Now. New York: Commission on Human Security, 2003.

Minow, Martha. *Between Vengeance and Forgiveness: Facing History after Genocide and Mass Violence.* Boston: Beacon Press, 1998.

Power, Samantha, and Graham T. Allison, eds. *Realizing Human Rights: Moving from Inspiration to Impact.* New York: St. Martin's Press, 2000.

Stremlau, John, and Helen Zille. "A House No Longer Divided: Progress and Prospects for Democratic Peace in South Africa." A Report to the Carnegie Commission on Preventing Deadly Conflict. New York: Carnegie Corporation of New York, 1997.

CHAPTER 7

Allison, Graham T. *Nuclear Terrorism: The Ultimate Preventable Catastrophe.* New York: Henry Holt/ Times Books, 2004.

Bundy, McGeorge, William J. Crowe, and Sidney D. Drell. *Reducing Nuclear Danger: The Road Away from the Brink.* New York: Council on Foreign Relations Press, 1993.

Bunn, Matthew. *Securing the Bomb 2007.* Cambridge, MA: Belfer Center, Harvard University, 2007. www.nti.org/securingthebomb.

Cirincione, Joseph. *Bomb Scare: The History and Future of Nuclear Weapons.* New York: Columbia University Press, 2007.

Cortright, David, ed. *The Price of Peace: Incentives and International Conflict Prevention.* Carnegie Commission on Preventing Deadly Conflict, Carnegie Corporation of New York. Foreword by David A. Hamburg and Cyrus R. Vance. Lanham, MD: Rowman and Littlefield, 1997.

Drell, Sidney. *Facing the Threat of Nuclear Weapons.* Seattle: University of Washington Press, 1983.

Drell, Sidney, and James Goodby. *The Gravest Danger: Nuclear Weapons.* Stanford: Hoover Institution Press, 2003.

George, Alexander, ed. *Avoiding War: Problems of Crisis Management.* Boulder: Westview Press, 1991.

Goodpaster, Andrew J. "When Diplomacy Is Not Enough: Managing Multinational Military Interventions." A Report to the Carnegie Commission on Preventing Deadly Conflict. New York: Carnegie Corporation of New York, 1996.

Hamburg, David. "Understanding and Preventing Nuclear War: The Expanding Role of the Scientific Community." In *The Medical Implications of Nuclear War*, edited by Frederic Solomon and Robert Marston, 1–11. Washington, DC: National Academy Press, 1986.

Hoffman, David E. *The Dead Hand: The Untold Story of the Cold War Arms Race and Its Dangerous Legacy.* New York: Doubleday, 2009.

McNeill, William H. *The Pursuit of Power. Technology, Armed Force and Society Since AD 1000.* Chicago: University of Chicago Press, 1982.

Perry, William J. "Preparing for the Next Attack." *Foreign Affairs* 8, no. 6 (November/December 2001): 31–45.

Shultz, George P., William J. Perry, Henry A. Kissinger, and Sam Nunn. "A World Free of Nuclear Weapons." *Wall Street Journal*, January 4, 2007, A15.

Solomon, Fredric, and Robert Marston, eds. *The Medical Implications of Nuclear War.* Foreword by Lewis Thomas. Washington, DC. Institute of Medicine, National Academy of Sciences, National Academy Press, 1986.

Taubman, Philip. *The Partnership: Five Cold Warriors and Their Quest to Ban the Bomb.* New York: HarperCollins, 2012.

CHAPTER 8

Allison, Graham T., and Hisashi Owada. *The Responsibilities of Democracies in Preventing Deadly Conflict: Reflections and Recommendations.* Paper presented at the Carnegie Commission on Preventing Deadly Conflicts Discussion, New York, July 1999.

Genocide Prevention Task Force. *Preventing Genocide: A Blueprint for U.S. Policymakers.* Washington, DC: United States Holocaust Memorial Museum, the American Academy of Diplomacy, and the Endowment of the United States Institute of Peace, 2008.

Lute, Douglas E. "Improving National Capacities for Response to Complex Emergencies." A Report to the Carnegie Commission on Preventing Deadly Conflict. New York: Carnegie Corporation of New York, 1997.

Stares, Paul B., and Micah Zenko. "Partners in Preventive Action: The United States and International Institutions." *Council Special Report* no. 62 (September 2011). Council on Foreign Relations: Center for Preventive Action.

CHAPTER 9

Annan, Kofi. *Towards a Culture of Prevention: Statements by the Secretary-General of the United Nations.* New York: Carnegie Commission on Preventing Deadly Conflict, 1999.

Chayes, Abram, and Antonia Handler Chayes, eds. *Preventing Conflict in the Post-Communist World: Mobilizing International and Regional Organizations.* Washington, DC: The Brookings Institution, 1996.

Cousens, Elizabeth M. "Conflict Prevention." In *The UN Security Council from the Cold War to the 21st Century*, edited by David M. Malone, 108–115. Boulder: Lynne Rienner Publishers, 2004.

Kennedy, Paul. *The Parliament of Man: The Past, Present, and Future of the United Nations.* New York: Random House, 2006.

Peck, Connie. "Special Representatives of the Secretary-General." In *The UN Security Council: From the Cold War to the 21st Century*, edited by David M. Malone, 325–339. Boulder: Lynne Rienner Publishers, 2004.

————. *Sustainable Peace: The Role of the UN and Regional Organizations in Preventing Conflict.* Lanham, MD: Rowman and Littlefield, 1997.

Vance, Cyrus R., and David A. Hamburg. "Pathfinders for Peace: A Report to the UN Secretary-General on the Role of Special Representatives and Personal Envoys." A Report to the Carnegie Commission on Preventing Deadly Conflict. New York: Carnegie Corporation of New York, 1997.

CHAPTER 10

Ash, Timothy G. *Free World: America, Europe, and the Surprising Future of the West.* New York: HarperCollins, 2003.

Behrman, Greg. *The Most Noble Adventure: The Marshall Plan and the Time When America Helped Save Europe.* New York: Free Press, 2007.

Cloos, Jim. "Conflict Prevention as an Instrument in the EU's Security Toolbox." In *Development, Security and Conflict Prevention, Anna Lindh Programme on Conflict Prevention,* 2005 ed., edited by Anders Mellbourn, 14–23. Hedemora, Sweden: Gidlunds Förlag, 2005.

Craig, Gordon. *Europe Since 1815.* New York: Holt, Rinehart and Winston, 1961.

Evans, Gareth. "Conflict Prevention and NGOs," in *Development, Security and Conflict Prevention: Anna Lindh Programme on Conflict Prevention,* 2005 ed., edited by Anders Mellbourn, 121–136. Hedemora, Sweden: Gidlunds Förlag, 2005.

Naimark, Norman M. *Fires of Hatred: Ethnic Cleansing in Twentieth-Century Europe.* London: Harvard University Press, 2001.

Preventing Violent Conflict and Building Peace: On Interaction between State Actors and Voluntary Organizations. European Centre for Conflict Prevention and Swedish Peace Team Forum. Stockholm: XBS Grafisk Service, 2002.

Youngs, Richard, ed. *The European Union and Democracy Promotion: A Critical Assessment.* Baltimore: Johns Hopkins University Press, 2010.

CHAPTER 11

Christopher, Warren. *Chances of a Lifetime: A Memoir.* New York: Scribner, 2001.

Daalder, Ivo, and James Goldgeier. "Global NATO." *Foreign Affairs* 85, no. 5 (September/October 2006): 105–113.

Ogata, Sadako. *The Turbulent Decade: Confronting the Refugee Crises of the 1990s.* New York: W. W. Norton, 2005.

CHAPTER 12

Beasley, Maurine H. *Eleanor Roosevelt: Transformative First Lady.* Lawrence: University Press of Kansas, 2010.

Coelho, George V., David A. Hamburg, and John E. Adams, eds. *Coping and Adaptation.* New York: Basic Books, 1974.

Cronin, Thomas E., and Michael A. Genovese. *Leadership Matters: Unleashing the Power of Paradox.* Boulder: Paradigm Publishers, 2012.

Davis, David Brion. *Inhuman Bondage: The Rise and Fall of Slavery in the New World.* New York: Oxford University Press, 2006.

De Cerreno, Allison L. C., and Alexander Keynan. *Scientific Cooperation, State Conflict: The Roles of Scientists in Mitigating International Discord.* New York: New York Academy of Sciences, 1998.

Foege, William H. *House on Fire: The Fight to Eradicate Smallpox.* Berkeley: University of California Press, 2011.

George, Alexander L. *On Foreign Policy: Unfinished Business.* Boulder: Paradigm Publishers, 2006.

George, Alexander, and David A. Hamburg. "Toward an International Center for Prevention of Genocide." *Foreign Policy Forum* 15/16 (2005): 85–89.

Glover, Jonathan. *Humanity: A Moral History of the Twentieth Century.* New Haven: Yale University Press, 2000.

Goldstein, Joshua S. *Winning the War on War: The Decline of Armed Conflict Worldwide.* New York: Dutton, 2011.

Gorbachev, Mikhail. "On Nonviolent Leadership." In *Essays on Leadership*, edited by David A. Hamburg and Cyrus R. Vance, 67–70. New York: Carnegie Commission on Preventing Deadly Conflict, 1998.

Hamburg, David A. "Human Aggressiveness and Conflict Resolution." In *World Change and World Security*, edited by Norman Dahl and Jerome Wiesner, 39–60. Cambridge, MA: MIT Press, 1978.

———. *Preventing Genocide: Practical Steps Toward Early Detection and Effective Action*, rev. and updated ed. Boulder: Paradigm Publishers, 2010.

Hamburg, David A., Alexander George, and Karen Ballentine. "Preventing Deadly Conflict: The Critical Role of Leadership." *Archives of General Psychiatry* 56 (November 1999): 971–976.

Hamburg, David A., and Cyrus R. Vance. *Essays on Leadership.* New York: Carnegie Commission on Preventing Deadly Conflict, 1998.

Hinde, Robert. *Changing How We Live: Society from the Bottom Up.* Nottingham, England: Spokesman, 2011.

Howard, Michael. *The Invention of Peace: Reflections on War and International Order.* New Haven: Yale University Press, 2000.

Janis, Irving. *Crucial Decisions: Leadership in Policy-Making and Crisis Management.* New York: Free Press, 1989.

Kiernan, Ben. *Blood and Soil: A World History of Genocide and Extermination from Sparta to Darfur.* New Haven: Yale University Press, 2007.

Kupchan, Charles A. *How Enemies Become Friends: The Sources of Stable Peace.* Princeton: Princeton University Press, 2010.

Peck, Connie. *Sustainable Peace: The Role of the UN and Regional Organizations in Preventing Conflict.* Carnegie Commission Series. Lanham, MD: Rowman and Littlefield, 1998.

Pinker, Steven. *The Better Angels of Our Nature: Why Violence Has Declined.* New York: Viking, 2011.

Preventing Violent Conflict: The Search for Political Will, Strategies and Effective Tools. Stockholm: Stockholm International Peace Research Institute, 2000.

Redlich, Fritz. *Hitler: Diagnosis of a Destructive Prophet.* New York: Oxford University Press, 1999.

Richardson, Louise. *What Terrorists Want: Understanding the Enemy, Containing the Threat.* New York: Random House, 2006.

Rock, Stephen R. *Why Peace Breaks Out: Great Power Rapprochement in Historical Perspective.* Chapel Hill: University of North Carolina Press, 1989.

Sandel, Michael. *What Money Can't Buy: The Moral Limits of Markets.* New York: Farrar, Straus and Giroux, 2012.

Schweitzer, Glenn E. *Scientists, Engineers, and Track-Two Diplomacy: A Half-Century of U.S.-Russian Interacademy Cooperation.* Washington, DC: National Academies Press, 2004.

Sennett, Richard. *Together: The Rituals, Pleasures and Politics of Cooperation.* New Haven: Yale University Press, 2012.

Staub, Ervin. *Overcoming Evil: Genocide, Violent Conflict, and Terrorism.* New York: Oxford University Press, 2011.

Sternberg, Robert, and Karin Sternberg. *The Nature of Hate.* Cambridge: Cambridge University Press, 2008.

Zartman, I. William, Mark Anstey, and Paul Meerts, eds. *The Slippery Slope to Genocide: Reducing Identity Conflicts and Preventing Mass Murder.* New York: Oxford University Press, 2012.

INDEX

About the Authors

David A. Hamburg, MD, is DeWitt Wallace Distinguished Scholar at Weill Cornell Medical College and visiting scholar at the American Association for the Advancement of Science (AAAS). He is president emeritus of the Carnegie Corporation of New York. He has been professor at Stanford University and Harvard University, president of the Institute of Medicine, National Academy of Sciences, and president of the AAAS. Dr. Hamburg's honors include the National Academy of Sciences Public Welfare Medal (its highest award) and the Presidential Medal of Freedom (the highest civilian award of the United States). Among his publications are *Preventing Genocide* (2010), *Today's Children* (1992), *No More Killing Fields* (2002), and *Learning to Live Together* (2004). He was cochair, with Cyrus Vance, of the Carnegie Commission on Preventing Deadly Conflict.

Eric Hamburg is writer, director, and producer of the documentary *Preventing Genocide* (2009). He is also coproducer of the films *Any Given Sunday* (1999) and *The Last Days of Kennedy and King* (1998), a Hermosa Beach Film Festival winner for best documentary, as well as the Oscar-nominated film *Nixon* (1995).